Research Methods
Laboratory Manual
for Psychology

THIRD EDITION

Research Methods
Laboratory Manual
for Psychology

William Langston

Middle Tennessee State University

WADSWORTH
CENGAGE Learning™

Australia • Brazil • Japan • Korea • Mexico • Singapore • Spain • United Kingdom • United States

WADSWORTH
CENGAGE Learning™

**Research Methods Laboratory Manual
for Psychology, Third Edition**
William Langston

Publisher/Executive Editor: Jon-David Hague

Acquisitions Editor: Timothy Matray

Editorial Assistant: Alicia McLaughlin

Marketing Manager: Jessica Egbert

Marketing Coordinator: Anna Andersen

Marketing Communications Manager:
Talia Wise

Content Project Management: PreMediaGlobal

Art Director: Vernon Boes

Print Buyer: Judy Inouye

Rights Acquisition Director: Bob Kauser

Rights Acquisition Specialist, Text/Image:
Dean Dauphinais

Production Service/Compositor:
PreMediaGlobal

Cover Designer: Lisa Henry

Cover Image: Paul Rice/Digital Vision

For product information and technology assistance, contact us at
Cengage Learning Customer & Sales Support, 1-800-354-9706

For permission to use material from this text or product,
submit all requests online at **www.cengage.com/permissions**
Further permissions questions can be emailed to
permissionrequest@cengage.com

Library of Congress Control Number: 2010926078

ISBN-13: 978-0-495-81118-3

ISBN-10: 0-495-81118-1

Wadsworth
20 Davis Drive
Belmont, CA 94002-3098
USA

Cengage Learning is a leading provider of customized learning solutions with office locations around the globe, including Singapore, the United Kingdom, Australia, Mexico, Brazil and Japan. Locate your local office at **www.cengage.com/global**

Cengage Learning products are represented in Canada by Nelson Education, Ltd.

For your course and learning solutions, visit **www.cengage.com**

Purchase any of our products at your local college store or at our preferred online store **www.cengagebrain.com**

Printed in the United States of America
1 2 3 4 5 6 7 14 13 12 11 10

To William Epstein,
whose target article approach to teaching research
methods inspired this manual

ABOUT THE AUTHOR

WILLIAM LANGSTON is a professor of psychology at Middle Tennessee State University. He has a bachelor's degree in psychology from the University of Houston and a Ph.D. in psychology from the University of Wisconsin–Madison. His graduate minor was in computer science. His teaching interests include research methods, cognitive psychology, human factors, the psychology of language, and science and pseudoscience in psychology.

Langston has published papers in a number of research journals in the areas of memory and language. He is a member of the Psychonomic Society, the Association for Psychological Science, APA Division 2—The Society for the Teaching of Psychology, the Society for Text and Discourse, and the Society for Personality and Social Psychology.

BRIEF CONTENTS

CONTENTS

PART **2** **Experimental Designs   91**

PREFACE

I wrote this manual to fill a need. There are plenty of textbooks for research methods classes. However, there are few options for textbooks in the laboratory. In my experience, students work at least as hard on their independent research in the laboratory as they work in the classroom. This manual is designed to help them with their laboratory work.

FEATURES FOR STUDENTS

This book offers several exciting features for students:

1. Each chapter is based on a target article that is a very good example of how the methodology in that chapter should be used. Students learn by seeing how some of the top people in the field have addressed similar questions.
2. The projects are educational. Several of the projects in the manual have been presented by students at regional conferences.
3. The chapters include a variety of project types. Students can conduct research in the laboratory or in the real world, using computers, paper and pencil, or observation sheets.
4. Most of what a student needs to conduct research is here in the manual. Students can focus more of their attention on asking (and answering) interesting questions and less on tracking down materials.

FEATURES FOR INSTRUCTORS

The book also offers exciting features for instructors:

1. All of the "big" design types for psychology research have been included (observation designs, surveys, and experiments). Instructors do not have to restrict their laboratory projects to experimental designs.

2. Whereas the topics chosen for this edition relate to the themes of skepticism and pseudoscience, many of the content areas in psychology have been sampled for projects (social psychology, personality, clinical psychology, cognition, perception). Students do not have to be future cognitive psychologists to find a project that interests them in this manual.

3. The appendixes cover getting approval for projects from institutional review boards, writing results sections, and presenting research. These topics help students overcome major roadblocks in their research projects; the manual is designed to walk students through each step.

4. Even though the manual offers a variety of potential projects, there is a common core that reduces the instructor's burden of supervising several totally unrelated projects simultaneously. Instructors can branch out from the areas they know best without tackling a major research project of their own.

5. Because of the variety of designs, students can rehearse their knowledge of all of the analyses covered in introductory statistics (from chi-square to factorial ANOVA).

6. Ethics notes remind students of the ethical rules in research and highlight situations where those rules may affect how research is conducted. Methodology notes highlight features of target articles and the methodological issues associated with the projects. Science notes highlight issues from the philosophy of science as they relate to real research questions.

FOR BOTH INSTRUCTORS AND STUDENTS

You can use this manual in one of two ways. If you have a methodology in mind (for example, "I want to do a survey"), then turn to the chapter covering that methodology. If you can choose any methodology, pick a topic that you like. If none of my project ideas interests you, the materials are generally flexible enough to let you strike out on your own. Here are some additional suggestions for how to use this manual:

1. The organization is the same for each chapter. A basic methodology is introduced, a target article that used that methodology is described, and projects are suggested. Some of the users of this book will need to pick a project topic early in the course, probably before any of the methodologies have been described. If that is the case for you, then start by choosing a topic that you like, and read the entire chapter related to that topic. The opening section should tell you enough about the method to help you understand the target article, which should help you decide if the topic is really right for you. If you have already read about a methodology before choosing a topic, skip the opening section. Your instructor and your textbook will already have prepared you to understand the target article (of course, it can never hurt to go over the basics one more time).

2. A large number of projects are suggested for each target article. Some of these are directly related to the studies in the target article; some are more

distantly related. Many of them have been tried by students in my classes. I will tell you up front that not all of the projects will "work." Some of the ideas go beyond the safe area where we know what the results will be. That is what makes them interesting. If you are concerned about conducting a project that does not provide the result you expect, stick to the first couple of suggestions in each chapter. If you are feeling brave, look farther down the list.

3. The suggested projects are in no way intended to limit what you do. Most of my students create projects that are similar to some of the suggestions but are not specifically the same as any one of them. The risks are higher if you do this, and you will work a little harder, but there is the potential to uncover a new fact about psychology.

CHANGES IN THE THIRD EDITION

- This manual was updated throughout to reflect the new edition of the *APA Publication Manual.*
- All new target articles were selected. All of the articles have a consistent theme related to pseudoscience and belief in the paranormal. The target articles still cover content from many subdisciplines within psychology.
- All of the suggested projects are new.
- Methodology sections were updated and revised.
- A new chapter was added for single-subject designs and more correlation research chapters were added.
- "Science Notes" highlight issues from the philosophy of science related to psychology research.
- Special comprehension check methodology notes at the end of each design description help students evaluate their understanding of the design.
- New Appendixes on evaluating sources and discriminating science from pseudoscience were added.

ACKNOWLEDGMENTS

My thanks to all of the students who have tested the projects that appear in the manual. Also, thank you to the reviewers of the second edition (Julie Feldman, Richard Beans, and Robert Weathersby) whose careful reading and valuable suggestions have greatly improved the quality of this manual as it transitioned to the third edition. The final version of this manual is much better due to the reviewers' efforts.

I would also like to acknowledge the incredible production team who made the finished book what it is. I was lucky to have the services of Dewanshu Ranjan and his team at PreMediaGlobal. I would also like to thank Pattie Stechschulte for copy editing and Jessica Egbert for her work in marketing.

Thanks also to the faculty at the University of Wisconsin–Madison, who instilled in me a love of methodology to go with my love of psychology and to my family for making it all possible.

William Langston

Single-Subject, Observation, Survey, and Correlation Research

The research techniques in Part 1 all involve measuring behavior or opinions without manipulating anything. Single-subject designs allow for careful study of one or a small number of participants. With naturalistic observation, the researcher observes what happens without intervening. With survey research, the researcher asks questions of participants. Correlation research is used to find relationships using observation or survey techniques.

CHAPTER 1

Single-Subject Designs

The elevator comes faster if I turn my back to it

Abstract

Psychology: The development of superstitious behavior is of interest to psychologists for a variety of reasons. For example, magical thinking can be used to predict and understand what people will do in a variety of contexts (see Chapter 11 for a discussion). Also, some forms of magical thinking have been associated with potential psychological problems (more information on this topic is presented in Chapter 5).

Skeptic/Pseudoscience: As a form of paranormal belief, understanding the development of superstition is of interest.

INTRODUCTION: SINGLE-SUBJECT DESIGNS

As you study psychology research methods you will discover that much psychology research is geared toward **nomothetic explanation** (describing people in general terms, usually based on group averages) as opposed to **ideographic explanation** (a detailed analysis of the behavior of an individual). For example, Lachman, Lachman, and Butterfield (1979) described nomothetic explanation as one of the fundamental commitments of cognitive psychology (along with empiricism and laboratory research, p. 39). However, there are benefits to a detailed analysis of a single case. For example, Ray (2009) used the case of H. M. (a patient who had his hippocampus removed as part of a surgery to control epileptic seizures) as an example of the value of single-subject designs. Data from a careful study of H. M.'s memory deficits as a result of his surgery were used to discourage future surgeries that involved damage to the hippocampus. It was not necessary to collect data from a large number of patients to reach the conclusion that the hippocampus plays an important role in forming new memories.

On the surface, it might seem that single-subject designs are most appropriate for situations in which detailed analysis of an individual is desired, rather than for making contributions to generalizable knowledge. However, it is possible to generalize from one case (or a small number of cases). A better way to think of the difference between single-subject designs and the other designs in this book is breadth versus depth. When detailed information about a phenomenon is what is desired, a careful analysis of one participant is appropriate.

In a way, the name single-subject design is misleading. Many studies using single-subject designs actually have more than one participant (as will the target article for this chapter). In fact, Ray (2009) suggested that the name small-N designs could be substituted for single-subject designs. The main difference between single-subject designs and other designs is that the data from individual participants are not averaged together (Ray).

As an example of a single-subject design, consider Haydon, Mancil, and Van Loan (2009). They were interested in the relationship between student opportunities to respond during a lesson and the performance of students with behavior disorders (acting out in class). The hypothesis was that providing students with more opportunities to respond would increase the amount of time they spent on task and would decrease the number of disruptive behaviors.

Haydon et al. (2009) identified the student in a class with the greatest number of behavior problems, and focused on that student for their research. In the beginning of the study, they observed the teacher's normal instruction. In the second phase, the teacher increased his rate of questions to at least three per minute. During this phase, the students were instructed to use choral responding (the entire class answered the question together). In a final phase, the teacher returned to his normal teaching practice.

At this point, we can ask ourselves what the advantages are of using a single-subject design in this kind of project. We can break these down into two sorts: pragmatic concerns and research concerns. On the pragmatic side, this kind of research is extremely difficult to conduct. First, a student-teacher pair had to be identified. Then, the teacher had to be trained in the technique used in the study. A detailed record of everything that happened in the classroom during the study period had to be made. Finally, the data for each of the target behaviors and the teacher's behavior had to be compiled from that record. Even with a single-subject design, the scheduling of observations (and the way they overlapped with the school calendar) prevented the authors from implementing the entire design as they would have liked. It would be difficult to collect data from a large sample. From the research concern perspective, this design provides much richer data than could be collected with other methods.

The data from Haydon et al. (2009) were compelling. First, the teacher was able to increase the number of questions he was asking to three per minute during the study period. During that phase of the study, the student's rate of disruptive behaviors changed from 1.90 per minute to 0.25 per minute. They increased to 2.00 per minute when the teacher returned to his normal instruction. At the same time, the student's on-task behavior went from approximately 35% of the time to 67%, and then returned to 38% when the teacher returned to normal instruction. Finally, the student's rate of correct responding went from 0.025 to 0.90 and then back to 0.20.

I should point out that the way that I have presented the data in the preceding paragraph is not in keeping with the single-subject approach. The value of the approach is in the details, and these are obscured by averaging. Looking at the graphs (in the original article) from the four baseline observations, the four observations during the treatment phase, and the four post-treatment observations provides a different perspective on the data. For example, with respect to disruptions, the student produced more in the baseline phase, but her performance was also highly variable. This could be a function of the degree to which the material held her attention. During the treatment phase, not only were there fewer disruptions, there was also less variability. The pattern for correct responding was also informative. During the treatment phase the student did increase her level of correct responding in a way that is very obvious from looking at the graph. However, her rate was declining during the treatment phase, and continued to decline in a consistent way into the post-treatment phase. It may be that the treatment was initially effective and the student then lost interest in the new method and started to return to baseline, or it may be that the treatment phase would have shown a continued increase in correct responding had it been carried on for more observation periods. This kind of information about patterns, and the impact that it has on the interpretation of the results, is obscured by focusing on averages.

One of the primary difficulties with single-subject designs is generalizing the results. As Haydon et al. (2009) pointed out, the data show that increasing opportunities to respond was effective for a first-year teacher with a fifth grade student, but it may not be effective in other situations. Given that their research replicated similar findings in other contexts, this may not be a significant problem. In general, however, concerns about how representative one person (or a small number of people) is of the general population will need to be addressed when single-subject designs are used. Speaking more broadly, this is a problem for **external validity** (the extent to which the results of a research project generalize to a population). One goal of research is to maximize external validity to increase the value of the data.

Another kind of validity is **internal validity** (related to the methodological quality of the study). This is also an issue for single-subject designs. To evaluate why, let us take as an example the simplest possible single-subject design, the one-shot case study. In this design, a single subject (or small group) is identified, given some sort of treatment, and then measured to determine if that treatment had an effect (Campbell & Stanley, 1963). Campbell and Stanley did not consider these designs to be of much use in research: "such studies have such a total absence of control as to be of almost no scientific value" (p. 6). The reason boils down to comparison. With nothing to compare to, how can the results of one-shot case studies be meaningful? Campbell and Stanley were particularly concerned about researchers making comparisons to hypothetical data that might have been found had a different treatment (or no treatment) been provided. Why is a comparison of some sort so important?

Campbell and Stanley (1963) listed seven specific confounds that are always of concern to researchers. You can think of confounds as uncontrolled sources of variation. If something in a study is changing (besides the treatment), it will be hard to decide whether the results were caused by the treatment or the confound (the thing that is changing along with the treatment). The seven confounds identified by Campbell and Stanley were:

1. History: What happens during the study (besides the manipulation of a treatment). This is the classic confound: Something that covaries with the treatment (e.g., changes in a regular way as the value of the treatment changes) and that could be expected to affect the results in the way the treatment would.
2. Maturation: There could be regular changes in the participants that affect the outcome of the study, but have nothing to do with the treatment.
3. Testing: Taking a test may, in and of itself, change performance on a subsequent test. For example, students may learn the procedure for taking the test, and that familiarity with the testing procedure could improve their performance, independent of the treatment.
4. Instrumentation: The instrument used to measure performance could change over time, making it look as though the treatment were having an effect. This is especially problematic with human observers coding the data because their familiarity with the coding system, boredom, etc., could affect the results.
5. Statistical regression: The basic phenomenon is that extreme scores tend to be less extreme when they are measured a second time. If participants are chosen on the basis of their extreme scores, a reasonable prediction would be that their scores would be less extreme on their next measurement, regardless of treatment.
6. Selection: Choosing different types of participants to receive different treatments could bias the results before any data are collected.
7. Mortality: If participants drop out of the study, and more participants drop out of one group than another, how does a researcher know that the different drop-out rates did not cause the result (instead of the treatment)?

Appropriate comparison groups allow researchers to evaluate the effects of these confounds on the data. It is completely out of line to do this (Campbell & Stanley, 1963, state as a footnote to their Table 1 that "it is with extreme reluctance that these summary tables are presented because they are apt to be 'too helpful' and to be depended upon in place of the more complex and qualified presentation in the text," p. 8), but a careful review of Campbell and Stanley's Table 1 shows how comparison groups allow researchers to get a handle on confounds.

Looking at Campbell and Stanley's (1963) "pre-experimental designs" section, one sees that adding a pretest to the one-shot case study allows a researcher some control over some of the confounds, but not others. For example, Campbell and Stanley placed a "+" under selection for the one-group pretest-posttest design. The reason for this is that the posttest results can be compared to the pretest results. If the researcher selected a group of partici-pants because they would do well on the posttest, that group would also do well on the pretest, and there would be no difference between the pretest and the posttest, showing that the treatment had no effect. In the one-shot case study, on the other hand, if the researcher selected participants who were likely to do well on the posttest (this biased selection is usually made without conscious intent to produce fraudulent results), the data would suggest that the treatment was effective. Without a comparison to a pretest, there would be no way to know that participants would have done well without the treatment.

Adding a control group (the static-group comparison design) allows for a handle on a complementary set of confounds. For example, Campbell and Stanley (1963) placed a "+" under history. By having a control group, it is possible to rule out changes besides the treatment. For example, if something happened at a school during a study, and that caused an improvement in per-formance, a person using a one-shot case study or a one-group pretest-posttest design would not be able to tell that that event changed the results (it would look like a treatment effect). However, with a control group, both groups would be affected by the confound, both would improve, and there would be no difference between the treatment and control groups.

Adding elements to the research design provides a way to minimize the effects of confounds on the data. As we will see in Part 2 of this book, experi-mental designs are one way to do this. Another way is to use quasi-experimental designs that allow a certain degree of control in settings in which experimental designs are not possible, but that also lack certain prop-erties of true experiments. Haydon et al. (2009) actually used a quasi-experiment design (under the general heading of single-subject designs). They used an equivalent time-samples (or reversal) design, in which they took mul-tiple measurements of the behaviors of interest, introduced a treatment, and took multiple measures, and then withdrew the treatment and measured again. This design allowed for some control over confounds. For example, in order to argue that a history confound caused the results (e.g., more time on task during the treatment phase), it would be necessary to identify a variable that changed at the same time treatment was introduced and then returned to its original value at the same time treatment was withdrawn. Using this type of a design, a researcher can make this possibility increasingly unlikely by in-troducing and withdrawing treatment multiple times (in fact, Haydon et al. would have liked to reintroduce the treatment, but they ran out of time).

We can sum up the section on internal validity by considering how to as-sess the internal validity of a study. First, I want to emphasize that the design chosen is not, in and of itself, a determining factor (e.g., an experiment can still have low internal validity if it is poorly conducted). However, the first consid-eration is to evaluate the extent to which the design chosen allowed researchers to at least measure the impact of confounds on the data. The second consider-ation is the amount of experimental control. For example, Haydon et al. (2009) were concerned that whereas they controlled the teacher's performance in the treatment phase very carefully, they did not control what he did during

METHODOLOGY NOTE **1.1**

As a check on your comprehension consider the following research situation. A researcher wants to evaluate the effectiveness of various tutoring methods on performance. The researcher is unsure which type of design would be more appropriate to address the research question. One approach would be to average performance for an entire class using each of the tutoring methods. A different approach would be to use a single-subject design to evaluate the tutoring methods. What would be the advantages of doing this research as a single-subject design? What possible disadvantages are there to using a single-subject design in this research? After you have considered these questions, you can check Madrid, Canas, and Ortega-Medina (2007) to see how they addressed these issues using a single-subject design.

the pretest and posttest periods, which may affect the internal and external validity. The final step in evaluating internal validity is to carefully think about the confounds with respect to the particular study being evaluated. Some studies will have more serious concerns with some confounds than others, and it will be most productive to focus on the relevant confounds as you evaluate your degree of confidence in any set of data. For example, mortality is not an issue for Haydon et al. since they only had one participant. The design they chose also reduced the extent to which history confounds would be a concern (although you should consider whether some history confound is possible, e.g., a change in the topic being covered). On the other hand, there may have been an instrumentation confound. The raters (who scored the student's behavior) might have been aware of which phase of the experiment they were rating, and that might have had an effect on the results. As you read a research report, you would want to look closely for how the researcher controlled any confounds that might have been present in the study.

Our target article for this chapter used a single-subject design to evaluate whether or not accidental reinforcement could lead to the development of superstitious behavior.

TARGET ARTICLE: SUPERSTITION

(Be sure to look at Appendix D to assist you in evaluating the sources cited in this chapter. Be especially aware of the guidelines for evaluating Internet and other non-peer reviewed sources.)

When I was in graduate school, one of the secretaries insisted that the elevators in the psychology building would come faster if you turned your back on them. In fact, if you were waiting for the elevator with her and you were looking at the elevators, she would ask you to turn around so that you would not slow them down. Obviously, the elevators did not "know" which direction the people waiting on them were facing, and that could not have affected the time it took for an elevator to arrive. Given that, how could such a behavior arise?

Many people engage in superstitious behavior. Vyse (1997) described research showing that 63% of adults have at least one superstition. People may vary in the extent to which they believe that their superstitious behaviors actually influence events. However, people may also be unwilling to forgo those behaviors and "take a chance." As Vyse pointed out, if the cost of doing the superstitious behavior is relatively small compared to the outcomes (either benefit from doing it or loss from not doing it), then most people would feel it was safer to go ahead with the behavior.

The general topic of superstition is large (e.g., Vyse, 1997), and overlaps with many of the topics covered in this book (for example, Chapter 11 will explicitly return to another aspect of superstitious behavior). For this chapter, I am going to narrowly focus on only one aspect of superstition: How might a superstitious behavior develop? I am also going to focus on just one answer to that question: A superstitious behavior might develop through the coincidental reinforcement of that behavior. For example, the secretary who turns her back on the elevator may have turned around for some reason (e.g., in response to a noise on the street behind her), and at just that moment the elevator may have opened. Once the link was established, she may have either coincidentally or intentionally turned around on other occasions, providing additional opportunities for reinforcement. Since the elevator always comes, once this behavior was established, it would always be reinforced. This is one of those superstitions that has little to no cost to perform, with a reasonably important outcome (less wait time), so why not?

Our target article, Skinner (1948), investigated the "coincidental reinforcement" hypothesis. Skinner's participants were pigeons, and the design of his study was relatively simple. During training sessions, each pigeon was placed in a cage. A food hopper was presented to the pigeons for five seconds at a fixed interval (every 15 seconds). The main feature of the design was that the presentation of the food was unrelated to whatever the pigeon happened to be doing (contrasted with more traditional operant conditioning designs in which a particular behavior, e.g., a peck, is required to get a food reinforcer).

This arrangement allowed the pigeons to develop "superstitious" responses. If they happened to be doing something when the food was made available, they could form an association between that behavior and the food. Depending on the delay until the next presentation of the food and how long they continued the behavior, a pigeon could get several reinforcements for a behavior that was originally exhibited by chance, and gradually increase the likelihood of repeating that behavior, as if the pigeon expected the behavior to influence the likelihood of getting the food.

Skinner (1948) found that six of his eight pigeons did develop a "superstitious" behavior in this situation. For example, one turned circles in the cage. Skinner interpreted these results as a way to explain superstitious behavior in people. For example, a bowler who continues to twist and turn as the ball rolls down the lane cannot actually influence the path of the ball, but might have been reinforced for doing so with successful hits. (See Staddon, 1992, and

Staddon & Simmelhag, 1971, for critiques of Skinner's study and explanation for the data)

Ono (1987) modified Skinner's (1948) task for human participants. He presented his participants with a booth that had three levers, a light, and a counter. Their goal was to get points on the counter. Specifically, participants were told, "The experimenter does not require you to do anything specific. But if you do something, you may get points on the counter. Now try to get as many points as possible" (p. 263). The counter added points on various reinforcement schedules, but the points were not associated with anything the participants were doing. Ono found that 3 of his 20 participants developed "superstitious" behaviors. For example, one participant was eventually jumping up to touch the ceiling with her slipper. Ono took his results to mean that humans can be conditioned to develop superstitious behaviors, but the rate is low.

One possible explanation for low rates of the development of superstitious behavior was proposed by Brugger and Graves (1997). Their hypothesis was that participants who scored high on a measure of magical thinking would test fewer hypotheses and would believe more hypotheses in a superstition-inducing task than participants who scored low on magical ideation. In other words, they expected individual differences in the likelihood of developing superstitions in this kind of study.

Brugger and Graves' (1997) task was to navigate a mouse through a grid to some cheese. If participants took longer than 4 seconds, they got the cheese. If they took less than 4 seconds, they got trapped. Brugger and Graves gave their participants 13 possible hypotheses that they might have considered to contribute to whether or not they got cheese (including the true one that time mattered), and asked them how many they tried. Brugger and Graves also asked their participants how many hypotheses were likely to contribute to whether or not the mouse got cheese. Therefore, they were able to test how many hypotheses participants considered and how many they accepted. Note that this is a different procedure from Ono (1987) in that Brugger and Graves were able to connect their participants' behavior to their participants' belief that it actually affected the results. For example, Ono's slipper-tapper might have just been filling time until the next reinforcement, and might not have believed that tapping her slipper to the ceiling actually affected the outcome.

Brugger and Graves (1997) found that their high magical ideation participants tested fewer hypotheses than their low magical ideation participants, and that these participants believed in more hypotheses that they had not tested than the low magical ideation group. Only 2 participants (of 40) actually figured out that time was all that mattered. The other 38 developed some form of superstition (in the sense that they believed something affected the outcome that did not). In spite of this, participants were able to learn in the task, improving over time.

At this point we have data that "superstitious" behaviors can arise due to accidental contingencies, that this can happen in people (but at a low rate), and that some individual difference measure (magical ideation) might account for why some people are more likely than others to develop superstitious behaviors. In the projects section, you will have an opportunity to use single-subject designs to investigate the development of superstitious behavior for yourself.

INFOTRAC® COLLEGE EDITION EXERCISES

You can use the InfoTrac College Edition to read about single-subject designs. Using the search string "single subject designs" with the boxes "in citation, title, abstract" and "to refereed publications" checked gave me a list of eight articles. One of these was Swain and Jones (1995). Their research investigated the effectiveness of goal-setting for improving the performance of basketball players, and they specifically discussed the advantages of using single-subject designs for this type of research. They also pointed out that single-subject designs could increase Hawthorne effects (that people try harder in research because they know they are being studied). If you vary the search string or parameters for your own searches, you can find additional information on single-subject designs. In general, reading the method sections of other people's research can be helpful as you plan your own study.

You can also use the InfoTrac College Edition to explore research about superstition. I found that typing in "psychology of superstition" (with the same boxes checked as previous) produced a list of seven articles. You could vary the search string and parameters of my search to find additional information.

IMPLEMENTING THE DESIGN

Materials

The primary material you will need is an experimental set-up that has a variety of irrelevant controls and some reward that is presented on a fixed schedule, independent of behavior. You will probably need to create this set-up yourself. In the literature (e.g., Ono, 1987) a careful record was kept of what the participants did, but out of the three participants in Ono's study who developed a superstitious behavior, one of them developed a behavior that was not recorded by the apparatus (tapping the ceiling with her slipper). You could evaluate whether or not superstitious behaviors occur by watching participants or by videotaping them for later analysis, and then looking for stereotypic patterns of responding. In other words, you would not need an expensive and highly technical recording device. You could also probably set up a regular reinforcement schedule without expensive equipment. For example, my cell phone alarm can be set to provide a "reward message" every minute.

To replicate aspects of Brugger and Graves (1997) you will need the magical ideation scale (Eckblad & Chapman, 1983) to divide participants based on magical ideation.

Suggested Projects

1. You could replicate aspects of Skinner's (1948) experiment. However, you would substitute human participants and change the experimental set-up as Ono (1987) did.
   a. One variable that Skinner (1948) expected to matter was the duration between reinforcements. He hypothesized that if it were too long, participants might not develop a superstitious behavior (the probability of getting a coincident reinforcement would be too low).

You could manipulate the interval in your project to see if this is the case.

    b. Keinan (2002) found that under stress (before an important exam), participants were more likely to engage in superstitious behavior. In particular, "knock wood" questions (e.g., "have you ever been involved in a fatal road accident?" p. 104) elicited more actual knocking on wood when students were stressed. If participants are more likely to engage in superstitious behavior when they are stressed, are they also more likely to develop superstitious behaviors when they are stressed? You could manipulate stress as Keinan did (e.g., test participants shortly before an exam) and see if more superstitious behavior results.

    c. Risen and Gilovich (2008) investigated participants' thoughts about "tempting fate." For example, participants rated how likely it would be for them to be called on by the professor in a large lecture class if they had not done the required reading. Participants rated not doing the reading as making it more likely that they would be called on (they tempted fate). In their Study 6, Risen and Gilovich added cognitive load to the task. Some participants had to count backwards by 3s from 564. Even more participants endorsed the "tempting fate by not reading is dangerous" hypothesis under load than those who were not counting backwards. Risen and Gilovich interpreted this as the operation of two-system processing. One system works fast and is subject to "irrational" influences, but usually works. However, a more rational second system can evaluate the output of the first system if it appears to be in error. In the case of superstitions, students can use the second system to edit the first system's response that being called on is more likely if they did not do the reading. Under cognitive load, the second system is interfered with, and "superstitious" thinking goes up. You could design a project to see if cognitive load increases the development of superstitious behaviors. Basically, will more superstitious behaviors occur when participants are counting backwards?

2. You could also follow Brugger and Graves' (1997) lead and investigate individual differences in susceptibility to the development of superstitions.

    a. Using your own task or creating a version of Brugger and Graves' (1997) task (again actual measurement of performance on the task is not necessary; the important dependent variables are the number of hypotheses tried and the number believed to be operating), evaluate the effect of magical ideation on the development of superstitious behavior.

    b. Other individual differences might also affect the formation of superstitious behavior. For example, Rudski and Edwards (2007) found that as need for control increased (e.g., the task being performed was more important), so did the use of superstitions. If you used a measure of intrinsic need for control in your participants, would the ones with a higher need for control be more likely to develop superstitious behavior?

REFERENCES

Brugger, P., & Graves, R. E. (1997). Testing vs. believing hypotheses: Magical ideation in the judgment of contingencies. *Cognitive Neuropsychiatry, 2,* 251–272. doi:10.1080/135468097396270

Campbell, D. T., & Stanley, J. C. (1963). *Experimental and Quasi-Experimental Designs for Research.* Chicago: Rand McNally.

Eckblad, M., & Chapman, L. J. (1983). Magical ideation as an indicator of schizotypy. *Journal of Consulting and Clinical Psychology, 51,* 215–225. doi:10.1037/0022-006X.51.2.215

Haydon, T., Mancil, G. R., & Van Loan, C. (2009). Using opportunities to respond in a general education classroom: A case study. *Education and Treatment of Children, 32,* 267–278. doi:10.1353/etc.0.0052

Lachman, R., Lachman, J. L., & Butterfield, E. C. (1979). *Cognitive psychology and information processing: An introduction.* Hillsdale, NJ: Lawrence Erlbaum Associates, Inc.

Keinan, G. (2002). The effects of stress and desire for control on superstitious behavior. *Personality and Social Psychology Bulletin, 28,* 102–108. doi:10.1177/0146167202281009

Madrid, L. D., Canas, M., & Ortega-Medina, M. (2007). Effects of team competition versus team cooperation in classwide peer tutoring. *Journal of Educational Research, 100,* 155–160. doi:10.3200/JOER.100.3.155-160

Ono, K. (1987). Superstitious behavior in humans. *Journal of the Experimental Analysis of Behavior, 47,* 261–271. doi:10.1901/jeab.1987.47-261

Ray, W. J. (2009). *Methods toward a science of behavior and experience* (9th Ed.). Belmont, CA: Wadsworth.

Risen, J. L., & Gilovich, T. (2008). Why people are reluctant to tempt fate. *Journal of Personality and Social Psychology, 95,* 293–307. doi:10.1037/0022-3514.95.2.293

Rudski, J. M., & Edwards, A. (2007). Malinowski goes to college: Factors influencing students' use of ritual and superstition. *The Journal of General Psychology, 134,* 389–403. doi:10.3200/GENP.134.4.389-404

Skinner, B. F. (1948). 'Superstition' in the pigeon. *Journal of Experimental Psychology, 38,* 168–172. doi:10.1037/h0055873

Staddon, J. E. R. (1992). The "superstition" experiment: A reversible figure. *Journal of Experimental Psychology: General, 121,* 270–272. doi:10.1037/0096-3445.121.3.270

Staddon, J. E. R., & Simmelhag, V. L. (1971). The 'superstition' experiment: A reexamination of its implications for the principles of adaptive behavior. *Psychological Review, 78,* 3–43. doi:10.1037/h0030305

Swain, A., & Jones, G. (1995). Effects of goal-setting interventions on selected basketball skills: A single-subject design. *Research Quarterly for Exercise and Sport, 66,* 51–63.

Vyse, S. A. (1997). *Believing in magic: The psychology of superstition.* New York: Oxford University Press.

Observation Research

Stop looking at me like that

Abstract

Psychology: Most people feel that they can tell when someone is staring at them, even if they cannot see that person. However, the evidence for this ability is mixed, and there is no plausible physical mechanism to explain this ability. One possibility is that the belief comes from confirmation bias: People remember when they turned around and someone was looking at them, they forget times that nobody was looking.

Skeptic/Pseudoscience: The "evidence" for staring detection is readily available in the phenomenological experience. However, does it mean what it seems to mean? This topic provides us with an opportunity to think about the role of phenomenological experience in evaluating pseudoscience and paranormal claims.

INTRODUCTION: OBSERVING BEHAVIOR

What makes psychological research so difficult to conduct? Basically, the thing we are trying to study (the human psyche) is not available for direct observation. You cannot open the top of a person's head and peer inside to find out about emotions, motivations, thought processes, or disorders. Instead, we observe behavior and use that to make inferences about the parts that cannot be observed.

One type of behavioral observation is to ask people what they are thinking or why they do what they do. Some psychological research is done using this technique (and we will see how in Chapters 3–6). A problem with this approach is that people often do not know why they do what they do or how they do what they do. Sometimes, people know why they do what they do, but social forces make them uncomfortable admitting their true motivation, and so they lie when asked.

When we are concerned that asking people about psychological activity will not yield useful information, we can observe people's behavior and use

15

that to infer their underlying motivations. The simplest way to do this is to use a technique called **naturalistic observation**. Basically, you observe what happens in a situation without the participants knowing that they are being observed. The observer does not intervene in the situation in any way. If you are a very careful observer of human behavior, and you record all of the events that transpire, you may be able to discover relationships that suggest the operation of underlying psychological variables.

One thing you have to be careful about when collecting observations is that you do not interfere with the situation. When you intervene, you can no longer be sure that the behavior you are observing is the same as the behavior that would normally be present.

Consider this example from an article in *Reader's Digest* (Ecenbarger, 1998). The title was "America's Worst Drivers," and the author went to various cities to see how badly people drive. In Boston, the author investigated people's reactions at a traffic circle by driving around it. The official policy at traffic circles is that incoming cars yield to cars in the circle. As the author described it, the first time around there were no problems, but after two or three laps, "things started happening." The "things" were that people started cutting in and getting hostile. Maybe people in Boston are hostile at traffic circles, but it is hard to separate that from people's hostility toward cars that just circle without turning anywhere. Crossing the line from naturalistic observation to participating in the event can make it difficult to interpret your results.

What can we learn from observation? The main thing is that we can uncover relationships that exist between behaviors and environmental variables. We can make statements like "if this event happens, a person is likely to respond in this way." We *cannot* say that a particular environmental event will cause a particular behavior. To make cause-and-effect statements will require an experiment (using techniques covered in Part 2). We also cannot say for certain that people will have a particular psychological reaction to a particular environmental event. However, based on their behavior, we can infer something about their mental state that led to the behavior.

ETHICS NOTE **2.1**

If you have already learned about research ethics, you might wonder how we can observe people without their permission, given that research participants should give informed consent before the research begins. Two factors are usually considered when deciding whether observational research is ethical. The first has to do with whether the observer is in any way involved in the situation. As long as people are acting in a public place and engaging in behaviors they would have engaged in whether the observer was present or not, it is usually considered acceptable to observe them. The second factor has to do with anonymity. Provided that the first concern is satisfied, if there is no way that any individual participant could be identified as having participated, the observation will probably be acceptable.

METHODOLOGY NOTE **2.1**

When collecting data, two kinds of validity are important. **Internal validity** has to do with the quality of the study. **External validity** has to do with how well the results will generalize to a larger population. Often, these two kinds of validity compete. To maximize internal validity a researcher needs to take control of the situation. To maximize external validity a researcher will try to collect data under conditions that approximate those in the real world. Increasing control necessarily makes conditions more artificial, hurting external validity. Giving up control to make conditions more natural hurts internal validity. Note that observation research errs on the side of maximizing external validity.

Why do observation research? There are three big reasons:

1. *To find out if relationships exist.* Observation research requires careful preparation and can be difficult to carry out, but it is simpler in some ways than doing surveys or experiments. Before investing time and resources in a project to find out why people respond in certain ways to certain events, it is always a good idea to find out if a relationship exists to be studied.
2. *Because observation designs are more natural.* Nothing could be less intrusive than naturalistic observation. Researchers use observation techniques to avoid **participant reactivity** (people act differently because they know they are being observed). This problem might be worse in psychology than in other sciences because the people we observe sometimes make conscious decisions to change their behavior when they are concerned about how they will be perceived by the researcher.
3. *As a check on information collected using other techniques.* Sometimes a researcher will ask people about their behavior in various situations and

METHODOLOGY NOTE **2.2**

As a check on your comprehension, you should consider how to use observation research to address the following research questions. The first question is: What will influence people's decision to litter? Is the behavior of others important? Is the amount of litter already in the environment important? Can you measure the effects of these variables using naturalistic observation, or would it be necessary to intervene and "set up" the environment? How do your choices affect internal and external validity? To see how researchers have addressed these issues, check Cialdini, Reno, and Kallgren (1990). The second question is: Could a sign suggesting that climbing stairs provides health benefits increase the number of people taking the stairs? Again, is this question amenable to naturalistic observation, or would you need to intervene? What are the internal and external validity implications of your decisions? To see how researchers have addressed these issues with respect to stair climbing, check Auweele, Boen, Schapendonk, and Dornez (2005).

then observe them in those situations to see if their self-reports match up with reality. Or a researcher will confirm that behavior in the artificial laboratory environment is consistent with behavior in the real world.

Our target article for this chapter used an observation design to determine if people can detect that they are being stared at.

TARGET ARTICLE: STARING DETECTION

(Be sure to look at Appendix D to assist you in evaluating the sources cited in this chapter. Be especially aware of the guidelines for evaluating Internet and other non-peer reviewed sources.)

If you ask children how vision works, you will discover that a large number of them subscribe to extramission theories, the idea that something comes out of the eyes and contacts the world during vision (Cottrell & Winer, 1994). Cottrell and Winer highlighted the long philosophical and popular tradition supporting extramission beliefs (e.g., the notion that the eyes can shoot daggers). Cottrell and Winer found that belief in extramission declines as children age. For example, in their first study approximately 58% of sixth graders supported extramission, but only 10% of college students held these views.

Cottrell and Winer's (1994) results on extramission beliefs stand in sharp contrast to results for the belief that people can tell when someone out of their line of sight is staring at them. Cottrell, Winer, and Smith (1996) found that 94% of sixth graders felt that they could detect when someone was staring at them, and 91% felt that other people could detect when someone was staring at them. The interesting result came from the college students in their study; 89% felt that they could detect stares, and 88% felt that other people could detect stares. Even more surprising was the finding that there was actually a strengthening of belief in the ability to detect unseen stares as people aged (even though the overall percentage of people believing stayed about the same). Cottrell et al. also asked their participants about extramission beliefs (assuming that some substance coming from the eyes during staring would be necessary in order for a person to detect that staring), and replicated the finding that belief in extramission theories of vision declined from sixth grade to college. Furthermore, belief in extramission was not correlated with belief in the ability to detect an unseen stare.

These results are puzzling for a variety of reasons. Irrational beliefs generally decline as people mature (as with belief in extramission). Yet, belief in the ability to detect unseen stares increases (even as belief in extramission, a mechanism to explain the ability, declines). This raises two possibilities. The first is that people actually are able to detect stares, and their belief in the ability comes from experience. The second possibility is that people cannot detect unseen stares, but that some aspect of their experience, combined with psychology, is causing them to believe that they can. What do the data say?

One of the earliest reports on stare detection came from Titchener (1898). He noted that many of his students believed in the ability, but that his laboratory studies with people who felt they possessed the ability showed that they could not detect staring. Titchener did not provide details of his studies, but he did provide an account of why people might feel that they have the ability. Basically, in a crowd, people are uncomfortable having their backs turned on the people behind them. Occasionally, this nervousness causes them to turn around. By turning around, they catch the attention of people behind them, causing those people to look at them. At this point, the person turning around sees someone staring at them and connects that experience with the feeling of nervous tension that caused them to turn around in the first place. Over time, people accumulate more and more experiences of this phenomenon, and increase their belief in their ability to detect stares.

Coover (1913) followed up on Titchener's study. In two samples, 68% and 86% of his students felt that they could detect stares. Coover tested whether people actually had the ability. He sat behind a person and either stared at them or not (choosing randomly for each trial) and had his participants guess whether or not he was staring at them. In a sample of 10 people who thought they had the ability, with 100 trials each, Coover found an accuracy rate of 50.2%, not different from chance. Coover noted that his participants had a better chance of detecting stares than of identifying no-stare trials. However, the participants also had a bias to say "yes," which elevated their accuracy on stare trials (as an example of this, a person who said "yes" on every trial would get 100% correct on stare trials, but 0% correct on no-stare trials). Correcting for this bias showed that the results were at chance levels. Coover provided an additional explanation for why people might believe in an ability that they do not have: they pay attention to the times when they "catch" someone staring at them in response to the feeling of being stared at, and ignore times that nobody is staring. In other words, they have a confirmation bias.

Other researchers have had better success in their studies. Sheldrake has produced a mountain of data in favor of the hypothesis that people can detect when they are being stared at (Sheldrake 1998, 1999, 2000). His basic procedure is to have people work in pairs, one member of the pair stares or not on the basis of a random sequence, the other records whether or not staring is taking place. In studies with school children, participants at conferences, Sheldrake's family, and a variety of other people from many different countries using multiple variations on the basic procedure, Sheldrake has consistently found a small but reliable effect, ranging from around 53% to 57% correct overall (these data are summarized in Sheldrake, 2005a).

Sheldrake (2000, 2001a) has also corrected for possible artifacts in the data (e.g., cheating, changes in starer behavior on different kinds of trials), using various corrections for artifacts in different studies. In some conditions, he had starers look at starees through windows (the starers were inside, the starees were outside). He also had the starees wear blindfolds in some conditions. Some conditions involved feedback, some did not have feedback (Sheldrake, 2008, specifically evaluated the effect of feedback on performance). Other controls were also instituted. In all cases, Sheldrake found an effect of staring. Sheldrake, Overby, and Beeharee (2008) were able to extend these results to tests using an automated procedure over the Internet.

Sheldrake (1998, 1999) also reanalyzed Coover's (1913) data and concluded that Coover actually found a positive effect for detecting staring. Sheldrake (1998, 1999) classified Coover's participants as "+" (more correct than incorrect), "−" (more incorrect than correct), or "=" (same number correct and incorrect). By Sheldrake's (1998, 1999) reckoning, for stare trials there were 7 +, 2 −, and 2 = (note that this is not possible since there were only 10 participants, the correct numbers are 7 +, 2 −, and 1 =). For stare and non-stare trials taken together, Sheldrake found 5 +, 3 −, and 2 =. Since he did not count = participants, Sheldrake concluded that there were more participants who detected staring than who did not. Keep in mind, however, that Coover's participants had a bias to say "yes" and the only legitimate comparison is in the overall data. The binomial probability of 5 successes in 8 tries is .22, which is not significant.

An alternative approach to investigating stare detection is to look for subtle differences in physiological variables that occur during stare trials. Braud, Shafer, and Andrews (1993a) pioneered these methods for stare detection. Their goal was to see if the relatively small effects obtained in studies using conscious guessing as the dependent variable would be larger with a more sensitive dependent variable. In their study, participants were in a different room from the starer and were being stared at (or not) on a television screen. Participants were instructed not to consciously try to detect staring, but rather to relax and allow unconscious reactions to have an effect. Braud et al. (1993a) did find changes in skin conductance as a result of being stared at. One group of participants who were untrained (in a program to help them connect to other people) showed increased arousal, and a second group of trained participants showed decreased arousal when being stared at. Braud et al. (1993a) concluded that staring detection did occur, and that physiological arousal was a more sensitive measure of the phenomenon.

Braud, Shafer, and Andrews (1993b) followed up on the Braud et al. (1993a) study and replicated the effect that participants showed decreased arousal for stare trials. They also included a control condition in which no staring took place on "stare" trials, and found no effect. Schlitz and LaBerge (1997) were also able to replicate this effect (that stare trials produced changes in physiological activity), but they found increased arousal during stare trials.

As part of a larger program investigating direct mental interaction between living systems (DMILS; e.g., trying to cause someone to become physiologically aroused through mental effort), Schmidt, Schneider, Binder, Burkle, and Walach (2001) and Schmidt and Walach (2000) described methodological improvements designed to bring parapsychological investigations using physiological measures up to the state-of-the-art in the field. These two guides could be used to evaluate previous research investigating DMILS in general, and remote staring detection as a subpart of that larger phenomenon. Essentially, Schmidt, Schneider, Utts, and Walach (2004) did just that in a meta-analysis of the DMILS literature, and a separate meta-analysis of the stare detection literature. Meta-analysis is a technique to combine the results of multiple studies into a single analysis to get an overall view of a field. As part of their meta-analyses Schmidt, Schneider, Utts, et al. created a methodological quality score based on the experimental procedure, appropriate use of physiological measurements, and general methodological issues. For the DMILS literature, they found that greater methodological rigor was associated with lower effect sizes. In other words, "some of the reported effects might be due to methodological shortcomings"

(p. 241). They attempted to overcome this issue in two ways. One way was to weight the impact of each study on the final outcome by its quality (so a lower quality study had less impact on the final result). Based on this analysis, they found a significant DMILS effect. The second approach was to focus only on the best quality studies. This procedure produced a non-significant effect. Overall, Schmidt, Schnieder, Utts, et al. noted that their effect size (however calculated) was lower than previous reports, partially due to weighting based on quality, and partially due to the fact that newer studies were producing smaller effects than the initial studies in the field.

Our concern is more with Schmidt, Schnieder, Utts, et al.'s (2004) remote stare detection meta-analysis. For that set of studies, there was not a correlation between quality and effect size. There was a significant remote stare detection effect in the meta-analysis. However, there were fewer studies in this meta-analysis, and they were of lower overall quality when compared to the DMILS studies.

At this point trying to synthesize the results from physiological measures of stare detection research is difficult because there is a little something for everyone in the data. A skeptic could conclude that there is no effect. As the Schmidt, Schnieder, Utts, et al. (2004) review illustrated, poor quality studies were more likely to show an effect. With respect to stare detection, there were no high quality studies (no 100% studies on the methodology scale), so there are no data available to determine if the significant effect that has been found is likely due to study quality, or if it is real. Based on the DMILS analysis, a skeptic could conclude that as better quality studies are done the effect is likely to go away. On the other hand, a proponent (as Schmidt, Schnieder, Utts, et al. were) could conclude that the effects are real. There was an effect when all of the DMILS studies were combined (weighted by quality), and there was a similar effect in the remote stare detection literature. As Schmidt, Schnieder, Utts, et al. said, the remote staring literature validates their conclusion that the DMILS effect is real, and that the data from the smaller subset of best-practices studies are the ones to discount.

In fact, differences in researcher expectations extend beyond interpretation of the data to the data themselves. A hint of this problem is already evident in the review above. Coover (1913) adopted a skeptical stance and found no effect. Sheldrake (e.g., 1998) was a proponent of stare detection ability and found positive results. Wiseman and Schlitz (1997) explicitly tested for experimenter effects. Schlitz (as in Schlitz & LaBerge, 1997) is a proponent of paranormal phenomena and stare detection, and has produced positive results. Wiseman is a skeptic. Working together using the same methodology and the same population of participants, Wiseman and Schlitz found mixed results. Wiseman found no effect, Schlitz found increased arousal during stare trials. Schlitz, Wiseman, Watt, and Radin (2006) were unable to replicate this effect (there was no evidence of stare detection for either researcher), however they were able to replicate the effect in other collaborations (Wiseman & Schlitz, 1999, cited in Schlitz et al.). Lobach and Bierman (2004) in their Study 2 (undertaken from a skeptical perspective) also failed to find an effect of staring on arousal. Again, the existence of stare detection ability appears to be a function of who is collecting the data.

Lobach and Bierman (2004) also attempted to replicate Sheldrake's (e.g., 1998, 1999) staring detection results. In their Study 1, there was actually a hint of staring detection for the skeptic starers, but not for the believing starers (contrary to the standard direction of experimenter effects). Overall, the results were very close to chance, and the size of the effect was much smaller than in Sheldrake's studies. After consulting with Sheldrake to improve their methodology, Lobach and Bierman in their Study 3 attempted to investigate whether close friends would produce better stare detection than strangers. It would be difficult to say what to expect from this manipulation since previous research found arousal for strangers (suggesting that the threat from a stranger staring at you would increase the chance of feeling it), but other studies (e.g., Sheldrake, 2001a) have reported stronger detection for pairs of people who are related. In the case of Lobach and Bierman's Study 3, there was no evidence of any ability to detect staring, so there was not a resolution to this issue.

Colwell, Schroder, and Sladen (2000) also attempted to replicate Sheldrake's results. Colwell et al. found that there was evidence for stare detection if feedback was given, but that the ability to detect staring improved over trials. There was no stare detection in the first block of trials. Because Sheldrake's sequences were not random, Colwell et al. concluded that his positive data were caused by participants learning the structure in the sequences as feedback was given. In their Experiment 2, when the sequences were truly randomized, there was no staring effect. Baker (2000), also a skeptic, was unable to replicate Sheldrake's results when staring through a one-way mirror.

Marks and Colwell (2000) also summarized their results in *Skeptical Inquirer* and Sheldrake (2001b) responded. The crux of Sheldrake's response for Colwell et al.'s (2000) Experiment 2 data was that the starer may have been a skeptic, a proposal disputed by Marks and Colwell (2001). However, Lobach and Bierman's (2004) results suggested that skeptical starers might actually be more effective at finding an effect, so this potential confound should not have made much of a difference. In an effort to summarize this literature, it seems that the primary points of dispute boil down to whether there is structure in the random sequences used to control stare and non-stare trials, whether violations of randomness are being learned by participants with feedback, and how response bias (primarily a bias to say "yes") could be influencing the outcome of the studies. Skeptics claim the entire effect in Sheldrake's studies comes from these kinds of experimental artifact, but Sheldrake responds that the volume of studies and the various conditions used in his studies counteract the possibility that all of the data arise from artifacts. Marks and Colwell (2001) pointed out that most of the data presented by Sheldrake were collected in uncontrolled conditions (e.g., as part of school projects), and that these data cannot be relied upon to determine whether or not there is an effect. They emphasized that it is the quality of the data that matters, not the quantity.

It seems at this point that if there is an effect it is at least partially explained by the experimental procedure used to collect the data. As indicated by the meta-analysis of Schmidt, Schneider, Utts, et al. (2004) higher

SCIENCE NOTE **2.1**

In a situation like the one we find ourselves in with stare detection, it might be useful to consider some of the resources in Appendix E to evaluate the science behind the phenomenon. For example, Sheldrake's studies (summarized in Sheldrake, 2005a) call to mind several of the features of pathological science (Langmuir & Hall, 1989).

1. "The maximum effect that is observed is produced by a causative agent of barely detectable intensity, and the magnitude of the effect is substantially independent of the intensity of the cause" (Langmuir & Hall, 1989, p. 44). There is no dose-response effect in the staring detection literature. All of Sheldrake's conditions produced roughly the same size effect (some of these data are summarized in Table 1 of Sheldrake, 2005a). Greater distance between starer and staree, intervening objects, and transmitting stares over various distances through closed-circuit television all produced similar results. Most physical variables show a relationship between the amount of input and the amount of output.

2. "The effect is of a magnitude that remains close to the limit of detectability, or, many measurements are necessary because of the very low statistical significance of the results" (Langmuir & Hall, 1989, p. 44). Sheldrake's data (e.g., Sheldrake, 2005a) do not meet this criterion. In fact, he reports data that are highly significant. However, as methodological improvements are made, the size of the effect diminishes (in many cases it goes away entirely). Due to the presence of experimenter effects (e.g., some strong, some non-existent), we can give this criterion half of a point.

3. "There are claims of great accuracy" (Langmuir & Hall, 1989, p. 44). Sheldrake (2005a) makes the sorts of claims considered by Langmuir and Hall.

4. "Fantastic theories contrary to experience are suggested" (Langmuir & Hall, 1989, p. 44). The explanation for stare detection is inconsistent with known laws. There is nothing that comes out of the eyes during vision. A theory that depends on extramission has a fundamental problem to overcome. Even Sheldrake (2005b) says his morphic fields hypothesis cannot explain the results from closed-circuit television studies: "It is difficult to imagine that perceptual fields first link the observer to the TV screen then extend backwards through the circuitry of the monitor, out through the input wires, out through the camera, and then project through the camera lens to touch the person being observed" (p. 44).

5. "Criticisms are met by *ad hoc* excuses thought up on the spur of the moment" (Langmuir & Hall, 1989, p. 44). *Ad hoc* explanations are provided for inconsistent data in the stare detection literature (e.g., Lobach & Bierman 2004, failed to find an effect because participants were using computers to enter their responses which Sheldrake, 2005a, felt might be distracting when contrasted to blindfolded participants, even though Sheldrake, 1998, did not have his participants wear

(continues)

Science Note **2.1** *(continued)*

blindfolds). Also, some of the *ad hoc* explanations undermine other aspects of the argument. Sheldrake (1999) proposed that the sense of being stared at could have evolved to help predators escape from prey, but he also claimed that anxiety (about receiving feedback or not, Sheldrake, 2008) could harm the effect. For an effect supposed to confer evolutionary advantage, it seems like it would be useful under conditions of anxiety or distraction (e.g., Becker, 2009, reported that for vision fear produced more efficient search even for non-threat related targets, and it seems that you would most need a "sixth sense" warning when your other senses are engaged).

6. "The ratio of supporters to critics rises up to somewhere near 50% and then falls gradually to oblivion" (Langmuir & Hall, 1989, p. 44). This criterion highlights the social nature of science. One key feature of pathological science is that people doing research in the area are not consciously committing misconduct, they are simply making a mistake in interpreting ambiguous data or have created an experimental procedure that is providing misleading data. Because of that, it is possible for many researchers to initially replicate the results before someone discovers the problem in the procedure. (A careful reading of Langmuir & Hall's examples from the history of physics would help to understand this point.) In the case of stare detection, the research enterprise is relatively new, so it is difficult to evaluate this criterion.

This kind of analysis does not prove or disprove the stare detection phenomenon. However, it does call attention to problems that proponents of stare detection must overcome, and it raises suspicions about the reality of the phenomenon. As Feynman said (quoted in Tavris & Bluming, 2008, p. 17), "If something is true, really so, if you continue observations and improve the effectiveness of the observations, the effects stand out more obviously, not less obviously."

---

quality studies have a tendency to produce smaller effects, but the data from those studies are not in yet for stare detection. A similar pattern can be seen in the conscious decision-making studies. As more quality studies are conducted, with tighter controls, the evidence is not as strong.

We are now ready for the target article for this chapter. In his first study, Baker (2000) took a different approach. Staring effects in laboratory conditions could arise due to errors in experimental procedure or they could be real, but either way they are not representative of the real world phenomenon of staring detection. Baker undertook an observation study in a natural setting to determine whether or not stare detection would occur. Technically, his study was not a naturalistic observation but a participant observation. To study stare detection using naturalistic observation, it would be necessary to

METHODOLOGY NOTE **2.3**

Note how observation research like Baker's (2000) is reasonably high in external validity. His research took place in a natural setting, with people engaged in routine activities that they would normally engage in in that setting. Baker's external validity was compromised slightly by the fact that he was staring as part of a research project rather than for the kinds of reasons people might be expected to stare at one another under ordinary conditions. Baker's internal validity was compromised to a greater extent. Each of his participants was engaged in a different kind of activity for different amounts of time with different levels of environmental distraction. Often you will see in research that increasing one kind of validity involves making sacrifices to the other kind of validity. For example, in Baker's case he could increase internal validity by standardizing the environment and the tasks performed by his participants, but this would harm his external validity.

observe instances in which some person in the environment spontaneously stared at some other person in the environment and then record whether or not the person being stared at detected that stare. Given the nature of the staring detection phenomenon, this would be complicated by the fact that the person doing the staring and the person being stared at would both be being stared at by the experimenter.

Baker (2000) modified the naturalistic observation procedure by intervening as a participant. He went to public settings (e.g., a university library) and stared at people for between 5 and 15 minutes. After the observation period, Baker approached his participants and asked them whether or not they felt that they were being stared at. Of the 40 participants, 35 did not detect that they were being stared at. Three of the remaining participants fidgeted during the staring and reported that they felt uncomfortable. Two of the participants were excluded by Baker. One was excluded for saying that she was always being stared at, and one was excluded for saying that he knew he was being observed due to his psychic abilities, but could not say where the observation was coming from. Sheldrake (2005a) took exception with excluding these participants. However, even with their data included, the results were 35 not detecting versus 5 detecting. This stands in sharp contrast to Sheldrake's (e.g., 2001a) data finding a highly replicable effect for conscious detection of staring. Under more natural conditions, there is no effect.

In the projects section, you will be able to use observation designs to evaluate the detection of staring for yourself.

INFOTRAC® COLLEGE EDITION EXERCISES

You can use the InfoTrac College Edition to read about additional studies using observational methodologies. For example, typing in "observation research" with "in title, citation, abstract" and "to refereed publications" checked gave me a list of 26 articles. One of those was by Olswang, Svensson, Coggins, Beilinson, and Donaldson (2006). They discussed a method for improving the coding of observations. Your study might benefit by reading about the methodology issues faced by other researchers and how they addressed those issues. Spend some time with InfoTrac College Edition reading method sections from a variety of articles using observation research before tackling your own project.

You can also use the InfoTrac College Edition to explore research about staring detection. I found that typing in "staring detection" with the same boxes checked produced a list of four articles discussed in this chapter. Experimenting with different search terms should yield additional information.

IMPLEMENTING THE DESIGN

Suggested Projects

1. You can replicate Baker's (2000) research using a participant observation design. Find a public place and stare at some participants, then ask them if they detected the staring (Baker included a copy of his questionnaire in his original article).

    a. Baker did not have a control group. However, it might be useful to have a group of people in similar circumstances who were not stared at to see if the level of "detection" in the non-staring condition matches the level in the stare condition.

    b. Sheldrake (2005a) discussed data he collected under natural conditions similar to Baker's (2000) and reported 27 detections versus 12 not. However, Sheldrake's participants knew that there was a chance they might be looked at. Lobach and Bierman (2004) in their Study 2 found that participants who knew they might be stared at showed more detection ability than participants who were unaware, so this difference might have influenced Sheldrake's results. It would require even more intervention, but you could notify some participants that surveillance might be taking place to see if that influences the results.

    c. A number of other variables have been proposed in the literature. For example, distraction, arousal, skill or belief of the starer, relationship between the starer and staree. You could design studies similar to Baker's (2000) to evaluate these variables. For example, Baker only chose participants actively engaged in a task (distracted). What would happen if participants were not engaged in a task?

    d. Titchener's (1898) proposal was that nervous tension (from a person having their back turned to a crowd) would cause people to turn around and accidentally create "stare detection" events. An alternative possibility is that heightened tension in these situations comes from the fact that people are really looking at a person's back. Either way, this suggests that tension could increase the likelihood of stare detection. Baker (2000) stared at people in more relaxed conditions. What would happen if participants were more tense? You could evaluate this by staring at people in different environments (e.g., Titchener's hypothesis suggests that a more crowded environment could be a source for increased tension).

2. It is not consistent with the methodological theme of this chapter (observation research), but you could design studies similar to Sheldrake's (summarized in Sheldrake, 2005a). There are a number of research questions, especially related to how random the sequences are. Additional questions relate to the presence of feedback, the beliefs of the starers and starees, the relationship between the starer and staree, the possibility of interaction, etc. Can you replicate Sheldrake's results, or will your data be more like Colwell et al.'s (2000, Experiment 2) results?

   a. Cottrell et al. (1996) evaluated a variety of factors that might affect stare detection using survey research to discover participants' naïve expectations about the phenomenon (e.g., looking through a one-way mirror, sheer curtain, window, etc.). It might be interesting to investigate "participant effects" similar to experimenter effects. If the results come about due to a bias from the participants (e.g., to say "yes" more often, or to attend more to feedback on "hit" trials), then the results of empirical investigations of stare detection might track Cottrell et al.'s survey data. Participants might unconsciously "make it come out right." To do this, you would need to give yourself the best chance to "detect" staring: Use pseudo random sequences with feedback and match the other conditions of the Colwell et al. (2000) Experiment 1.

   b. You could also investigate experimenter effects. In addition to the standard "skeptics usually find nothing and proponents find detection" effects, other types of effects might be present. For example, Sheldrake (2001a) described a study carried out by non-identical Irish twins. Their results were that strangers produced the poorest results, and non-identical twins produced the best. It seems on the surface that the relationship ought to be "more strongly related leads to more effect," suggesting identical twins as the best. Perhaps the results were influenced by the non-identical twin experimenters rooting for non-identical twins to be the most special (note that with experimenter effects the standard explanation is not fraud but rather subtle aspects of the interaction between the experimenter and participants). Will experimenters given various hypotheses produce data that conform to those hypotheses? Again, to have the best shot at success, you should use an experimental paradigm most likely to produce an effect (even if that effect is entirely due to experiment artifacts). Schlitz et al.'s (2006) procedure of varying the person giving the instructions to the participants (and thereby communicating experimenter expectations) and the person doing the staring (affecting the actual results) suggests a nice design for this type of research.

3. Making the assumption that the staring detection phenomenon is, in fact, due to experiment artifacts, you could try to design a project to understand why so many people believe in it. For example, you could evaluate

Titchener's (1898) hypothesis by videotaping a crowd of people and then coding the number of times people turn around when someone was actually looking at them versus the number of times someone looked at them after they turned around (possibly causing them to feel that they turned around in response to being stared at). Technically, this could be done as a naturalistic observation, but the coding would have to be done from videotape to connect turning around behavior with what was happening before people turned around. To evaluate whether or not belief in stare detection is due to confirmation biases would be even more difficult. You would have to count how many times someone turned around and nobody was looking at them and how many times they turned around when someone was looking at them, then find out how many times the person remembered. The confirmation bias hypothesis would be that people would remember more of the times when someone was really looking. This design would require you to combine observation and survey approaches.

REFERENCES

Auweele, Y. V., Boen, F., Schapendonk, W., and Dornez, K. (2005). Promoting stair use among female employees: The effects of a health sign followed by an email. *Journal of Sport and Exercise Psychology, 27*, 188–196.

Baker, R. A. (2000). Can we tell when someone is staring at us? *Skeptical Inquirer, 24*, 34–40.

Becker, M. W. (2009). Panic search: Fear produces efficient visual search for nonthreatening objects. *Psychological Science, 20*, 435–437. doi:10.1111/j.1467-9280.2009.02303.x

Braud, W., Shafer, D., & Andrews, S. (1993a). Reactions to an unseen gaze (remote attention): A review with new data on autonomic staring detection. *Journal of Parapsychology, 57*, 373–390.

Braud, W., Shafer, D., & Andrews, S. (1993b). Further studies of autonomic detection of remote staring: Replication, new control procedures, and personality correlates. *Journal of Parapsychology, 57*, 391–409.

Cialdini, R. B., Reno, R. R., and Kallgren, C. A. (1990). A focus theory of normative conduct: Recycling the concept of norms to reduce littering in public places. *Journal of Personality and Social Psychology, 58*, 1015–1026. doi:10.1037/0022-3514.58.6.1015

Colwell, J., Schroder, S., & Sladen, D. (2000). The ability to detect unseen staring: A literature review and empirical tests. *British Journal of Psychology, 91*, 71–85. doi:10.1348/000712600161682

Coover, J. E. (1913). "The feeling of being stared at": Experimental. *The American Journal of Psychology, 24*, 570–575. doi:10.2307/1413454

Cottrell, J. E., & Winer, G. A. (1994). Development in the understanding of perception: The decline of extramission perception beliefs. *Developmental Psychology, 30*, 218–228. doi:10.1037/0012-1649.30.2.218

Cottrell, J. E., Winer, G. A., & Smith, M. C. (1996). Beliefs of children and adults about feeling stares of unseen others. *Developmental Psychology, 32*, 50–61. doi:10.1037/0012-1649.32.1.50

Ecenbarger, W. (1998). America's worst drivers. *Reader's Digest, 152*, 108–114.

Langmuir, I., & Hall, R. N. (1989). Pathological Science. *Physics Today, 42*, 36–48. doi:10.1063/1.881205

Lobach, E., & Bierman, D. J. (2004, August). *The invisible gaze: Three attempts to replicate Sheldrake's staring effects.* Paper presented at the Parapsychological Association Convention, Vienna, Austria. Retrieved from http://m0134.fmg.uva.nl/publications/2004/Staring_PA2004.pdf

Marks, D. F., & Colwell, J. (2000). The psychic staring effect: An artifact of pseudo randomization. *Skeptical Inquirer, 24*, 41–49.

Marks, D., & Colwell, J. (2001). Fooling and falling into the feeling of being stared at. *Skeptical Inquirer, 25*, 62–63.

Olswang, L. B., Svensson, L., Coggins, T. E., Beilinson, J. S., & Donaldson, A. L. (2006). Reliability issues and solutions for coding social communication performance in classroom settings. *Journal of Speech, Language, and Hearing Research, 49,* 1058–1071. doi:10.1044/1092-4388(2006/075)

Schlitz, M. J., & LaBerge, S. (1997). Covert observation increases skin conductance in subjects unaware of when they are being observed: A replication. *The Journal of Parapsychology, 61,* 185–196.

Schlitz, M., Wiseman, R., Watt, C., & Radin, D. (2006). Of two minds: Sceptic-proponent collaboration within parapsychology. *British Journal of Psychology, 97,* 313–322. doi:10.1348/000712605X80704

Schmidt, S., Schneider, R., Binder, M., Burkle, D., & Walach, H. (2001). Investigating methodological issues in EDA-DMILS: Results from a pilot study. *The Journal of Parapsychology, 65,* 59–82.

Schmidt, S., Schneider, R., Utts, J., & Walach, H. (2004). Distant intentionality and the feeling of being stared at: Two meta-analyses. *British Journal of Psychology, 95,* 235–247. doi:10.1348/000712604773952449

Schmidt, S., & Walach, H. (2000). Electrodermal activity (EDA)—State-of-the-art measurement and techniques for parapsychological purposes. *The Journal of Parapsychology, 64,* 139–163.

Sheldrake, R. (1998). The sense of being stared at: Experiments in schools. *Journal of the Society for Psychical Research, 62,* 311–323. Retrieved from http://www.sheldrake.org/Articles&Papers/papers/staring/

Sheldrake, R. (1999). The "sense of being stared at" confirmed by simple experiments. *Biology Forum, 92,* 53–76. Retrieved from http://www.sheldrake.org/Articles&Papers/papers/staring/

Sheldrake, R. (2000). The "sense of being stared at" does not depend on known sensory clues.

Biology Forum, 93, 209–224. Retrieved from http://www.sheldrake.org/Articles&Papers/papers/staring/

Sheldrake, R. (2001a). Experiments on the sense of being stared at: The elimination of possible artefacts. *Journal of the Society for Psychical Research, 65,* 122–137. Retrieved from http://www.sheldrake.org/Articles&Papers/papers/staring/

Sheldrake, R. (2001b). Research on the feeling of being stared at. *Skeptical Inquirer, 25,* 58–61.

Sheldrake, R. (2005a). The sense of being stared at: Part 1: Is it real or illusory? *Journal of Consciousness Studies, 12,* 10–31. Retrieved from http://www.sheldrake.org/Articles&Papers/papers/staring/

Sheldrake, R. (2005b). The sense of being stared at: Part 2: Its implications for theories of vision. *Journal of Consciousness Studies, 12,* 32–49. Retrieved from http://www.sheldrake.org/Articles&Papers/papers/staring/

Sheldrake, R. (2008). The sense of being stared at: Do hit rates improve as tests go on? *Journal of the Society for Psychical Research, 72,* 98–106. Retrieved from http://www.sheldrake.org/Articles&Papers/papers/staring/

Sheldrake, R., Overby, C., & Beeharee, A. (2008). The sense of being stared at: An automated test on the Internet. *Journal of the Society for Psychical Research, 72,* 86–97. Retrieved from http://www.sheldrake.org/Articles&Papers/papers/staring/

Tavris, C., & Bluming, A. (2008). Taking the scary out of breast cancer stats. *Observer, 21,* 16–17.

Titchener, E. B. (1898). The 'feeling of being stared at.' *Science, 8,* 895–897. doi:10.1126/science.8.208.895

Wiseman, R., & Schlitz, M. (1997). Experimenter effects and the remote detection of staring. *The Journal of Parapsychology, 61,* 197–207.

Survey Research

Tell me something (vaguely) good

Abstract

Psychology: The Forer effect (or Barnum effect) is well known in psychology: People will tend to accept vague, positively worded statements as being descriptive of them if they are supposed to be personally relevant. How does this affect our ability to evaluate psychological measurements?

Skeptic/Pseudoscience: This effect has been proposed to explain people's belief in a variety of pseudoscientific topics (e.g., astrology and graphology). It is possible that the Forer effect can be used to explain why there is a disconnect between empirical evidence showing that an assessment is not valid and widespread public acceptance of that procedure as valid.

INTRODUCTION: CONDUCTING A SURVEY

How can we find out about the sources of human behavior? One way is to watch people and infer why they do what they do (see Chapter 2). Another way is to ask people why they do what they do. That is the topic of this chapter. How are surveys used to understand human behavior?

There are two main uses of surveys. You are familiar with practical uses of surveys. Politicians conduct polls to find out which issues are popular with voters. News organizations conduct polls to find out how people feel about politicians. Businesses conduct polls to find out how people feel about products and services. These results are used for practical purposes. If consumers will not buy an instant bacon product that squeezes out of a tube like toothpaste, nobody will waste time and money manufacturing it.

There are also research applications for surveys. For example, *Consumer Reports* commissioned a survey investigating the effectiveness of psychotherapy (Seligman, 1995; *Consumer Reports*, 1995, November). These data have a practical value to the readers of *Consumer Reports*, but they also serve to demonstrate whether or not psychotherapy is an effective treatment for mental disorders. The results can be used by therapists to optimize their interventions. (As an aside, Seligman's discussion of the methodology of the *Consumer Reports* survey illustrates nicely how to determine if the results of a survey are sound.) Surveys that are particularly relevant for the topic of this book are those measuring belief in the paranormal. For example, Musella (2005) reported the results of a Gallup poll conducted in the summer of 2005. We will consider the various survey methodology issues in light of this type of survey.

When planning and carrying out a survey, a number of methodological decisions must be made. How researchers handle these issues will have a large impact on the usefulness of their results. Basically, we are trying to get as much information from people as we can without allowing any biases to affect that information. The big issues include:

1. Who will participate in the survey? You start with a **population**. This is a theoretical entity that corresponds to everyone to whom you want to generalize. Sometimes the population is very large (Nielsen ratings should generalize to the entire country). Sometimes the population is very small (if I want to know whether students in a class would like to postpone an exam, the results should generalize to the class). For many surveys investigating belief in the paranormal, the population is everyone in the country. From this population, you select a **sample**. These are the people you actually survey. You have to be careful to avoid selection biases when choosing a sample. How do you get the sample?

One way is to use **random sampling**. With this technique, every person in the population has an equal chance of being in the sample. It is like throwing all the names in a hat and then drawing them out until you get the number of people you want. For a university population, you could get a random sample by numbering every name in the directory and using a random number table to pick names. If the sample is random, there is a good chance that it will also be **representative**. In other words, its makeup will mirror that of the population. If the sample is representative, you can be confident that the results of your survey will apply to everyone in the population. If your sample is biased, you can only generalize to the people who participated.

Keep in mind that the number of people sampled is usually not the issue but rather how they were chosen. Even if 100,000 people visit a news show's website and express the same opinion, the results will probably not apply to the population at large. Chances are that only a special subset of the population will vote in a television poll (at the simplest level, only people watching the show will even know that a survey is being conducted). The goal of any survey is usually to collect a representative sample from the population of interest.

For surveys about belief in the paranormal to have any value, a representative sample is necessary. For example, Musella (2005) reported that 73% of the population believes in some type of paranormal phenomenon. It is

METHODOLOGY NOTE **3.1**

Whenever you conduct research, you want the results to be valid. Two important kinds of validity are internal and external validity. **Internal validity** has to do with the design of the study. Your goal is to have high internal validity to assure the quality of the data. You can achieve internal validity by increasing researcher control, by using measures that are reliable and valid, and by using sound research design. **External validity** (also called generalizability) has to do with your ability to extend the findings to a population. No matter how interesting your results are, if they only apply to a tiny subset of people in very specialized circumstances, they will not be very valuable. The two kinds of validity usually compete. To get high internal validity, you need control over the situation. Control makes the situation less natural, lowering external validity. Survey research often involves a compromise between the two kinds of validity: we sacrifice a certain amount of control to get results that have the highest generalizability.

much more interesting if this applies to the entire country than to just the people who participated in the survey. Also, representative samples allow comparisons over time. If the samples are not representative, then changes in percentage of belief could arise due to the samples contacted and not due to change over time.

2. How do you contact the sample? There are four basic ways: personal interview, phone survey, mail, and Internet. Each has its merits and its problems. Interviews and phone surveys can yield rich data, but they can also be expensive and difficult to carry out. Mail surveys are relatively cheap and easy to conduct but often have a problem with a low response rate. A potential solution to these problems is to collect data via the Internet. According to Buchanan (2000), Internet research can be easier for researchers because surveys can be distributed and scored automatically. At the same time, users can benefit from the fact that the survey they complete is tailored to them (e.g., a section for car owners is presented only to participants who own cars). This might increase response rates by decreasing participant frustration. Also, a researcher can get access to a larger and more diverse sample than the typical psychology department research pool. Finally, participants might be more honest completing Internet-based surveys (possibly because they feel more anonymous). Buchanan was interested in whether or not using the Internet would produce a valid outcome (see Methodology Note 3.1). His results showed that an Internet version of a survey could produce similar results to paper-and-pencil methods, with the benefits discussed before. This issue might be especially important for surveys of belief in the paranormal. For example, people may not want to tell someone on the telephone that they believe in ghosts (to avoid appearing foolish), but they might be willing to respond that way on the Internet.

METHODOLOGY NOTE **3.2**

Two important issues in any measurement situation are reliability and validity. A measure is reliable if it produces a consistent result every time someone completes it (assuming that the thing being measured has not changed). For example, if IQ is a stable property of my psyche, then my IQ score should be the same every time I take an IQ test. Reliability is important if we are to make sense of differences in people's scores on a survey. If the measure is unreliable, then we have no way of knowing if the differences we find reflect real differences between people or if they are simply the result of a poor instrument. If we were using a survey to measure change over time (e.g., to evaluate the effectiveness of therapy), an unreliable measure would make it hard to tell whether changes reflect real change or simply an unreliable instrument. Reliability can be assessed in a number of ways, but one of the easiest is to use a test-retest procedure. In this procedure, people are given a test, and then they are tested again later. If the test is reliable, then performance on the first test will be strongly correlated with performance on the second test.

Validity has to do with how well a test measures what it is supposed to measure. For example, a survey instrument that is supposed to measure anxiety but actually measures depression would not be valid. Obviously, a measure that is not valid is of little use in research, so it is important to use instruments that actually measure what they claim to measure. Unfortunately, assessing validity can sometimes be difficult (if we are trying to find out if an instrument measures some psychological attribute, how do we measure that attribute to see if our instrument is accurately assessing it?). As a general rule in research methods classes, it is wise to find surveys for which other people have already collected data on reliability and validity. If you need to construct your own instrument, you can get some benefit by modeling it on an existing instrument.

3. How do you ask the questions? Generally, the more specific the questions, the better. You want to avoid asking questions that are open to interpretation. If you cannot be sure what a person meant by a response, you will not be able to make sense of the results. For mail, phone, and Internet surveys, **closed questions** (multiple choice) work best. For example, on a product survey, you might ask which types of soup participants eat by having them put a check by each item on a list of soups that they have eaten in the past. Closed questions make all of the answers consistent. If you are unsure of what the answers will be, you can use **open questions** (essay). Instead of giving participants choices of how to answer, let them say whatever they want. For open questions, the interview format works best.

As an example of the influence of question wording on responses in paranormal belief surveys, consider the issue of alien contact. Clancy, McNally, Schacter, Lezenweger, and Pitman (2002) defined contact as an alien abduction, including experiences of being touched and seeing alien beings. French,

Santomauro, Hamilton, Fox, and Thalbourne (2008) defined contact as UFO sightings, telepathic communication, device implantation, etc. If a survey asked "Have you had contact with aliens?" participants could have any subset of these things or all of these things in mind when responding. For example, a person might consider telepathic communication to be contact, but a researcher might not. The wording of a question like this could have a big impact on the results.

You also need to be sensitive to the ordering of the questions. Arrange them from general to specific to avoid fixing participants' responses early on. For example, ask about general paranormal belief before asking about specific aspects of belief. If you have several similar questions, mix them up so that you have several orderings over the whole set of surveys. Finally, use filter questions to cut down on the work of respondents (for example, "Do you own a car? If yes, then answer this set of car questions ...").

It is especially important to avoid bias in the wording of the questions. Consider this item from a Democratic National Committee (DNC) survey (1999): "Do you favor or oppose Republican plans to give parents tuition vouchers that would take tax dollars away from our public schools and use this money to subsidize tuition at private schools and academies?" The wording makes a "favor" response sound bad, which may push respondents into saying "oppose." The authors of this survey were probably more interested in energizing the party faithful than in collecting real data (a significant amount of material in the brochure is devoted to appeals for money). That is fine as long as no attempt is made to generalize from the results to policy. If the DNC really wanted to know how people felt about school vouchers, a less biased wording would be more appropriate. From a paranormal belief perspective, participants might be inclined to say "no" to avoid endorsing viewpoints they expect to be unpopular. Poorly worded questions could enhance this bias.

4. How can you be sure that people are responding truthfully? Sometimes, people will feel pressure to lie to look good (a problem with **social desirability**; see Methodology Note 3.3). Other times, people may not know how to answer the question because they do not understand their own behavior. Any time you collect data using a survey, you have to worry about the accuracy of people's responses.

Ruback and Juieng (1997) investigated territorial behavior in the parking lot. They found that people take longer to back out of a space if someone is waiting. In their Study 3, they used a survey technique to determine if people are aware of their own territoriality. Previous research has suggested that they are not. For example, Ruback, Pape, and Doriot (1989) found that people did not *think* they would take longer at a pay phone when someone was waiting, even though, in fact, they *did* take longer. For the parking lot study, Ruback and Juieng presented people with four questions about their behavior in the parking lot.

For themselves, people said intrusion would have more of an effect if the intrusion were more severe (if the waiting driver honked the horn). When

METHODOLOGY NOTE **3.3**

One solution to the problem of social desirability is to build in questions to explicitly measure whether or not a person is trying to look good for the survey. For example, someone who strongly endorses a statement like "I never swear," may be trying to look good for the researcher. A set of these types of questions could be used to identify people who may be more concerned with making a good impression than with responding truthfully.

METHODOLOGY NOTE **3.4**

As a check on your comprehension, consider how design decisions will affect the validity of the survey. Random sampling affects which validity more, internal or external? Using filter questions affects which validity more, internal or external? What is the relationship between response rate and validity?

thinking about another driver, the same pattern was present. Overall, people thought another driver would be more affected by intrusion than they would.

One interesting aspect of the questionnaire results is that the average response for a mild intrusion (no honking) was 2.35. That is on the "faster" end of the scale, suggesting that people think they will hurry up when another car is waiting. This aspect of their responding does not match with behavior, because people actually take longer. This may be due to a problem with social desirability. People know they take longer when someone is waiting, but they do not want to admit that to a researcher. It may also be a problem with people's self-knowledge. They may not be consciously aware of their behavior, and so they believe they are responding truthfully when they are not.

Again, in the area of paranormal belief it might be useful to have some independent confirmation of participants' responses. There could be biases to conceal paranormal belief, or biases to affirm it if it is vital to a respondent's self-concept. As a researcher, your goal is to minimize these influences as much as possible, and to collect evidence that converges on a consistent answer to increase your confidence in the results.

Our target article (Forer, 1949) used a survey methodology to investigate the "fallacy of personal validation."

TARGET ARTICLE: THE FORER EFFECT (OR BARNUM EFFECT)

(Be sure to look at Appendix D to assist you in evaluating the sources cited in this chapter. Be especially aware of the guidelines for evaluating Internet and other non-peer reviewed sources.)

A common theme in this book will be how to evaluate paranormal or pseudoscientific claims. For example, how do we know if predictions from astrology about a person's personality are accurately describing that person? The simplest thing would be to present that person with the astrological profile and ask them how well it describes them. Unfortunately, those judgments are contaminated by a problem called "personal validation" (Forer, 1949). Basically, when a person is asked to evaluate statements made about them, they are not good at distinguishing things that would be universally true of everyone from things that are actually diagnostic. Therefore their judgment contributes nothing to our evaluation of the procedure that produced the description. As Forer points out, this can also increase a clinician's (or other practitioner's) belief in the validity of a procedure. For example, if all of my clients endorse my astrological profiles, that would increase my belief in my own skills as an astrologer, even if I am only providing information that everyone would endorse (and therefore is not diagnostic of any individual).

One important note: The Forer effect is also often called the Barnum effect (Meehl, 1956). Meehl proposed this name specifically to "stigmatize those pseudo-successful clinical procedures in which personality descriptions from tests are made to fit the patient largely or wholly by virtue of their triviality" (p. 266). Supposedly the name comes from P. T. Barnum's description of his show as having "a little something for everyone" (Andersen & Nordvik, 2002, p. 539).

How can we get around the problem of personal validation when evaluating claims? One way would be to avoid it entirely. Rather than have people judge the fit between themselves and profiles, try to find an objective measure to compare against our predictions (we will see some of this when discussing graphology in Chapter 6). Another approach would be to use the fallacy of personal validation as a research tool. Unlike some chapters in this book, this chapter is primarily a methodology chapter. I have two goals: a) how can we evaluate the ways in which the fallacy of personal validation is affecting our research results? and b) how can we use this phenomenon to our advantage?

Forer's (1949) study was conducted as a classroom demonstration. He allowed his students to take a personality inventory that they had discussed ("a list of hobbies, reading materials, personal characteristics, job duties, and secret hopes and ambitions of one's ideal person," p. 119). One week later, the students were provided with what they thought were personality descriptions prepared for them based on an analysis of their questionnaires. The personality sketches had 13 statements, and all students received the same personality sketch (their own names were on them to make them look personalized).

Forer (1949) had his students rate the personality instrument, the extent to which the personality sketch described them, and to check off which statements (out of 13) were true of them. Ratings were made on a 0–5 scale, on which 5 indicated a good instrument or an accurate personality sketch. Overall, students had a high opinion of the instrument (the average rating was 4.31) and felt that their personality sketches were accurate (the average rating was 4.26). On average, students accepted 10.2 statements as true of them. These results highlight the problem of personal validation. On the basis of very little evidence (one bogus personality sketch), students developed a high confidence in the measurement instrument that was used to produce the sketch. They failed to notice (until they were told) that the statements were so vague and general as to apply to almost anyone.

Forer (1949) also provided data on which statements were most effective. Dividing the range of the number of true responses (from 12–38) into three parts, we find that students strongly endorsed a tendency to be critical of themselves, the ability to compensate for some personality weaknesses, being disciplined on the outside but worried on the inside, having doubts about decisions, preferring change and variety, being independent thinkers, not being too frank in revealing themselves, and being extroverted at times and introverted at other times. To a moderate extent they endorsed having a need for others to like and admire them, having unused capacity, and having security as a major life goal. They were less likely to endorse that their sexual adjustment had presented problems and that they had unrealistic aspirations.

Forer (1949) followed up his study by asking students to report their ratings of the instrument and ratings of the sketch from memory three weeks later. He found that the ratings of the instrument did not change, but that participants' ratings of the accuracy of the sketch were significantly lower when students reported them from memory. Forer interpreted this to mean that memory changes tend to be in the direction of improving self-esteem (being tricked is bad, so remembering being tricked less is good).

Forer's (1949) conclusion was that "validation of a test instrument or of a personality sketch by means of personal validation is a fallacious procedure" (p. 122). In the projects section, you will have an opportunity to explore this issue further.

INFOTRAC® COLLEGE EDITION EXERCISES

You can use the InfoTrac College Edition to read about additional studies using survey methodologies. For example, typing in "survey research" and checking the box for "in title, citation, abstract" gave me a list of 1,513 articles (you would ordinarily want to narrow your search to a more specific topic if you got that many results, but my goal here was to look at people's use of the method, so I kept a broad list). There are two large uses of survey research: practical (e.g., market research) and empirical (e.g., psychology research). One research article in my list was "Survey research looks at attitudes, obstacles to walking and biking to work" (2009). The research investigated people's feelings about walking and biking to work at a university. They found that students were more likely to walk or bike than faculty and staff, and also that 20 minutes of walking or biking was the maximum amount most people would do. In general, reading a variety of method sections can help you with ideas for your own project. As an aside, there are also a number of articles in InfoTrac College Edition presenting market research (including research about market research). For example, I discovered that using websites to collect data from consumers is most useful for marketing departments and least useful for human resources departments (McMains, 2009).

You can also find information about the Forer effect using the InfoTrac College Edition. When I typed "barnum effect" into the search box and checked the box for "in entire article content," I received a list of 23 articles (I got no relevant hits for "Forer effect"). One of those articles was about a procedure called Personalysis (Radford, 2009). Radford was answering a question about a product that "takes the guesswork out of understanding people" (p. 33). He contends that much of the product's success stems from using Barnum statements in people's profiles (" 'You need freedom to explore ideas and act,' and 'You are frustrated when having to deal with repetitious details or needless bureaucracy.' This is of course in stark contrast to the rest of us, who don't need freedom to explore ideas, and who enjoy dealing with needless bureaucracy," p. 34). It is always useful to evaluate systems claiming to prepare a profile "just for you" by comparing that profile to other people. If it fits everyone, it is not going to provide much insight into your own personality.

IMPLEMENTING THE DESIGN

Materials

You will need two basic materials for a Forer effect project: A personality test that has **face validity** (appears to the participants to be a real assessment of personality) and a personality profile that is general enough to describe almost anyone. There are a number of sources for personality tests. For example, Donnellan, Oswald, Baird, and Lucas (2006) presented a 20-item scale for measuring the big-five personality factors. You can also search for personality tests on the Internet. In this instance, since you are not actually trying to find out about real personality information (the profile will be unrelated to the answers on the test), you do not need an instrument that has been tested for reliability and validity, it just needs to look real to the participants. When I typed "free personality test" into Google, I received a list of possible tests, including the color quiz (http://www.colorquiz.com/). The test does not provide any explanation of how clicking color patches will reveal personality, nor does it explain why you have to wait 120 seconds and choose colors again. However, the description it provided was startlingly accurate.

As for Barnum statements, the original Forer (1949) article provides guidance. However, there a number of other Barnum effect projects available in the literature. You can locate one of those or make your own (varying them in particular ways) as suggested in the projects section.

Suggested Projects

1. You can replicate the original Forer (1949) study. You will need to substitute your own personality instrument, but Forer's statements are available. Will your participants have unwarranted confidence in an evaluation instrument that seems to be able to describe them? You can also vary Forer's procedure:
   a. If you look closely at the statements that Forer's participants endorsed (and failed to endorse), you find that people did not want to

ETHICS NOTE **3.1**

Many of the projects in this section involve at least a small amount of deception (participants will be told that they are receiving personalized feedback when they are not). Even though this type of deception is mild, it can contribute to suspicion about research. Institutions will vary in how they evaluate research using deception (see Appendix A). It is wise to consult with your professor or Institutional Review Board when planning your study, and to minimize deception as much as possible. Also, you will need to pay special attention to your debriefing procedure when doing research involving deception. (See Beins, 1993 for a classroom demonstration of the Barnum effect designed to inform students about the ethical implications of deception.)

claim problems in sexual adjustment and unrealistic aspirations. Will people be less likely to endorse vague, but negative information when compared to vague, but positive information? In other words, is there a limit on the effect of personal validation? Snyder and Newburg (1981) manipulated the valence of the feedback (along with other variables) and found that participants endorsed positive feedback more strongly than negative feedback (however, this was qualified by an interaction with the status of the person providing feedback). MacDonald and Standing (2002) also evaluated the effect of positive and negative feedback in the area of personality testing. Their participants rated positive characteristics in a personality report as being more like them than negative personality characteristics. Hamilton (2001) found that some astrological signs have a tendency to receive more favorable analyses from astrologers than others, and that people with those signs were also more likely to believe, suggesting that belief is influenced by how favorable astrology is to a person. Glick, Gottesman, and Jolton (1989) manipulated the valence of the feedback for participants who did and did not believe in astrology. Believers rated both positive and negative astrological descriptions as accurate, non-believers rated negative astrological descriptions as less accurate than positive descriptions. An interesting effect of personal validation also happened in this study. Non-believers increased in belief in astrology the most after receiving a horoscope, especially if that horoscope was positive. So, Barnum statements led to an increased sense of the validity of astrology, even for skeptics.

METHODOLOGY NOTE **3.5**

Note that some of the projects are actually using a hybrid design combining elements of experiments with survey research.

b. Does the source of the information make a difference? Snyder, Larsen, and Bloom (1976) told participants that their reports were from a psychological test (they wrote what they saw in an inkblot), a graphology test (they signed a piece of paper and copied a sentence), and an astrology evaluation (they provided their birth date). Snyder et al. found that the source of the report did not matter. On the other hand, all participants, regardless of source, increased their faith in the procedure and their perception of the diagnostician's skill after receiving a report. In other words, the Barnum effect occurs just from receiving a report, regardless of the procedure used to generate it. You might investigate if other sources might produce a difference, or if the validity of the source might matter (e.g., whether the handwriting specimen is collected under controlled conditions). Similarly, Rogers and Soule (2009) found that Chinese students were just as accepting of horoscopes using Western astrological techniques as Chinese astrological techniques. Rosen (1975) did find an effect of source when the comparison was between a psychologist using "a valid psychological test" and an astrologer. Perhaps participants were already skeptical of the inkblot procedure, and treated all three assessments in the Snyder et al. study as equivalent.

c. Snyder (1974) manipulated the specificity of the information that was requested from participants to determine their astrological profile. Some participants were given a general horoscope (without providing information about themselves), some provided their birth year and month, and some provided their birth year, month, and day. The more information participants provided to the "astrologer" preparing the report, the more they endorsed the profile provided as true of them. You could manipulate the amount of information collected from participants to evaluate the extent to which that variable affects their support for the profiles generated.

d. Handelsman and McLain (1988) investigated the effect of intimacy (couples who were intimately acquainted or strangers) on acceptance of Barnum statements. They found that intimate couples were more accepting of their reports and showed a greater increase in their belief in the assessment procedure. You could manipulate the degree to which participants know one another and evaluate its impact on Barnum statements. Handelsman and McLain suggest that the effect arises from a desire not to appear to be revealing personal information to a stranger. That is another avenue to explore: Why do intimate couples accept Barnum statements more than strangers?

e. DiClementi and Handelsman (1987) manipulated participants' sophistication with psychology. One group was told that they were very experienced and knowledgeable about psychology because they had been exposed to it in their introduction to psychology class. They thought that the other group would be high school sophomores with no knowledge of psychology. This was the sophisticated group. The non-sophisticated group was told that they were being compared to advanced graduate students. DiClementi and Handelsman also manipulated the perceived validity of the test, telling one group the test was highly valid, and another group that it was not. The expectation was that non-sophisticated participants would unquestioningly accept any feedback, regardless of validity, but that sophisticated participants would pay attention and only accept feedback from valid tests. However, the opposite pattern emerged. Non-sophisticated participants were more likely to accept feedback from a valid test, sophisticated participants accepted all feedback. DiClementi and Handelsman proposed a variety of explanations for this result, and evaluating those explanations empirically would be an interesting project.

2.   You can also use the Barnum effect to investigate what we will call the "gap problem": Why is there such a large gap between empirical evidence showing that an assessment procedure does not work and public acceptance of that procedure? The Barnum effect has been proposed to explain belief in a number of phenomena: fortune telling (Hughes, Behanna, & Signorella, 2001), Rorschach inkblot tests, psychics, astrologers (Wood, Nezworski, Lilienfeld, & Garb, 2003), mediums (Greasley, 2000), and graphology (King & Koehler, 2000). You can design a project to evaluate the extent to which people's belief in these types of phenomena is based on Barnum effects.

3.   The Barnum effect can also be used as a research methods tool. For example, Logue, Sher, & Frensch (1992) used the Barnum effect to evaluate whether or not there is a personality profile that is characteristic of adult children of alcoholics. To do this, they had people who were adult children of alcoholics, and people who were not, evaluate the extent to which personality statements described them. Both people who were and were not adult children of alcoholics accepted statements that were supposed to be true only of adult children of alcoholics, and they also rated Barnum statements as equally descriptive of them. In other words, belief in a particular personality associated with adult children of alcoholics may arise entirely from the fact that the personality descriptions used could apply to anyone (a Barnum effect). On the other hand, Wyman and Vyse (2008) found that personality statements generated from the NEO-FFI (a personality inventory measuring the big five personality factors) were not accepted solely due to Barnum effects. They used astrological charts as a control (which they expected a priori to be accepted due to the Barnum effect). What they found was that they could substitute a participant's real astrological chart with someone else's and they would still accept it as accurate. On the other hand, participants rated their real NEO profile as more accurate than someone else's substituted at random. Participants also showed significant Barnum effects (all of the profiles were rated as significantly better than chance at describing the participants' personality). However, the design of the study allowed Wyman and Vyse to show that the NEO had validity beyond Barnum effects. These studies suggest a variety of projects.

a.   Basically, if you want to assess the validity of an evaluation instrument, the appropriate control is a Barnum statement. If the instrument being evaluated shows effects beyond basic Barnum effects, that can give you some confidence in its validity. For example, it might be that astrology has validity, but only in certain circumstances. Generic predictions made by daily horoscopes are intentionally vague because they have to apply to everyone with a given sign. A profile generated for a specific person with their specific information might be more valid. You could substitute a person's generic profile with someone else's and have them rated, and try the same procedure with a personally prepared profile. Is there a difference between specific and generic astrology profiles?

b.   Alternatively, you could evaluate any measuring instrument (personality, astrology, graphology, or Tarot) by having one reading done by following the rules and a second reading done while breaking the rules (e.g., respond randomly to a personality scale). If participants can tell the "correct" and "incorrect" readings apart, that suggests that the scale is measuring more than Barnum effects.

4.   Forer (1949) suggested that Barnum effects might account for a practitioner's confidence in a procedure (since clients say it works, the practitioner has increased confidence in it). Handelsman and McLain (1988) suggest that the Barnum effect could be used to increase buy-in for therapy (e.g., couples counseling), and possibly increase its effectiveness. This suggests two sorts of projects. First, how does success with a technique (produced by the Barnum effect) change a practitioner's confidence in it? As an example, you might have skeptics of astrology use an astrology system to generate personality profiles, and have their "clients" provide feedback to them on the accuracy of the profiles. If the feedback is positive, will that change them from skeptics to believers? A second project would be to evaluate the effect of Barnum statements provided to a person on their belief. Glick et al. (1989) found that positive personality statements increased skeptics' belief in astrology.

5.   Forer (1949) found that memory was influenced by knowledge of the deception. You could investigate this more explicitly. For example, what happens to memory for people who were made aware of the deception and people who were not (you would eventually need to debrief all participants)? Or, does the perceived validity of the procedure influence memory changes? For example, if participants were "tricked" with astrology, would they be more motivated to misremember than participants "tricked" with a valid psychology test?

REFERENCES

Andersen, P., & Nordvik, H. (2002). Possible Barnum effect in the five factor model: Do respondents accept random NEO Personality Inventory—Revised scores as their actual trait profile? *Psychological Reports, 90*, 539–545. doi:10.2466/PR0.90.2.539-545

Beins, B. C. (1993). Using the Barnum effect to teach about ethics and deception in research. *Teaching of Psychology, 20*, 33–35. doi:10.1207/s15328023top2001_6

Buchanan, T. (2000). Internet research: Self-monitoring and judgments of attractiveness. *Behavior Research Methods, Instruments, and Computers, 32*, 521–527.

Clancy, S. A., McNally, R. J., Schacter, D. L., Lenzenweger, M. F., & Pitman, R. K. (2002).

Memory distortion in people reporting abduction by aliens. *Journal of Abnormal Psychology, 111,* 455–461. doi:10.1037//0021-843X.111.3.455

Democratic National Committee. (1999). *1999 presidential agenda survey* [brochure]. Washington, DC: Author.

DiClementi, J. D., & Handelsman, M. M. (1987). Effects of perceived sophistication and test validity on acceptance of generalized feedback. *Journal of Clinical Psychology, 43,* 341–345. doi: 10.1002/1097-4679(198705)43:3<341::AID-JCLP2270430307>3.0.CO;2-7

Donnellan, M. B., Oswald, F. L., Baird, B. M., & Lucas, R. E. (2006). The Mini-IPIP scales: Tiny-yet-effective measures of the big five factors of personality. *Psychological Assessment, 18,* 192–203. doi:10.1037/1040-3590.18.2.192

Forer, B. R. (1949). The fallacy of personal validation: A classroom demonstration of gullibility. *The Journal of Abnormal and Social Psychology, 44,* 118–123. doi:10.1037/h0059240

French, C. C., Santomauro, J., Hamilton, V., Fox, R., & Thalbourne, M. A. (2008). Psychological aspects of the alien contact experience. *Cortex, 44,* 1387–1395. doi:10.1016/j.cortex.2007.11.011

Glick, P., Gottesman, D., & Jolton, J. (1989). The fault is not in the stars: Susceptibility of skeptics and believers in astrology to the Barnum effect. *Personality and Social Psychology Bulletin, 15,* 572–583. doi:10.1177/0146167289154010

Greasley, P. (2000). Management of positive and negative responses in a spiritualist medium consultation. *Skeptical Inquirer, 24,* 45–49.

Hamilton, M. (2001). Who believes in astrology? Effect of favorableness of astrologically derived personality descriptions on acceptance of astrology. *Personality and Individual Differences, 31,* 895–902. doi:10.1016/S0191-8869(00)00191-4

Handelsman, M. M., & McLain, J. (1988). The Barnum effect in couples: Effects of intimacy, involvement, and sex on acceptance of generalized personality feedback. *Journal of Clinical Psychology, 44,* 430–434. doi:10.1002/1097-4679 (198805) 44:3<430:: AID-JCLP2270440319>3.0.CO;2-V

Hughes, M., Behanna, R., & Signorella, M. L. (2001). Perceived accuracy of fortune telling and belief in the paranormal. *The Journal of Social Psychology, 14,* 159–160. Retrieved from http://www.heldref.org/pubs/soc/about.html

King, R. N., & Koehler, D. J. (2000). Illusory correlations in graphological inference. *Journal of Experimental Psychology: Applied, 6,* 336–348. doi:10.1037/1076-898X.6.4.336

Logue, M. B., Sher, K. J., & Frensch, P. A. (1992). Purported characteristics of adult children of alcoholics: A possible "Barnum effect." *Professional Psychology: Research and Practice, 23,* 226–232. doi:10.1037/0735-7028.23.3.226

MacDonald, D. J., & Standing, L. G. (2002). Does self-serving bias cancel the Barnum effect? *Social Behavior and Personality, 30,* 625–630. doi:10.2224/sbp.2002.30.6.625

McMains, A. (2009, April 20). Customers deliver brand insights online: Survey shows social media useful in creation of marketing concepts. *AdWeek, 50,* 6.

Meehl, P. E. (1956). Wanted—A good cookbook. *American Psychologist, 11,* 263–272. doi:10.1037/h0044164

Mental health: Does therapy help? (1995, November). *Consumer Reports,* 734–739.

Musella, D. P. (2005). Gallup poll shows that Americans' belief in the paranormal persists. *Skeptical Inquirer, 29,* 5.

Radford, B. (2009). The pseudoscience of Personalysis. *Skeptical Inquirer, 33,* 33–34.

Rogers, P., & Soule, J. (2009). Cross-cultural differences in the acceptance of Barnum profiles supposedly derived from Western versus Chinese astrology. *Journal of Cross-Cultural Psychology, 40,* 381–399. doi:10.1177/0022022109332843

Rosen, G. M. (1975). Effects of source prestige on subjects' acceptance of the Barnum effect: Psychologist versus astrologer. *Journal of Consulting and Clinical Psychology, 43,* 95. doi:10.1037/h0076289

Ruback, R. B., & Juieng, D. (1997). Territorial defense in parking lots: Retaliation against waiting drivers. *Journal of Applied Social Psychology, 27,* 821–834. doi:10.1111/j.1559-1816.1997.tb00661.x

Ruback, R. B., Pape, K., & Doriot, P. D. (1989). Waiting for a phone: Intrusion on callers leads to territorial defense. *Social Psychology Quarterly, 52,* 232–241. doi:10.2307/2786718

Seligman, M. E. P. (1995). The effectiveness of psychotherapy: The Consumer Reports study. *American Psychologist, 50,* 965–974. doi:10.1037/0003-066X.50.12.965

Snyder, C. R. (1974). Why horoscopes are true: The effects of specificity on acceptance of astrological interpretations. *Journal of Clinical Psychology, 30,* 577–580.

doi:10.1002/1097-4679(197410)30:4<577::
AID-JCLP2270300434>3.0.CO;2-8

Snyder, C. R., Larsen, D. L., & Bloom, L. J. (1976).
Acceptance of general personality interpretations
prior to and after receipt of diagnostic feedback supposedly based on psychological, graphological, and
astrological assessment procedures. *Journal of Clinical Psychology, 32,* 258–265. doi:10.1002/1097-
4679(197604)32:2<258::AID-JCLP2270320211>
3.0.CO;2-O

Snyder, C. R., & Newburg, C. L. (1981). The Barnum
effect in a group setting. *Journal of Personality
Assessment, 45,* 622–629. doi:10.1207/
s15327752jpa4506_10

Survey research looks at attitudes, obstacles to walking
and biking to work. (2009, May 14). *Women's
Health Weekly, 335.*

Wood, J. M., Nezworski, M. T., Lilienfeld, S. O., &
Garb, H. N. (2003). The Rorschach Inkblot Test,
fortune tellers, and cold reading. *Skeptical Inquirer,
27,* 29–33, 61.

Wyman, A. J., & Vyse, S. (2008). Science versus the
stars: A double-blind test of the validity of the NEO
five-factor inventory and computer-generated astrological natal charts. *The Journal of General
Psychology, 135,* 287–300. doi:10.3200/
GENP.135.3.287-300

Correlation Research 1

Pseudoscience is for people who are bad at math

Abstract

Psychology: People are notoriously bad at understanding probability. Could this difficulty account for differences in belief in the paranormal (e.g., are believers poorer at understanding probability)?

Skeptic/Pseudoscience: Not understanding probability might make people think things are miraculous even though those things are actually quite likely (coincidences). In general, cognitive differences between believers and non-believers might explain belief in the paranormal.

INTRODUCTION: FINDING RELATIONSHIPS

One goal of research in any scientific discipline is to find out what relationships exist between variables in the world. In Chapter 2, we looked at how observation of naturally occurring behavior could be used to uncover relationships. In Chapter 3, we looked at how survey data could be used to uncover relationships.

Correlation research is a special case of observation and survey research. Three things characterize correlation research. The first characteristic is that all of the variables are measured variables. The investigator does not manipulate anything that is being studied. The second characteristic is that the variables being measured must be capable of being expressed numerically, and the more values the variables can take on, the better. Ideally, the variables will be **continuous**. A continuous variable has an infinite number of possible values. The third characteristic is the computation of a correlation coefficient once the data are collected. A correlation coefficient can tell us the strength and direction of a relationship.

Let's consider an example of a correlational study. Daneman and Carpenter (1980) were interested in the relationship between one's ability to understand

METHODOLOGY NOTE **4.1**

Correlation research involves measuring variables. Two important issues in any measurement situation are **reliability** and **validity**. A measure is reliable if it produces a consistent result every time someone completes it (assuming that the thing being measured has not changed). Reliability is important if we are to make sense of differences in people's scores in a study. If the measure is unreliable, then we have no way of knowing if the differences we find reflect real differences between people, or if they are simply the result of a poor instrument. For the target article in this chapter, we will be concerned with a reliable way to measure variables like belief in the paranormal.

Validity has to do with how well a test measures what it is supposed to measure. For example, a survey instrument that is supposed to measure anxiety but actually measures depression would not be valid. Obviously, a measure that is not valid is of little use in research, so it is important to use instruments that actually measure what they claim to measure.

written text passages and a variable called "reading span." To measure reading span, a person is given a list of sentences to read out loud and then has to memorize the last word in each sentence. After a set of sentences, the person has to report the last words. For example, a set of two sentences would be:

1. According to the results of the survey, Robert Redford is the most-liked Hollywood star.
2. The weather was unpredictable that summer, so no one made plans too far in advance.

A person being tested would read the sentences and then recall "star" and "advance." The sentences can be presented in sets of 2, 3, 4, 5, or 6; a person's reading span is the largest number of sentences for which he or she can recall the final words.

The goal of developing the reading span test was to find a quick method of assessing a person's working memory capacity. Then, the test could be used to sort participants in reading experiments into high- and low-capacity groups or to control for differences in capacity. To assess reading comprehension, Daneman and Carpenter (1980) had participants read short stories and answer questions about them. To see if the span test was related to this measure of comprehension ability, Daneman and Carpenter computed the correlation between reading span and people's ability to answer the questions correctly. This correlation was $r = .72$. What does that mean?

First, a correlation can range between -1 and $+1$. A positive correlation means that a positive relationship exists. As the score on one measured variable increases, so does the score on the other. In the case of reading span and comprehension, there is a positive relationship, so as reading span gets higher, so does comprehension. A negative correlation would mean that a negative relationship exists between two variables. As the score on one increases, the score on the other decreases. For example, we would expect a negative relationship between reading disabilities and reading comprehension (as degree of reading disability goes up, reading comprehension should go down).

A large correlation has an absolute value close to 1. So .72 is relatively large (note that −.72 would be just as large; the sign is irrelevant when considering the size of a correlation). The larger the correlation, the stronger the relationship.

What we can say, then, is that a strong, positive relationship exists between reading span and text comprehension. Does this mean that a big reading span causes improved comprehension? No. You need to commit this fact to memory and keep it fresh in your mind: Correlation does not imply causation. All we know after we compute a correlation is that a relationship exists. Causally, there are three possible situations. In terms of span and comprehension:

1. High spans cause good comprehension (high-span people have so much mental room that they can simultaneously read and hold more ideas from a text, improving comprehension).
2. People who comprehend well have high spans (maybe because they are not working so hard to understand the sentences, they have room left over to hold the words).
3. Some third factor causes people to have high spans and comprehend well (for example, a good diet helps all cognitive capacities to improve).

With just a correlation, each possibility is equally likely to be true, and we have no way of telling which is correct. We cannot use a correlation to establish causality.

So, correlation research can be used to determine the strength and direction of relationships between variables. But you cannot use correlation research to uncover information about the causes of behavior. You may be asking yourself, "Why would anyone do correlation research if a causal statement cannot be made at the end of the study?" There are three good reasons:

1. *Ethics.* If I wanted to investigate the relationship between self-esteem and body image, I could randomly assign one group to be low in self-esteem, but that would require me to lower their self-esteem. This would violate ethical principles. Similarly, it would not be possible to manipulate childhood sexual abuse to investigate its effect on adult psychological well-being. To investigate these questions, we would have to do correlational research.

ETHICS NOTE **4.1**

Measuring such variables as childhood sexual abuse helps you avoid the ethical issues associated with manipulating these variables, but other ethical issues are still involved. Whenever you collect sensitive information from participants, you need to take extra precautions to ensure confidentiality and anonymity. In addition, most ethics review boards will expect to see a clear need for this information to be collected before letting a project continue.

METHODOLOGY NOTE **4.2**

As a check on your comprehension, consider the following cases. If a researcher were investigating the relationship between marijuana use and the development of psychosis, would that person expect a positive or negative relationship? Assuming a relationship were found, why would it be difficult to conclude that marijuana use was causally related to the development of psychosis (Semple, McIntosh, & Lawrie, 2005)? Suppose a researcher were interested in the relationship between working (hours worked per week) and high school achievement. Would that researcher be more likely to expect a positive or negative relationship? Assuming a relationship were found, why would it be difficult to conclude that there was a causal relationship between the two variables (Singh, Chang, & Dika, 2007)?

2. *Generalizability.* A good experiment requires careful control by the experimenter. Achieving this control can reduce the naturalness of the task. If a researcher wants the conditions of the research to closely match those in the real world, a correlation design may be chosen.
3. *Feasibility.* Experiments can be difficult and expensive to conduct. The corresponding correlation research might be simpler (e.g., because participant populations are readily available). In those cases, researchers do correlation research to fully explore the relationship between two variables. Once the relationship is understood, it might then be possible to do an experiment to determine causality.

Correlation research has been used to explore a variety of relationships between variables in the realm of paranormal beliefs and pseudoscience. In Chapter 5, we will look for a correlation between paranormal belief and personality. In Chapter 6, we will look for a correlation between handwriting variables and personality. Our target article for this chapter used a correlation approach to investigate the relationship between paranormal belief and reasoning ability.

TARGET ARTICLE: REASONING AND PARANORMAL BELIEF

(Be sure to look at Appendix D to assist you in evaluating the sources cited in this chapter. Be especially aware of the guidelines for evaluating Internet and other non-peer reviewed sources.)

Although the topics for this book have been chosen because they relate to topics in the paranormal and pseudosciences, this is primarily a psychology book. One problem that will appear in most of the chapters can be called the "gap problem": Why is it that even when the empirical evidence in favor of some phenomenon might be very poor, the level of belief in that phenomenon remains high? (For example, Musella, 2005, reported that 41% of the population believes in ESP in spite of the poor evidence for it.) This is fundamentally a psychology question, and the answer to this question can be very informative. One possible answer to the question is that people believe in paranormal phenomena because they believe that they have had a paranormal experience (Blackmore & Troscianko, 1985).

Blackmore and Troscianko (1985) proposed two explanations for why people might believe that they have had a paranormal experience: a) they have actually had a paranormal experience, or b) they have misinterpreted something normal as being a paranormal experience (e.g., thinking about someone that you have not seen in a long time and then bumping into that person the next day could be taken as an experience of psychic precognition). One explanation for people misinterpreting non-paranormal events as paranormal is the probability misjudgment hypothesis. Loosely speaking, if people are poor at judging the probability of things happening (e.g., coincidences), then when those things do happen people search for an explanation, and those explanations are often of the paranormal variety.

Blackmore and Troscianko's (1985) hypothesis was that belief arises from a poorer ability to estimate the probabilities of things, meaning that believers should be worse at estimating probabilities. One problem with this explanation for the gap problem is that people are generally bad at understanding probability (e.g., Kahneman & Tversky, 1972). Is there room within this generally poor performance for believers to do significantly worse?

Blackmore and Troscianko (1985) measured participants' ability to produce and judge random strings of numbers. Generally, people expect:

> More irregular sequences to be more likely (e.g., HHTHTH looks like a more likely outcome of tossing a coin six times than HTHTHT, Hahn & Warren, 2009).

> More alternation to be more likely (HHHTTT seems less likely than HHTHTH, Hahn & Warren, 2009).

Kahneman and Tversky (1972) argued that this pattern of expectations arises due to a heuristic called representativeness. Basically, the sequences people think are more likely appear to be more representative of the random process that was supposed to produce those sequences. This is an error because all possible outcomes of six tosses of a fair coin are equally likely.

Blackmore and Troscianko (1985) also measured participants' sensitivity to the impact of sample size on probabilities. Basically, as the number of coin flips increases, the less likely it is that a 50–50 ratio of heads to tails could come from a biased coin. On the other hand, as the number of coin flips increases, the more likely it is that a 75–25 ratio comes from a biased coin (e.g., three heads and one tail is reasonably likely to happen when flipping a fair coin four times, but 15 heads and 5 tails is less likely when flipping a fair coin 20 times). Kahneman and Tversky (1972) found that even though an "extreme outcome is more likely to occur in a smaller sample" (p. 443), their participants were most likely to conclude that outcomes were equally likely, regardless of sample size (e.g., when comparing the number of days that a large hospital with 45 births per day and a small hospital with 15 births per day would have more boys than girls, the correct answer is

SCIENCE NOTE **4.1**

Hahn and Warren (2009) foreshadow the surprising turn that this chapter is going to take. They took as their starting point the basic facts about people's judgments of randomness discussed in the chapter. Much has been made of people's poor performance at judging and producing random sequences (I will refer you to Hahn & Warren for a discussion). However, when one looks more closely at people's actual experience, and when one takes into account such well-understood psychological phenomena as a limited short-term memory capacity, one finds that people's expectations about randomness are actually pretty accurate. For example, the wait time ("the average number of coin tosses that one has to wait before encountering a particular substring," p. 455) is 14 for HHH, but only 8 for HHT. If one is limited to 20 coin flips in a row, there is approximately a 53% chance of never encountering HHHH, but only a 25% chance of never encountering THHH. Given that people's experience is more likely to come from finite sequences of flips than from infinite sequences, and given the additional constraint that comes from having a limited short-term memory capacity, people's expectations about randomness suddenly do not seem so bad (e.g., some sequences *are* more likely). From a more global perspective this makes more sense than the "people are really bad at understanding randomness" position. As Hahn and Warren put it "Can people's undoubted sensitivity to the structure of the environment be reconciled with these seeming errors of judgment?" (p. 454). The answer is "yes." People's performance only looks poor if they are being compared to an arbitrary model.

the smaller hospital, but participants were most likely to say the chances were equal). Again, this can be explained in terms of representativeness.

Blackmore and Troscianko (1985) also included problems similar to Kahneman and Tversky's (1972) problems investigating posterior probability estimates. Basically, they took problems for which there was a likely reasoning error and packaged them together into a measure they called "sampling questions."

The logic of Blackmore and Troscianko's (1985) study was simple: construct a survey with a variety of problems with known outcomes (people are generally not very good at answering these types of problems), present them to believers and non-believers, and see if believers are worse at these problems than non-believers. The results were somewhat mixed. In the first experiment, they found that believers were worse at understanding the impact of sample size in the coin tossing problem. In their second experiment, believers were worse at answering the sampling questions. This seems to answer the original question in the affirmative. People may be more likely to believe because they are poorer at judging probability and therefore interpret more normal experiences as paranormal. But, a closer look at the data suggests a more cautious conclusion. First, Blackmore and Troscianko (1985) failed to replicate their own findings within their own study. The effect of sample size did not replicate in Experiment 2, and the sampling questions did not differ in Experiment 1. Furthermore, the sample size problem difference found in Experiment 1 is less impressive when one notices that the average score for both groups was below zero, suggesting that none of the participants understood the impact of changing sample size on probabilities.

This chapter will now take a somewhat unexpected turn. The hypothesis that people who believe in the paranormal are different from non-believers on cognitive tasks has actually received little empirical support. For example, Blackmore (1997) argued against the probability misjudgment hypothesis proposed by Blackmore and Troscianko (1985). One concern raised in Blackmore's (1997) study was the artificial nature of the tasks being used. Instead of laboratory measures of reasoning ability, she tried to relate probability judgments to a real-world context. In particular, if someone were to visit a psychic and that psychic were to make a statement like "you own a CD or tape of Handel's water music," that would seem to most people to be a pretty remarkable "hit." However, if it is actually very likely for people to own that piece of music, then the psychic's performance seems much less remarkable.

Blackmore (1997) asked her participants to rate whether 10 statements of the sort typically made by psychics would be true of them and the likelihood that they would be true of others. Blackmore's expectation from the probability misjudgment hypothesis was that believers would be more likely to underestimate the extent to which the statements were true of others than non-believers. In other words, if being bad at estimating probability supports belief in the paranormal, people who believe should be worse at guessing probabilities. The data did not support this expectation. In fact, believers and non-believers *overestimated* the extent to which the statements would be true of others. They did not differ in these overestimates. As Blackmore put it "misjudgments of probability are not likely to be an important factor in the determination of paranormal belief" (p. 688).

A similar pattern emerges when considering other possible differences between believers and non-believers: initial research suggests a difference, but additional studies undermine that conclusion. Wiseman and Watt (2006) presented a comprehensive review of a number of possible differences between believers and non-believers. I am going to summarize their conclusions here, but I strongly suggest that you consult their original review for a complete description.

The first hypothesis considered by Wiseman and Watt (2006) was that believers and non-believers differ in general cognitive ability (e.g., academic outcomes or critical thinking). The results were mixed, but Wiseman and Watt were able to conclude that there was no difference between believers and non-believers (there was one exception to this conclusion that we will explore more fully in the projects section). We can consider critical thinking as representative of this area of research. Roe (1999), after critically evaluating previous research in the area, presented believers and non-believers with research articles to evaluate. This was a real-world example of critical thinking skill; if believers are poor at critical thinking then they should be worse at evaluating research papers. In addition, Roe manipulated the content of the papers. One report was pro-ESP and one was anti-ESP. This allowed Roe to assess whether believers and non-believers would be more critical of papers with which they disagreed. Roe found that there was no significant difference between believers and non-believers in judging the quality of the papers (but believers were actually a little *more* critical). Roe did find a congruency effect: participants were more critical of papers that did not match their own position. Similar to Blackmore (1997), when a real world task was used, believers and non-believers did not differ. (Note that the results are not purely a function of real world versus laboratory measures. Hergovich & Arendasy, 2005, using a more traditional measure of critical thinking, also found no relationship between critical thinking and belief in the paranormal.)

Wiseman and Watt (2006) also reviewed the probability misjudgment literature discussed before. One interesting conclusion was that there may be a major contribution of task type. Artificial tasks tend to produce an effect, whereas more natural tasks do not. However, this conclusion must be classified as tentative because there are not many studies using ecologically valid materials and tasks. We will revisit this issue in the projects section. Also, Wiseman and Watt reviewed two areas of the literature for which there were differences between believers and non-believers. I have reserved discussion of those parts of the review for the projects section.

We can now turn our attention to the target article for this chapter. Bressan (2002) had two goals for her study. The first was to evaluate the probability misjudgment hypothesis with a larger sample. As noted previously, the literature in this area is mixed. Bressan's second purpose was to incorporate the frequency with which people experience coincidences into this research. The probability misjudgment hypothesis predicts that being poor at understanding random sequences should cause a person to perceive more coincidences in their life (things perceived as nonrandom will appear to be surprising coincidences). Will there be a relationship between the number of coincidences people experience and their ability to estimate randomness?

Bressan (2002) conducted two studies; the second was essentially a replication of the first. She collected data from a diverse population that included university students and "regular workers" who had completed either middle school or high school. She collected data on three dependent variables. The first was probabilistic reasoning (e.g., the sampling questions from Blackmore & Troscianko, 1985, and problems requiring the generation of random sequences). The second dependent variable measured the number of coincidences people experienced (e.g., "thinking of someone and running unexpectedly into that person soon afterwards," p. 32). The final dependent variable was a belief in the paranormal questionnaire.

We will begin by considering the probabilistic reasoning items. There were no differences between believers and non-believers on the probability problems in Study 1. There were some differences in Study 2. Performance on Bressan's (2002) coin tossing problem (similar to the problem in Blackmore & Troscianko, 1985) was negatively correlated with belief, but only for the workers (e.g., more belief was associated with poorer performance). For a

METHODOLOGY NOTE **4.3**

One problem with studies finding no difference between believers and non-believers is accepting the null hypothesis. The logic of statistical hypothesis testing makes accepting the null hypothesis difficult. The basic idea is that there are only two possible outcomes to a statistical test: there is a difference or there is not a difference. By showing that it is unlikely that there is *not* a difference, we conclude that there must be a difference. If we cannot show that it is unlikely that there is *not* a difference, we cannot automatically conclude that there is not a difference. It is possible that a lack of a difference occurred due to methodological errors or low statistical power. One solution to this problem is to be clever in designing studies such that we will expect a difference (as opposed to expecting the means to be the same). Roe (1999) illustrated this nicely in the construction of his sample research papers that participants evaluated. The pro-ESP paper described a procedure in which a significant difference would support the existence of ESP (an experimenter pretended to show cards briefly, but in fact only transmitted them telepathically). The anti-ESP paper described a procedure in which a significant difference would work against the existence of ESP (the experimenter actually showed the cards briefly, in addition to transmitting them telepathically). So, even when no ESP effect was expected (a null result), there would still be a significant difference. Another way to validate null results is to build in a condition in which a difference is expected in addition to a condition in which no difference is expected. This will typically be done in a factorial design, which is the topic of Chapter 9. Researchers can also argue that a significant difference with one dependent variable validates a null effect for another variable (as in "the experiment was sufficiently well-designed to find this, so not finding that means it really is not there").

A related issue is the bias in science against null results. If something is supposed to be there, but is not, that is still news. Imagine looking for your car in the parking lot and not finding it where you left it. Technically, that is a null result, but you will probably perceive it as important. In this case, finding no difference between believers and non-believers is meaningful. It suggests a more nuanced understanding of belief in the paranormal: believers are not somehow defective; rather understanding psychology allows us to predict that some people will believe certain kinds of things. That does not excuse belief in things that are not true, but it does help us to understand how people think and how to think about things like the paranormal.

problem in which participants judged which of a set of dice rolls was more likely (e.g., 4 6 6 6 3 5 versus 4 3 2 5 4 1), there was a significant negative correlation with paranormal belief for both workers and students.

Bressan (2002) provided a possible reason for why there are few differences between believers and non-believers on these kinds of tasks. Performance is so poor overall that there is no room for a difference to emerge (a **floor effect**). This might be a partial explanation for the mixed results reviewed by Wiseman and Watt (2006). Some of the problems (e.g., ones with extreme deviations) are easier, and in those problems differences emerge.

There was a significant negative correlation between performance and belief in the paranormal for all but one of the generation of random strings tasks, but in all cases the correlation only held for the workers. In a sense, education may be creating a **ceiling effect** within the data. As people learn about probability, differences between believers and non-believers disappear. To sum up, the effects of varying education levels and problem difficulty could both be contributing to the mixed results found in previous studies.

Bressan's (2002) primary interest was in the correlation between the number of coincidences perceived and reasoning. Part of the probability misjudgment hypothesis is that a poor understanding of probability causes a lot of normal events to be classified as paranormal. In this case, poorer reasoning should be associated with perceiving more coincidences. This prediction was not supported by the data. On the other hand, there was a strong correlation between paranormal belief and the number of coincidences experienced. Even though belief is correlated with the experiencing of coincidences, the experiencing of coincidences is not correlated with a poorer understanding of probability, undermining a critical assumption of the probability misjudgment hypothesis.

Bressan (2002) proposed an alternative to the probability misjudgment hypothesis. Believers have "an inclination to connect events causally" (p. 29). Because of this, they have a stronger belief in the paranormal and experience more coincidences. Strong pattern-finders will also have a different model of randomness from weak pattern-finders. The expression of this difference depends on a variety of factors (e.g., education, problem difficulty). However,

METHODOLOGY NOTE **4.4**

Bressan's (2002) data have the possibility of shedding light on the mixed results of previous studies, but there are a number of assumptions built into the explanation. In cases like these, it is useful to search for independent confirmation of the assumptions. For example, if education removes differences between believers and non-believers, then a larger number of articles finding a difference should have used less-educated participants, and a larger number of articles not finding a difference should have used more-educated participants. Another approach to evaluating the assumptions would be to build them into a study as variables. For example, in the projects section one suggestion is to manipulate problem difficulty within a survey and evaluate the impact of problem difficulty on the correlation between belief and performance.

in the right circumstances believers will be poorer at understanding random-ness than non-believers.

It is not possible to make causal conclusions at the end of correlation studies like Bressan's (2002) because no variables have been manipulated. However, it is informative to consider the possible causal relationships. The probability misjudgment hypothesis is that poor understanding of probability will cause the perception of more coincidences (paranormal experiences), which will cause a higher belief in the paranormal. With respect to the first two variables in that chain, Bressan's results were that they are not related, so we can dispense with concerns about which causes which. For number of coincidences and paranormal belief, it could be that more coincidences cause higher paranormal belief, higher paranormal belief leads to the experiencing of more coincidences, or some third factor causes both. Bressan prefers the third explanation as being more parsimonious. For the first possibility, how could something appear to be a meaningful coincidence without a belief structure that would cause a person to label it as such? For the second, where would belief come from in the first place? For Bressan, a predisposition to be a pattern seeker is a valuable skill, and one that can vary in the population. More of it leads to a higher number of perceived coincidences and greater be-lief in the paranormal. As she puts it, "The condition we are genetically equipped for is the search for bonds, patterns, meanings: paranormal belief represents its byproduct at least as much as the ability to classify, the love for music, or the gift for scientific discovery" (p. 30).

The projects will allow you to explore these variables for yourself, and will also allow you to test other possible relationships between reasoning abil-ity and belief in the paranormal.

INFOTRAC® COLLEGE EDITION EXERCISES

You can use the InfoTrac College Edition to read about additional studies using a correlation methodology. For example, typing in "correlation re-search" and checking the box for "in entire article content" gave me a list of 204 articles. Many of these did not seem related to my goal to find articles using a correlation methodology. Checking the box for "to refereed publica-tions" allowed me to reduce that set to peer-reviewed journals. That returned 87 articles. One of those was "The 'window problem' in studies of children's attainments: A methodological exploration" (Wolfe, Haveman, Ginther, & An, 1996). The authors discussed the effect of limited time frames on correla-tions. Their conclusion was that it can be misleading to base a correlation re-lating childhood events to eventual outcomes on only a limited data window (of one year or less). In general, you can learn a lot of methodological infor-mation from reading other people's research. Spend some time with the Info-Trac College Edition reading method sections from a variety of articles using correlation research before tackling your own project.

You can also find additional information about people's understanding of probability using the InfoTrac College Edition. When I typed "probability and paranormal" with the box for "in title, citation, abstract" checked, I got a list of four articles. This included Blackmore (1997). When I checked the box for "in entire article content," I got a list of 82 articles. This list included Wiseman and Watt (2006), which is a great starting point for research. This search also included a greater diversity of articles related to skepticism, the paranormal, and reasoning.

IMPLEMENTING THE DESIGN

Materials

One nice feature of Bressan's (2002) article is that she included most of her materials. You can reconstruct the probabilistic reasoning sections of her surveys with her Appendix B and Appendix C. A perusal of the literature will provide you with other examples of problems. Bressan also included her coincidences measure in Appendix A.

You will also need a scale to measure belief in the paranormal. Bressan's (2002) specific scale was not included. However, as part of their review Wiseman and Watt (2006) discussed the primary measures used in previous research. Many studies also included the items that they used to measure belief in the paranormal. Here is a partial list:

> Thalbourne and Delin (1993) presented the 18-item Australian Sheep-Goat Scale. (Sheep are believers in the paranormal; goats are non-believers.)

> Tobacyk and Milford (1983) presented a 25-item paranormal beliefs scale with seven dimensions of paranormal belief.

> Wiseman and Morris (1995) presented a 6-item Belief in the Paranormal Questionnaire for use in a study with "genuine psychic claimants" as an important component.

Suggested Projects

1. You can replicate aspects of Bressan's (2002) study. Create a questionnaire including probabilistic reasoning problems, a measure of coincidences, and paranormal belief. Present this questionnaire to participants and look at the various correlations.

    a. Bressan (2002) highlighted the importance of the population in research of this type. The convenience sample most readily available to college students is generally other students. However, Bressan found that level of education affected the relationship between performance on probability judgment tasks and paranormal belief. You could include different education levels as a variable in your study. Alternatively, Musch and Ehrenberg (2002) measured general cognitive ability (a weighted grade average used to determine university admissions in Germany) and found that once this was controlled for, differences in reasoning between believers and non-believers disappeared. Instead of looking for a different population, you could measure some aspect of cognitive ability within your sample. (See also Dagnall, Parker, & Munley, 2007 for a failure to replicate Bressan. Their participants were all first-year psychology majors, but they found a difference in belief correlated with perception of randomness. It might matter how far along in their education students are, which program they are in, or how homogenous the sample is.)

b. Bressan (2002) suggested that easier problems led to finding differences between believers and non-believers. One example was her coin tossing problem. As the deviation became more extreme, participants did better overall and there was a difference between believers and non-believers. She also pointed out that more alternatives allowed for differences in repetition avoidance in random generation problems to manifest themselves and, therefore, for differences between believers and non-believers to show up. Finally, Wiseman and Watt (2006) proposed that ecological validity in the problems might lead to better performance (but decrease differences between believers and non-believers). You could explicitly manipulate problem types within your survey to assess these effects.

c. Bressan (2002) suggested that degree of pattern seeking underlies both belief in the paranormal and experiencing of coincidences. You could explicitly measure this variable and look for correlations to support that hypothesis. For example, Blackmore and Moore (1994) found a tendency for believers to be more likely to identify something in a noisy image, and a significant correlation between belief and the number of times participants mistake a stranger for someone they know (see Wiseman & Watt, 2006 for a review of this literature). This latter variable is a more ecologically valid measure of the likelihood of making false identifications. Incorporating a measure like this into a replication of Bressan's study would allow you to explicitly test her hypothesis.

d. Wiseman and Watt (2006) discussed problems associated with measures of paranormal belief. Instead of using a paranormal belief scale, perhaps it would be better to classify participants into believers and non-believers on the basis of experience. Bressan (2002) found that paranormal belief was correlated with number of coincidences, suggesting number of coincidences as an experience-based measure of belief. Blagrove, French, and Jones (2006) found that the number of precognitive dreams experienced was correlated with paranormal belief, suggesting that as a measure of paranormal experience. Do other experiences with the paranormal also divide participants into believers and non-believers?

2. There is not strong evidence to support hypotheses that believers have different cognitive abilities from non-believers, nor is there strong evidence for the probability misjudgment hypothesis. However, there are other differences that do appear to be reliable. You could investigate these differences. These projects could go in two directions: Is there a

difference between believers and non-believers? Is that difference affected by the kinds of variables that affect probability misjudgment?

a. Wiseman and Watt (2006) found that there was good evidence for a difference between believers and non-believers in syllogistic reasoning. For example, Wierzbicki (1985) found that believers made more errors on conditional reasoning problems than non-believers. Further, he found that these errors were more likely on modus tollens and affirming the consequent problems than on modus ponens and denying the antecedent problems. Wierzbicki expected that believers would err more on problems with parapsychological content, but this hypothesis was not supported. These results were essentially replicated by Roberts and Seager (1999). (Roberts & Seager included measures of probabilistic reasoning and found that those did not distinguish between believers and non-believers, replicating Bressan, 2002.) You could design a project to investigate conditional reasoning more fully and include other variables that have been shown to affect conditional reasoning (e.g., permission situations, Cheng & Holyoak, 1985). Bressan implied that easier problems would make differences between believers and non-believers more apparent (e.g., permission situations), but the data from Wierzbicki suggest the opposite (modus tollens and affirming the consequent are the harder problems).

b. Wiseman and Watt (2006) reviewed the literature on fantasy proneness and found that believers were more fantasy prone. For example, Irwin (1990) found a correlation between fantasy proneness and a variety of paranormal beliefs. You could design a project to investigate this relationship or to connect fantasy proneness to other reasoning tasks used by Bressan (2002).

c. Langer and Roth (1975) had participants either call a series of coin flips or observe another person calling coin flips. They had three levels of feedback. In the descending condition, participants scored a lot of successes early. In the ascending condition, successes came later. There was also a random condition. They found that participants reported greater control for situations in which they were calling the coin flips and for the descending condition (early success made it seem more like a skill). Note that since participants had no actual control, Langer and Roth were measuring an illusion of control. Blackmore and Troscianko (1985) included a measure of the

METHODOLOGY NOTE **4.5**

Note that some of the projects are actually using a hybrid design combining elements of experiments with correlation research. Projects of this sort will help to answer Wiseman and Watts' (2006) call for more experimentation in this research area to move from purely correlational studies to studies allowing a causal conclusion.

illusion of control in their Experiment 3. They found that believers did report higher illusions of control in a task like Langer and Roth's. You could carry out a project investigating differences in illusions of control between believers and non-believers, or to evaluate how illusions of control interact with the sorts of variables measured by Bressan (2002).

d. Nickerson (1998) reviewed the literature on confirmation biases (a tendency to seek evidence that supports a belief that a person already holds). He related confirmation bias to a variety of potentially paranormal phenomena (e.g., number mysticism). Rudski (2002) investigated the extent to which paranormal belief correlated with performance on a telepathy task when a hindsight bias was possible and when one was not possible. He found that there was a correlation in the hindsight possible condition, suggesting a confirmation bias. You could design projects to investigate the extent to which confirmation biases support paranormal beliefs.

3. A couple of other interesting projects could be inspired from research into cognitive differences between believers and non-believers.

a. Wierzbicki (1985) found that content did not affect reasoning errors (abstract or paranormal content did not produce a significant difference in number of errors). Roe (1999) did find that participants rated papers that were incongruent with their beliefs to be of poorer quality than papers that were consistent with their beliefs (see also Russell & Jones, 1980, for data on believers and non-believers when provided with inconsistent information). An interesting project would be to do more carefully controlled studies into the effect of content on performance (e.g., instead of Kahneman and Tversky's, 1972, hospital

SCIENCE NOTE **4.2**

Rudski (2002) was concerned about studies that imply "value judgments on the intelligence of the participants' beliefs" (p. 904) and pointed out that hindsight biases can actually be adaptive. Similarly, Hahn and Warren (2009) were concerned about the natural leap researchers make from poor perception of randomness in studies to the conclusion that participants' reasoning is faulty. With respect to Blackmore and Moore's (1994) study showing that believers are more likely to see patterns in ambiguous data, one can hardly argue that not being able to find patterns in data is objectively better than finding patterns. What these have in common is that research into differences between believers and non-believers may be investigating a small, quantitative difference in a cognitive skill (e.g., Bressan's, 2002, pattern seeking variable) rather than a qualitative difference in cognitive ability. The goal of psychology research is to understand the whys of behavior, not to pass judgment on the conclusions people come to from the data they have collected, even if people conclude from their experience that a paranormal explanation is the best.

problem, turn it into a problem with paranormal content) and the effect of materials in agreement with a person's previous position on performance (e.g., will believers be more likely to discount contrary evidence, or will non-believers show more of an effect?).

b. Blackmore (1997) found surprising results in her survey of facts about people. Believers endorsed more of the facts and were significantly higher than non-believers on several of them (e.g., having a scar on their knee and owning a cat). Do believers fit a different profile than non-believers? Also, what kinds of facts are endorsed more by people and which are more rare? This kind of information could be used to provide a baseline for evaluating psychics' predictions about people (e.g., over 25% of Blackmore's sample had been to France, so it would not be so surprising if a psychic predicted that someone had been to France and they had been). Finally, Blagrove et al. (2006) noted that believers may respond "yes" to questions of this type due to an affirmative bias. If they are more likely to say "yes" overall, then this could inflate correlations between belief and other variables. It would be interesting to see if there really is a difference in affirmative bias between believers and non-believers.

REFERENCES

Blackmore, S. J. (1997). Probability misjudgment and belief in the paranormal: A newspaper survey. *British Journal of Psychology, 88*, 683–689.

Blackmore, S., & Moore, R. (1994). Seeing things: Visual recognition and belief in the paranormal. *European Journal of Psychology, 10*, 91–103.

Blackmore, S., & Troscianko, T. (1985). Belief in the paranormal: Probability judgments, illusory control, and the 'chance baseline shift.' *British Journal of Psychology, 76*, 459–468.

Blagrove, M., French, C. C., & Jones, G. (2006). Probabilistic reasoning, affirmative bias and belief in precognitive dreams. *Applied Cognitive Psychology, 20*, 65–83. doi:10.1002/acp.1165

Bressan, P. (2002). The connection between random sequences, everyday coincidences, and belief in the paranormal. *Applied Cognitive Psychology, 16*, 17–34. doi:10.1002/acp.754

Cheng, P. W., & Holyoak, K. J. (1985). Pragmatic reasoning schemas. *Cognitive Psychology, 17*, 391–416. doi:10.1016/0010-0285(85)90014-3

Dagnall, N., Parker, A., & Munley, G. (2007). Paranormal belief and reasoning. *Personality and Individual Differences, 43*, 1406–1415. doi:10.1016/j.paid.2007.04.017

Daneman, M., & Carpenter, P. A. (1980). Individual differences in working memory and reading. *Journal of Verbal Learning and Verbal Behavior, 19*, 450–466. doi:10.1016/S0022-5371(80)90312-6

Hahn, U., & Warren, P. A. (2009). Perceptions of randomness: Why three heads are better than four. *Psychological Review, 116*, 454–461. doi:10.1037/a0015241

Hergovich, A., & Arendasy, M. (2005). Critical thinking ability and belief in the paranormal. *Personality and Individual Differences, 38*, 1805–1812. doi:10.1016/j.paid.2004.11.008

Irwin, H. J. (1990). Fantasy proneness and paranormal beliefs. *Psychological Reports, 66*, 655–658.

Kahneman, D., & Tversky, A. (1972). Subjective probability: A judgment of representativeness. *Cognitive Psychology, 3*, 430–454. doi:10.1016/0010-0285(72)90016-3

Langer, E. J., & Roth, J. (1975). Heads I win, tails it's chance: The illusion of control as a function of the sequence of outcomes in a purely chance task. *Journal of Personality and Social Psychology, 32*, 951–955. doi:10.1037/0022-3514.32.6.951

Musch, J., & Ehrenberg, K. (2002). Probability misjudgment, cognitive ability, and belief in the paranormal. *British Journal of Psychology, 93*, 169–177. doi:10.1348/000712602162517

Musella, D. P. (2005). Gallup poll shows that Americans' belief in the paranormal persists. *Skeptical Inquirer, 29,* 5.

Nickerson, R. S. (1998). Confirmation bias: A ubiquitous phenomenon in many guises. *Review of General Psychology, 2,* 175–220. doi: 10.1037/1089-2680.2.2.175

Roberts, M. J., & Seager, P. B. (1999). Predicting belief in paranormal phenomena: A comparison of conditional and probabilistic reasoning. *Applied Cognitive Psychology, 13,* 443–450. doi: 10.1002/(SICI)1099-0720(199910)13:5 <443::AID-ACP592<3.0.CO;2-K

Roe, C. A. (1999). Critical thinking and belief in the paranormal: A re-evaluation. *British Journal of Psychology, 90,* 85–98. doi:10.1348/ 000712699161288

Rudski, J. M. (2002). Hindsight and confirmation biases in an exercise in telepathy. *Psychological Reports, 91,* 899–906.

Russell, D., & Jones, W. H. (1980). When superstition fails: Reactions to disconfirmation of paranormal beliefs. *Personality and Social Psychology Bulletin, 6,* 83–88. doi:10.1177/014616728061012

Semple, D. M., McIntosh, A. M., & Lawrie, S. M. (2005). Cannabis as a risk factor for psychosis: Systematic review. *Journal of Psychopharmacology, 19,* 187–194. doi: 10.1177/0269881105049040

Singh, K., Chang, M., & Dika, S. (2007). Effects of part-time work on school achievement during high school. *The Journal of Educational Research, 101,* 12–22. doi:10.3200/JOER.101.1.12-23

Thalbourne, M. A., & Delin, P. S. (1993). A new instrument for measuring the sheep-goat variable: Its psychometric properties and factor structure. *Journal of the Society for Psychical Research, 59,* 172–186. Retrieved from http://www.spr.ac.uk/ expcms/index.php?section=41

Tobacyk, J., & Milford, G. (1983). Belief in paranormal phenomena: Assessment instrument development and implications for personality functioning. *Journal of Personality and Social Psychology, 44,* 1029–1037. doi:10.1037/0022-3514.44.5.1029

Wierzbicki, M. (1985). Reasoning errors and belief in the paranormal. *The Journal of Social Psychology, 125,* 489–494.

Wiseman, R., & Morris, R. L. (1995). Recalling pseudo-psychic demonstrations. *British Journal of Psychology, 86,* 113–125.

Wiseman, R., & Watt, C. (2006). Belief in psychic ability and the misattribution hypothesis: A qualitative review. *British Journal of Psychology, 97,* 323–338. doi:10.1348/000712605X72523

Wolfe, B., Haveman, R., Ginther, D., & An, C. B. (1996). The "window problem" in studies of children's attainments: A methodological exploration. *Journal of the American Statistical Association, 91,* 970–982. doi:10.2307/2291716

CHAPTER 5

Correlation Research 2

The "paranormal" personality

Abstract

Psychology: Research has investigated the relationship between belief in the paranormal and psychopathology. Rather than focus on negative aspects of belief in the paranormal, the target article for this chapter asks the question: Are there differences in personality between believers and non-believers?

Skeptic/Pseudoscience: A personality difference could explain why some people are more susceptible to paranormal belief than others. Additionally, considering the adaptive nature of paranormal belief might help explain how those beliefs persist.

INTRODUCTION: FINDING RELATIONSHIPS

The target article for this chapter uses a correlation design. Correlation designs were discussed at length in the opening section of Chapter 4. If you have not already done so, you may want to read that section before continuing with this chapter.

TARGET ARTICLE: THE PERSONALITY OF PARANORMAL BELIEVERS

(Be sure to look at Appendix D to assist you in evaluating the sources cited in this chapter. Be especially aware of the guidelines for evaluating Internet and other non-peer reviewed sources.)

In Chapter 4, we addressed the question of whether believers in the paranormal have different cognitive abilities from non-believers (e.g., do they differ in critical thinking). The goal was to find a psychological variable to explain what we are calling the "gap problem": in spite of overwhelming evidence against a variety of paranormal phenomena, people continue to believe in those phenomena. Another possible explanation for the gap problem is that people who believe in the paranormal have different personalities from people who do not believe.

There is ample evidence for the gap problem. Musella (2005) discussed the results of a Gallup poll finding that 73% of respondents believed in at least one paranormal phenomenon. For some representative phenomena: 41% believed in ESP, 37% believed in haunted houses, and 25% believed in astrology. Farha and Steward (2006) presented similar questions to a sample of college students and found: 28% believed in ESP, 40% believed in haunted houses, and 17% believed in astrology. Some researchers have looked at data like these and concluded that there must be something wrong with people who believe in paranormal phenomena.

However, as Russell and Jones (1980) pointed out, paranormal beliefs may serve a functional role helping people to deal with experiences outside of their control. This may explain why belief in the paranormal has not changed as access to education has increased. Also, it may explain apparently contradictory findings like Farha and Steward's (2006) data showing that as education level increased within their sample, belief also increased. Instead of seeking evidence of pathology associated with belief in the paranormal, the aim of this chapter is to review research into ordinary personality differences between believers and non-believers.

Our target article for this chapter, Auton, Pope, and Seeger (2003), reflected this approach to the question. They broke research investigating individual differences between believers and non-believers into two camps. The *skeptical view* is "that paranormal believers are psychologically dysfunctional (i.e., psychotic, neurotic, and depressive)" (p. 712). The *nonskeptical view* is

METHODOLOGY NOTE **5.1**

One problem that we are going to encounter in this chapter is that there is no agreed upon measure of paranormal belief (see Wiseman & Watt, 2006). Some see paranormal belief as unitary, some see it as having multiple facets (e.g., traditional religious belief, witchcraft, psychic ability, superstition, spiritualism, extraordinary life forms, and precognition, Tobacyk & Milford, 1983). When we are looking for correlations between personality variables and paranormal belief, it will be important to consider how the researcher has **operationally defined** belief (their precise definition), as this may impact the data. As an example, Wiseman and Watt (2004) noted that the Paranormal Belief Scale only measures superstition with negative items (e.g., breaking a mirror brings bad luck). Correlations between this measure and negative psychological traits might arise from the kind of superstitions considered, and not from superstition itself. At the same time, there are a variety of scales for measuring personality, and many personality dimensions have been identified. Again, the operational definition of personality chosen by a researcher may affect the data.

to look for "the relationship between belief in the paranormal and those personality traits that are broadly relevant to the normal functioning of individuals" (p. 712). Another way to classify these two research enterprises is the functional role assigned to paranormal belief. The skeptical view essentially sees paranormal beliefs as maladaptive, whereas the nonskeptical view is more interested in the ways in which paranormal beliefs may themselves be adaptive, or may arise from personality characteristics that are adaptive.

Auton et al. (2003) began with a review of research from the skeptical camp. There are a number of associations between paranormal belief and potentially maladaptive personality characteristics. For example, Hergovich, Schott, and Arendasy (2008) described schizotypy "as a milder form of schizophrenia"

SCIENCE NOTE **5.1**

One goal of science is objectivity. Scientists are supposed to put their biases aside when they do research, and report just the facts. However, true objectivity is never possible. One of the challenges of doing science is finding a place along the continuum from pure objectivity (uninfluenced by anything but data) and pure subjectivity (being unable to see reality through the veil of your biases). If I may be allowed to trivialize these complex issues (see Longino, 1990, for a comprehensive discussion of this problem), we know pure objectivity is impossible because of obvious influences on the scientific process (e.g., funding opportunities can dictate which questions scientists choose to investigate). On the other end of the continuum, pure subjectivity accounts of science cannot be correct because we have obvious verifications of science all around us (e.g., the planes rarely fall from the sky). This issue is relevant to Auton et al.'s (2003) discussion of skeptical and nonskeptical approaches to research investigating differences between believers and nonbelievers. A person who seeks evidence of pathological differences between believers and nonbelievers is going to use measures that will highlight pathology, and will be biased to find evidence in support of that position. A person with a nonskeptical approach will do the opposite. These biases may affect the data collected (experimenter expectancies have been shown to affect the results, e.g., Rosenthal & Fode, 1963). However, the more interesting issue lies in the interpretation of the data. Longino's proposal is that scientists should make their biases known and take them into account when interpreting the results of studies. By having a variety of perspectives with relatively equal access to the conversation, the truth can emerge. In this case, a researcher in the nonskeptical camp can accept the results that paranormal belief is associated with schizotypy, but still evaluate the extent to which that personality type might be adaptive as opposed to maladaptive. In other words, we can try to minimize the influence of expectancies on the actual data collected while acknowledging their role in how we interpret those data. Given the inherent biases evident in research into paranormal and pseudoscientific phenomena (on both sides of the issue), this is a really important consideration.

(p. 119) that may predict psychosis. However, only a small percentage of people with schizotypy actually develop schizophrenia. Hergovich et al. found that in adolescents there was a strong link between schizotypy and aspects of paranormal belief (belief in precognition, psychic ability, witchcraft, and spiritualism). They interpreted their results as potentially important for people who work with adolescents because "belief in the components of paranormal belief strongly associated with schizotypy brings with itself the potential danger of a larger delusional system and the involvement of a partial psychotic component" (p. 124).

Houran, Irwin, and Lange (2001) also found that schizotypy was more strongly associated with some aspects of paranormal belief in adults. They divided the Paranormal Belief Scale into two factors: New age philosophy (allowing "control over external events on an *individual level* ... reinforced by personal experience", with items such as psychic ability, reincarnation, and astrology) and traditional paranormal beliefs ("which are effective in maintaining control over external events on a *social level* and which are largely reinforced by the individual's culture", with items such as the devil, Heaven and Hell, and witchcraft) (p. 374). They summarized a number of differences between believers who are of primarily new age philosophy and those who are of primarily traditional paranormal belief. In part, they suggested that the scale can be used by clinicians because new age philosophy is more closely associated with psychopathology.

McCreery and Claridge (2002) argued for "healthy schizotypy" in out-of-body experiences. People who have out-of-body experiences, in contrast to schizophrenics with hallucinations, often enjoy the experience, suggesting that schizotypy is not inherently maladaptive. In fact, schizotypy can be adaptive, contributing to creativity; out-of-body experiences, in particular, can help reduce pain after surgery. Goulding (2004) extended this finding (that schizotypy is not necessarily maladaptive) to other forms of paranormal experience. In other words, even though paranormal belief is associated with schizotypy, schizotypy is not inherently pathological. There may be a relationship between psychopathology and paranormal beliefs, but if there is, it will be more complicated than a simple correlation, and it will be between certain types of beliefs and certain dimensions of schizotypy.

Auton et al. (2003) adopted a nonskeptical approach to the question of personality differences between believers and non-believers. They measured personality using a scale that was not seeking psychopathology, the Personality Research Form. They measured belief in the paranormal using the Paranormal Belief Scale. Their participants were both believers and non-believers.

The main question for Auton et al. (2003) was whether there would be differences between believers and non-believers on personality dimensions. The answer was mostly "no." For the 20 scales of the Personality Research Form, there were only four significant differences (at the alpha = .05 level). Believers scored lower on abasement (meekness) and higher on aggression, defendence (defensiveness), and sentience (sensitivity) (adjectives describing the scales were taken from Fekken, Holden, Jackson, & Guthrie, 1987). However, given the number of comparisons (20), Auton et al. decreased the alpha level for significance (with an alpha = .05, their true probability of a Type I error for 20 comparisons was around .64). Based on this, only defendence was significant.

The main conclusion from Auton et al. (2003) is that when comparing believers and non-believers on a personality scale used to measure normal adults, there were not any real differences. They pointed out that some of the scales measured negative traits, and these also did not differ (e.g., attention seeking or a need to be held in high regard by others).

Auton et al. (2003) did find that there were differences in other areas. Basically, believers had more social support for their beliefs. They watched more television programs about the paranormal, read more books about the paranormal, and had more friends who believe. Auton et al. suggested that social support might be a better explanation for belief than a pathological personality.

The projects will allow you to explore the relationship between personality and belief in the paranormal more fully.

INFOTRAC® COLLEGE EDITION EXERCISES

You can use the InfoTrac College Edition to read about additional studies using correlational methodologies. This was discussed in Chapter 4. You can also find a lot of information about paranormal beliefs and personality using the InfoTrac College Edition. When I typed "paranormal personality" into the search box with "in title, citation, abstract" checked, I only found one article (Thalbourne & Delin, 1994). Whereas there was only one article with these particular terms, it was very appropriate to the issues addressed in this chapter, and had a very useful reference list. You could explore other possible search terms to generate additional articles (e.g., "Thalbourne" generated a list of 19 articles, one of which was Thalbourne, 1998, which presented additional data on paranormal belief in psychotics).

IMPLEMENTING THE DESIGN

Materials

Personality measures:

You may have trouble locating some of the specific personality scales used in the articles reviewed in this chapter. Although you cannot safely substitute personality scales without having a possible effect on the data, you can search for valid and reliable measures of personality to incorporate into your own projects. Some potentially useful personality measures are described here.

The Personality Research Form is not in the public domain. However, Fekken et al. (1987) presented 20 adjectives corresponding to Personality Research Form subscales that their participants rated on a 9-point scale. You could substitute the adjective rating task for the full form. However, there are some limitations on this procedure. Fekken et al. were norming the Personality Research Form in a sample of Filipino students. It is possible that their results may not generalize to other populations (in fact, the responses to the Infrequency scale suggested that the Filipino sample was different). Also, the

METHODOLOGY NOTE **5.2**

Keep in mind the importance of **reliability** and **validity** when choosing measures. Reliability refers to consistent measurement. It is important that a measure have internal consistency and that it produce the same result each time it is used to measure someone. Unreliable measures make it difficult to interpret a person's score. Valid measures are ones that measure what they are supposed to be measuring. Obviously, if your measures are not valid then it will be difficult to interpret people's scores. When choosing measures, you should look for those that are both reliable and valid. Usually, studies of reliability and validity will be available in the literature.

overall validity between the adjective task and the Personality Research Form was not as high as it might have been. That being said, the scale-adjective pairs were:

> Abasement—meek; Achievement—ambitious; Affiliation—sociable; Aggression—
> aggressive; Autonomy—independent; Change—changeable; Cognitive
> Structure—seeks definitiveness; Defendence—defensive; Dominance—dominant;
> Endurance—persistent; Exhibition—attention-seeking; Harmavoidance—
> thrill-seeking (reversed); Impulsivity—impulsive; Nurturance—supporting;
> Order—orderly; Play—fun-loving; Sentience—sensitive; Social Recognition—seeks
> approval; Succorance—seeks help; Understanding—curious (p. 401).

Wiseman and Watt (2004) and Williams, Francis, and Robbins (2007) measured neuroticism. Wiseman and Watt measured this using a single-item scale in their first study ("I tend to worry about life"). This produced similar results to their Study 2 with a more formal measure of neuroticism, suggesting that it may be a valid measure. Some measures of neuroticism can be found on the Internet. For example, the free personality test at trans4mind.com (http://www.trans4mind.com/personality/) claims to be based on Eysenck's test. Similarminds.com (http://similarminds.com/index.html) provides a variety of personality tests, including a version of Eysenck's test that gives scores on Eysenck's dimensions of extroversion (sociability), neuroticism (emotionality), and psychoticism (rebelliousness). If you choose to substitute one of these tests, you should search for information about their reliability and validity first, and try to choose the best instrument possible.

Other personality measures are available in the literature. For example, Donnellan, Oswald, Baird, and Lucas (2006) presented a 20-item scale for measuring the big-five personality factors.

Eckblad and Chapman (1983) presented a scale for measuring magical ideation. This was used in some studies as a measure of schizotypy. Mason, Claridge, and Jackson (1995) presented a scale for measuring four dimensions of schizotypy. Their article only contained sample items for each subscale, but the entire scale is available from the author. Complete shorter versions of the scales, with instructions for scoring, were presented by Mason, Linney, and Claridge (2005). The SPQ-B can also be used as a brief measure of schizotypy and is described in Raine and Benishay (1995).

Measures of belief in the paranormal:

As discussed in Methodology Note 5.1, there is a great deal of disagreement regarding an adequate measure of belief in the paranormal. You will find that many of the studies in this area have used their own scale. Some of these are described in enough detail that you can use them in your research, some will be difficult to replicate without writing the author. Some scales are used in a variety of research and are readily available. Three of these are:

The Australian Sheep-Goat Scale: Thalbourne and Delin (1993).

The Paranormal Belief Scale: Tobacyk and Milford (1983).

The Belief in the Paranormal Questionnaire: Wiseman and Morris (1995).

Note that you probably cannot substitute these measures for one another. In fact, in the projects section, one project is to evaluate the impact of different measures of belief in the paranormal on the relationships found with personality variables.

Alternatively, the Anomalous Experiences Inventory (Gallagher, Kumar, & Pekala, 1994) can be used to identify participants' paranormal experiences, beliefs, and abilities. This would be a useful scale to divide participants based on paranormal experience rather than belief.

Other scales:

Wiseman and Watt (2004) wanted a measure of positive psychological functioning to relate to superstition. They used the Satisfaction With Life Scale that was presented in Diener, Emmons, Larsen, & Griffin (1985). The items and instructions for presenting the test are provided.

Schutte et al. (1998) presented a measure of emotional intelligence that could be used in studies looking at the adaptive nature of paranormal beliefs.

Zuckerman (1971) presented a measure of sensation seeking that could be used to explain differences in paranormal belief.

A variety of measures of locus of control are provided at http://wilder dom.com/psychology/loc/Measures.html.

Suggested Projects

1. You could replicate Auton et al.'s (2003) study. The materials section provides most of the tools that you would need for a replication.
   a. It might also be interesting to investigate other potential personality differences between believers and non-believers (e.g., the big five). There are a variety of personality scales for adult populations with no psychopathology that could be used.
   b. You could also look at different measures of the paranormal. The aspects of the paranormal that you measure may influence whether or not there are differences. For example, Houran et al. (2001) divided the subscales of the Paranormal Belief Scale into new age philosophy and traditional paranormal belief categories. Perhaps if participants are classified this way, differences between believers and non-believers may manifest themselves.

    c. Following the theme that Auton et al.'s (2003) nonskeptical research category is related to research investigating whether or not a particular personality feature is adaptive (even if it is potentially pathological), Wiseman and Watt (2004) presented a study that is a hybrid of projects 1a and 1b. Their main personality variable was neuroticism (potentially pathological), and they modified the Paranormal Belief Scale's superstition measure to include both negative (walking under a ladder is bad luck) and positive (carrying a lucky charm) superstitions. Because there were differences between positive and negative superstitions, Wiseman and Watt raised the possibility that some superstitious beliefs may be adaptive (e.g., positive superstitions provide a sense of control), whereas others may be maladaptive. Without incorporating both into models of the relationship between belief and personality, there is no way to know.

        i. An interesting project might be to take adaptive features of belief into account. For example, Williams et al. (2007) found a relationship between neuroticism and belief. However, they suggested that the correlation arose because belief allows people high in neuroticism to have a sense of control and reduce their over-emotionality. You could include items on your survey to investigate explicitly what belief does for people who believe.

        ii. Wiseman and Watt (2004) also called for a better understanding of positive superstitions. Perhaps there are other paranormal beliefs that can be broken into positive and negative categories (or that can be taken by participants as positive or negative). For example, traditional religious belief (e.g., life after death) could be comforting. Is there a difference between believers who endorse more positive aspects of belief and believers who endorse more negative aspects of belief?

2. You could look at other variables that might differ between believers and non-believers:

    a. Whereas it is not entirely consistent with the theme of this chapter, you could replicate research on the relationship between schizotypy and belief (e.g., aspects of Hergovich et al., 2008). Your project

METHODOLOGY NOTE **5.3**

Wiseman and Watt (2004) used an Internet sample in their first study. They were concerned that this sample might not be representative. To validate the sample, they compared their participants to previous research using their measures. Their participants showed that women had more belief than men and neuroticism correlated with belief. Since these patterns in their sample were consistent with previous research, they argued that their participants were representative of the kind of participants usually used in this type of research. As we will see in project 3, the population used in a study can have an effect.

SCIENCE NOTE **5.2**

Groth-Marnat and Pegden (1998) expected paranormal belief to be associated with an external locus of control. With respect to superstition, they found that it was actually related to an internal locus of control. In a sense, it is reasonable to expect superstition to be related to an external locus of control because superstitions relate to outside forces controlling your life. On the other hand, superstitious behaviors provide a way to influence events that are normally out of your control, and could be related to an internal locus of control. For exploratory research of the sort usually seen with surveys, the goal is to find out what is there, and it is somewhat acceptable to have hypotheses that can account for the data no matter how they come out. For hypothesis testing research, it is necessary to make a commitment up front.

might include elements to investigate the potentially adaptive nature of schizotypy and belief.

b. Groth-Marnat and Pegden (1998) found relationships between aspects of paranormal belief and locus of control and sensation seeking (e.g., spirituality was associated with an external locus of control). You could replicate these results or extend them with additional measures.

c. Rogers, Qualter, Phelps, & Gardner (2006) investigated differences between coping styles, emotional intelligence, and paranormal belief. They found that believers were no different in coping styles (contrary to expectation). They also found no overall effect of emotional intelligence. Keeping with the theme that operational definitions matter, they argued that a behavioral measure of emotional intelligence might have worked better. Perhaps there were other problems with the scales chosen. An interesting project would be to look at a more fine-grained analysis of paranormal belief to see if it is related to specific components of emotional intelligence or coping (similar to Hergovich et al., 2008).

d. Hergovich (2003) investigated the relationship between belief, field dependence (people who are field dependent are more influenced by their surroundings), and suggestibility. Superstitious thinking was related to field dependence and suggestibility. There were also other relationships. Again, how could paranormal belief be adaptive for people who are field dependent or suggestible?

e. Gow, Lang, and Chant (2004) examined the relationship between fantasy proneness and belief (in people who had or had not had out-of-body experiences). Bartholomew, Basterfield, and Howard (1991) investigated the relationship between fantasy proneness in a population of UFO abductees and contactees. Gow et al. found that fantasy-proneness was associated with paranormal belief in people with out-of-body experiences. Bartholomew et al. argued that the reason that abductees and contactees appear to have no psycho-pathology is that they are simply higher on fantasy proneness. This suggests projects investigating possible differences between believers and non-believers on fantasy proneness.

3. Thalbourne and Delin (1994) found no difference in paranormal belief between populations of manic-depressives, schizophrenics, and students. Thalbourne (1998) was concerned that students were not the appropriate control group for this research. Using a more representative control group (support-givers for people having panic attacks), he found that there was a difference. This suggests an important feature of research into personality differences between believers and non-believers: the population tested can make a difference. How might the results of prior studies be affected by the population chosen?

   a. Alternatively, how does a paranormal experience (e.g., a UFO contact, Clancy, McNally, Schacter, Lenzenweger, & Pitman, 2002) affect the relationship between paranormal belief and personality variables? Within the subpopulation of people who have had a paranormal experience, are there personality differences based on type of experience? Is the more meaningful personality comparison between people with and without experiences (as in Gow et al., 2004), rather than between believers and non-believers?

   b. Otis and Alcock (1982) also varied the population taking their survey on beliefs (people of different educational backgrounds). They found differences in belief based on background. These differences could be correlated to personality differences as well.

REFERENCES

Auton, H. R., Pope, J., & Seeger, G. (2003). It isn't that strange: Paranormal belief and personality traits. *Social Behavior and Personality, 31,* 711–720. doi:10.2224/sbp.2003.31.7.711

Bartholomew, R. E., Basterfield, K., & Howard, G. S. (1991). UFO abductees and contactees: Psychopathology or fantasy proneness? *Professional Psychology: Research and Practice, 22,* 215–222. doi:10.1037/0735-7028.22.3.215

Clancy, S. A., McNally, R. J., Schacter, D. L., Lenzenweger, M. F., & Pitman, R. K. (2002). Memory distortion in people reporting abduction by aliens. *Journal of Abnormal Psychology, 111,* 455–461. doi:10.1037//0021-843X.111.3.455

Diener, E., Emmons, R. A., Larsen, R. J., & Griffin, S. (1985). The satisfaction with life scale. *Journal of Personality Assessment, 49,* 71–75. doi:10.1207/s15327752jpa4901_13

Donnellan, M. B., Oswald, F. L., Baird, B. M., & Lucas, R. E. (2006). The Mini-IPIP scales: Tiny-yet-effective measures of the big five factors of personality. *Psychological Assessment, 18,* 192–203. doi:10.1037/1040-3590.18.2.192

Eckblad, M., & Chapman, L. J. (1983). Magical ideation as an indicator of schizotypy. *Journal of Consulting and Clinical Psychology, 51,* 215–225. doi:10.1037/0022-006X.51.2.215

Farha, B., & Steward, G., Jr. (2006). Paranormal beliefs: An analysis of college students. *Skeptical Inquirer, 30,* 37–40.

Fekken, G. C., Holden, R. R., Jackson, D. N., & Guthrie, G. M. (1987). An evaluation of the validity of the Personality Research Form with Filipino university students. *International Journal of Psychology, 22,* 399–407. doi:10.1080/00207598708246781

Gallagher, C., Kumar, V. K., & Pekala, R. J. (1994). The anomalous experiences inventory: Reliability and validity. *The Journal of Parapsychology, 58,* 402–428. Retrieved from http://www.rhine.org/journal.shtml

Gow, K., Lang, T., & Chant, D. (2004). Fantasy proneness, paranormal beliefs and personality features in out-of-body experiences. *Contemporary Hypnosis, 21,* 107–125. doi:10.1002/ch.296

Groth-Marnat, G., & Pegden, J. A. (1998). Personality correlates of paranormal belief: Locus of control and sensation seeking. *Social Behavior and Personality, 26,* 291–296. doi:10.2224/sbp.1998.26.3.291

Goulding, A. (2004). Schizotypy models in relation to subjective health and paranormal beliefs and experiences. *Personality and Individual Differences, 37,* 157–167. doi:10.1016/j.paid.2003.08.008

Hergovich, A. (2003). Field dependence, suggestibility, and belief in paranormal phenomena. *Personality and Individual Differences, 34,* 195–209. doi: 10.1016/S0191-8869(02)00022-3

Hergovich, A., Schott, R., & Arendasy, M. (2008). On the relationship between paranormal belief and schizotypy among adolescents. *Personality and Individual Differences, 45,* 119–125. doi: 10.1016/j.paid.2008.03.005

Houran, J., Irwin, H. J., & Lange, R. (2001). Clinical relevance of the two-factor rasch version of the Revised Paranormal Belief Scale. *Personality and Individual Differences, 31,* 371–382. doi:10.1016/S0191-8869(00)00143-4

Longino, H. E. (1990). *Science as social knowledge: Values and objectivity in scientific inquiry.* Princeton, NJ: Princeton University Press.

Mason, O., Claridge, G., & Jackson, M. (1995). New scales for the assessment of schizotypy. *Personality and Individual Differences, 18,* 7–13. doi: 10.1016/0191-8869(94)00132-C

Mason, O., Linney, Y., & Claridge, G. (2005). Short scales for measuring schizotypy. *Schizophrenia Research, 78,* 293–296. doi:10.1016/j.schres.2005.06.020

McCreery, C., & Claridge, G. (2002). Healthy schizotypy: The case of out-of-the-body experiences. *Personality and Individual Differences, 32,* 141–154. doi:10.1016/S0191-8869(01)00013-7

Musella, D. P. (2005). Gallup poll shows that Americans' belief in the paranormal persists. *Skeptical Inquirer, 29,* 5.

Otis, L. P., & Alcock, J. E. (1982). Factors affecting extraordinary belief. *The Journal of Social Psychology, 118,* 77–85.

Raine, A., & Benishay, D. (1995). The SPQ-B: A brief screening instrument for schizotypal personality disorder. *Journal of Personality Disorders, 9,* 346–355.

Rogers, P., Qualter, P., Phelps, G., & Gardner, K. (2006). Belief in the paranormal, coping and emotional intelligence. *Personality and Individual Differences, 41,* 1089–1105. doi:10.1016/j.paid.2006.04.014

Rosenthal, R., & Fode, K. L. (1963). Psychology of the scientist: V. Three experiments in experimenter bias. *Psychological Reports, 12,* 491–511.

Russell, D., & Jones, W. H. (1980). When superstition fails: Reactions to disconfirmation of paranormal beliefs. *Personality and Social Psychology Bulletin, 6,* 83–88. doi:10.1177/014616728061012

Schutte, N. S., Malouff, J. M., Hall, L. E., Haggerty, D. J., Cooper, J. T., Golden, C. J., et al. (1998). Development and validation of a measure of emotional intelligence. *Personality and Individual Differences, 25,* 167–177. doi:10.1016/S0191-8869(98)00001-4

Thalbourne, M. A. (1998). The level of paranormal belief and experience among psychotics. *The Journal of Parapsychology, 62,* 79–81. Retrieved from http://www.rhine.org/journal.shtml

Thalbourne, M. A., & Delin, P. S. (1993). A new instrument for measuring the sheep-goat variable: Its psychometric properties and factor structure. *Journal of the Society for Psychical Research, 59,* 172–186. Retrieved from http://www.spr.ac.uk/expcms/index.php?section=41

Thalbourne, M. A., & Delin, P. S. (1994). A common thread underlying belief in the paranormal, creative personality, mystical experience, and psychopathology. *Journal of Parapsychology, 58,* 3–38. Retrieved from http://www.rhine.org/journal.shtml

Tobacyk, J., & Milford, G. (1983). Belief in paranormal phenomena: Assessment instrument development and implications for personality functioning. *Journal of Personality and Social Psychology, 44,* 1029–1037. doi:10.1037/0022-3514.44.5.1029

Williams, E., Francis, L. J., & Robbins, M. (2007). Personality and paranormal belief: A study among adolescents. *Pastoral Psychology, 56,* 9–14. doi:10.1007/s11089-007-0094-x

Wiseman, R., & Morris, R. L. (1995). Recalling pseudo-psychic demonstrations. *British Journal of Psychology, 86,* 113–125.

Wiseman, R., & Watt, C. (2004). Measuring superstitious belief: Why lucky charms matter. *Personality and Individual Differences, 37,* 1533–1541. doi:10.1016/j.paid.2004.02.009

Wiseman, R., & Watt, C. (2006). Belief in psychic ability and the misattribution hypothesis: A qualitative review. *British Journal of Psychology, 97,* 323–338. doi:10.1348/000712605X72523

Zuckerman, M. (1971). Dimensions of sensation seeking. *Journal of Consulting and Clinical Psychology, 36,* 45–52. doi:10.1037/h0030478

CHAPTER 6

Correlation Research 3
My hand is no good at keeping secrets

Abstract

Psychology: Proponents of graphology claim to be able to predict a wide variety of variables from handwriting. Many of these variables overlap with the interests of psychologists (e.g., personality). Can graphology predict the sorts of things it is supposed to predict? Could it be a useful tool for psychology?

Skeptic/Pseudoscience: If graphology works (e.g., helping employers to select the best employee) then it ought to correlate with variables like intelligence and personality. Since graphology is also touted as a way to surreptitiously identify criminal behavior or tendencies (Lilienfeld & Landfield, 2008), it is especially important that it be on a firm empirical foundation. Given that there is little empirical evidence to support the claims of graphology, why do so many people believe in it?

INTRODUCTION: FINDING RELATIONSHIPS

The target article for this chapter uses a correlation design. Correlation designs were discussed at length in the opening section of Chapter 4. If you have not already done so, you may want to read that section before continuing with this chapter.

TARGET ARTICLE: GRAPHOLOGY AND PERSONALITY

(Be sure to look at Appendix D to assist you in evaluating the sources cited in this chapter. Be especially aware of the guidelines for evaluating Internet and other non-peer-reviewed sources.)

The Skeptic's Dictionary defines graphology as "the study of handwriting, especially when employed as a means of analyzing character" (Carroll, 2009,

Graphology, para. 1). Goodwin (2009) proposes that handwriting is really "brainwriting." He attributes variations in handwriting styles to "the unconscious mind" revealing itself. This information is what is really in the person's mind, and can therefore provide a rich source of information. Graphology is touted as being useful in: choosing employees to determine traits such as honesty or being a hard worker (Goodwin, 2009; Grapho-Guides, 2009; however, see Simner & Goffin, 2003 for a skeptical position statement by the International Graphonomics Society on the use of graphology in choosing employees), lie detection, comparing changes across the lifespan, solving criminal cases, finding out things that children may not express in other ways (Goodwin, 2009), planning relationships, parents trying to determine whether their children's development represents normal changes or problems, people looking for career guidance, and doctors trying to make diagnoses (Grapho-Guides, 2009). A search of Internet graphology websites would probably turn up additional uses of graphology. I can safely state that people who believe in graphology's usefulness see value in its application to a wide variety of tasks.

A review of graphology websites on the Internet suggests that graphology rests on a strong empirical foundation. Goodwin (2009) claims that graphology is a science with over 130 years of research support. He claims that graphology is 90% accurate, whereas Rorschach tests are only 63% accurate (however, see Dawes, 1994 for a review of the validity of Rorschach testing; it is possible that the 63% estimate is itself too high). Additionally, Goodwin claims that graphologists can uncover 300 personality traits. Unfortunately, he provides no citations for these claims. Handwriting Research Corporation (2009) provides a "facts and history" page on their website. They claim that Chinese scholars have been aware of the importance of graphology for centuries and that "there are more than 2,200 published works on handwriting analysis" (para. 15). They also quote a book (Lester, 1981) claiming that since published studies have shown the validity of graphology that we must accept it as valid. Even though they cite the book making that claim, they do not cite any of the studies that the claim was based on. Furthermore, their "library of resources" section is described as "under construction," making it difficult to locate these sources. As is the case with many of the topics considered in the book, grand claims are made (including claims of incredible accuracy and empirical validation), but the resources needed to evaluate those claims are not provided. That leaves us with the burning question: Can graphology do the things it is supposed to be able to do? We will not be able to evaluate all of the claims here, but the answer is going to be: no.

Let's begin with an overview of graphology techniques and evidence related to it. One problem that we will encounter is that there are a number of graphology analysis systems that emphasize different handwriting features, and these systems make various inferences based on those features from a variety of theoretical perspectives. My bias has been to stick as closely as possible to the peer-reviewed literature in which details of the analysis system and assumptions about the connection between features and personality have been clearly stated. However, in fairness to graphology proponents, some of the issues raised here should not be generalized to any particular system without evaluating the degree of overlap between the system being evaluated and the system for which data were collected. Also, some of the graphology systems are secret technology (Greasley, 2000), and specific details cannot be provided. Still, we can make some general statements about evaluating graphological systems: (a) empirical evidence on the reliability and validity of inferences made using the system should be provided, (b) details of the methodology used to collect those data should be available, and (c) to the extent that it is possible, the analysis and evaluation should come from an independent source that is not invested in a particular technology.

Klimoski and Rafaeli (1983) provided an overview of graphological techniques and identified three schools of graphology: the trait school focusing on handwriting features, the gestalt school focusing on overall analysis, and the Graphoanalysis approach combining features of the trait and gestalt schools. As with any psychological measurement, we can evaluate graphology by considering its **reliability** (consistency of measurement) and **validity** (ability to measure what it claims to measure). The good news for graphology is that within an individual, there is a great deal of reliability in handwriting features over time (Klimoski & Rafaeli, 1983). Unfortunately, the literature on the more important reliability question, i.e., do graphologists agree in their analysis of handwriting, was harder to come by. Klimoski and Rafaeli described the results of a number of studies investigating this question, but many of these studies had methodological problems. In a study that they conducted (Rafaeli & Klimoski, 1983), they found correlations with a median value around .45. Even though a number of their interjudge correlations were significant (i.e., different raters came to similar conclusions based on handwriting), only one correlation reached the .80 level that is typically taken as an indicator of reliability. However, given their procedure and the fact that the graphologists who participated may have come from different schools, they took these results to provide "a qualified yes" to the reliability question (p. 216).

Galbraith and Wilson (1964) had better success, finding an average interjudge correlation of .78. They also found that experience with the analysis system and the interpersonal interaction between the judges using the system affected the results. Basically, more experience with the system and more experience with one another improved the reliability between judges. Since their judges were trained in Graphoanalysis which has a "standardized training course" and a focus on "evaluation of writing strokes rather than letter formations as such" (p. 615), a relatively high interjudge reliability would be expected, and training with the system should improve reliability.

To sum up, reliability studies of handwriting within an individual indicate that handwriting is stable over time, and interjudge reliability studies suggest that regardless of the system, graphologists show some similarities in their ratings of handwriting. The next question is to evaluate the validity of the graphologists' inferences (e.g., do they accurately predict the things that they are supposed to predict?). These results suggest a very different conclusion.

METHODOLOGY NOTE **6.1**

Note that whereas Klimoski and Rafaeli's (1983) article might seem a bit dated, Greasley (2000), using a different approach toward the evaluation of graphology, reached the same conclusion. Also, Klimoski and Rafaeli's conclusions reaffirmed the conclusions of Fluckinger, Tripp, and Weinberg (1961). Fluckinger et al.'s review covered the period back to 1933. Note the pattern that is emerging: Approximately every 20 years a review of the recent empirical data related to graphology comes to the same conclusions. Some people may have a bias to focus only on recent research, but in this case the most recent article is not the most comprehensive, and the pattern that emerges from a long-term perspective is, in itself, very informative. For at least 85 years, extraordinary claims have been made for graphology, and those claims are not supported by carefully controlled empirical studies. In fact, this situation is very similar to Dawes' (1994) concern about "arguments from the vacuum" in which possible empirical results are used as positive evidence after actual empirical results showing problems with a technique have been dismissed for a variety of reasons.

The results from studies employing rigorous methodology do not support the claim that graphologists can predict the things they claim to be able to predict.

Rafaeli and Klimoski (1983) compared graphological predictions of sales success to supervisors' ratings, self ratings, monthly commission, number of monthly listings, number of monthly sales, the dollar amount of monthly sales, and a global measure of performance. Graphological inferences did not predict performance. In fact, there were no significant correlations with any of the objective measures of performance. Tett and Palmer (1997) found no evidence for Graphoanalysis as a valid predictor of personality traits. Furnham and Gunter (1987) also found that graphology did not predict personality using a different graphological technique and a different personality measure. Neter and Ben-Shakhar (1989) conducted a meta-analysis of validity studies investigating graphology. They concluded that "graphologists are not better than non-graphologists in predicting future performance on the basis of hand-written scripts" and that "graphologists' results were much better when they analyzed content-laden material" (p. 743). With respect to job performance, Ben-Shakhar et al. (1986) found that graphologists performed no better than non-graphologists when their evaluation was compared to supervisors' ratings, and graphologists were not able to predict professions based on handwriting.

Our target article for this chapter (Furnham, Chamorro-Premuzic, & Callahan, 2003) used a correlational design to evaluate the effectiveness of graphology to predict personality and intelligence. Furnham et al. also made an effort to identify and eliminate as many of the methodological concerns discussed above as possible. In particular, they used a standardized personality test that is one of the most used in the field (the NEO PI-R). Using a test with known

SCIENCE NOTE **6.1**

One problem highlighted by Klimoski and Rafaeli (1983) was the variability in the emphasis on methodology employed in graphology research. When research results do not support the claims of graphology, a number of issues are typically brought forward: (a) the system used is not correct (e.g., the researchers used one school, but a different school would have produced positive results), (b) the system used has been applied incorrectly (e.g., the raters were not trained in the system or had too little experience), (c) the handwriting samples were not spontaneous, but involved copied script, (d) the objective measures being correlated to predictions from graphologists measured different things (e.g., the graphologists were working with different operational definitions from those used by the other measures), (e) other general methodological errors were made (e.g., small sample sizes were used, there are problems with self-report measures), and (f) graphology measures *true* characteristics that may not match on to objective measures like a person's actual profession (e.g., just because a person is a plumber does not mean that that person does not have a different true calling). (I also relied on Tett & Palmer, 1997, and Ben-Shakhar, Bar-Hillel, Bilu, Ben-Abba, & Flug, 1986, in generating this list.) As Klimoski and Rafaeli put it "Many of the studies suffer, in particular, from a curious lack of interest in control when it comes to obtaining script samples. This is despite the fact that practicing graphologists are quick to emphasize the preferred conditions under which handwriting samples should be gathered" (p. 200). To put it plainly, positive results are accepted without question, and negative results are subjected to a methodological rigor that allows any findings to be dismissed. It is a good idea to evaluate research findings by paying careful attention to methodology; however, it is also a good idea to apply the same standards to findings that you agree with as to findings with which you disagree.

validity that measures a wide variety of factors allowed them to make a more careful comparison to predictions from graphology. Also, they used handwriting from exams as the writing sample. This offered several advantages: it was spontaneous and not copied, the content contained no personal information, the content was reasonably standardized, and participants were not trying to conceal anything because they were focused on the exam.

A coder (who was not a graphologist) coded 14 variables from the handwriting samples (such as connectedness, crossed t's, dotted i's). A second coder produced very similar results, with interjudge correlations ranging from .87 to 1.00. In other words, the coding was very reliable; it is possible to have a high degree of confidence in the scores for these variables.

SCIENCE NOTE **6.2**

An interesting question to consider at this point is why there is such a gap between research evidence (suggesting that graphology is not valid) and practice (a pattern of increasing use over time). This issue appears again and again in the empirical literature related to graphology. For example, "employers should be informed of the gap between the public impression and the limited predictive efficiency ... Awareness of this gap may contribute to a more restricted use of handwritten scripts in determining a person's compatibility to a given profession or job" (Neter & Ben-Shakhar, 1989, p. 744), but Thomas and Vaught (2001) note that "the use of graphology remains widespread in Europe and is actually on the increase in the United States" (p. 31). We will explore this topic more fully in the projects section.

In addition to the personality measure, participants also took a reasoning test and a mental rotation test. These were measures of two aspects of intelligence. In sum, there were five personality dimensions and two measures of intelligence correlated with 14 handwriting features.

The logic behind graphology is relatively straightforward. Handwriting is stable over time. Not everyone makes their letters in the same way; perhaps those variations in writing styles are meaningful. Personality is also stable over time and if variations in handwriting are meaningful, then those handwriting styles might correspond to aspects of personality, revealing "insider" information about a person. The question for Furnham et al. (2003) was simple: Do we see associations between handwriting features and personality and intelligence?

The analysis Furnham et al. (2003) performed was straightforward, but complicated by the number of correlations being computed. Rather than describe all of the correlations, I am going to focus on a subset of their analyses. Furnham et al. subjected 12 of the graphology variables to a principal components analysis that allowed them to reduce them to two dimensions. These were: dimension (with variables such as size and percentage of space used) and details (with variables such as i's dotted and crossed t's). Basically, they were able to "boil down" the 12 variables into two handwriting factors. When they correlated these two handwriting dimensions to the five personality traits and the two measures of intelligence, they found no significant correlations. In other words, handwriting features were unrelated to personality and intelligence. They also conducted regression analyses to see if handwriting dimensions could be used to predict personality and intelligence. They could not.

At this point, the news looks pretty bad for graphology. Handwriting features that can be very reliably coded do not correlate with standardized measures of personality or intelligence. However, in the larger analysis with the 14 variables considered separately, there were a few significant correlations (e.g., there was a significant correlation between extraversion and frequency of crossed t's). Therefore, Furnham et al. (2003) replicated the study with a new set of participants and a different measure of intelligence.

Again, I will focus on a subset of the results. After repeating the principal components analysis and correlating with the personality measures and the new measure of intelligence, they found that the dimension factor did correlate significantly with their measure of intelligence ($r = -.23$). No other correlations were significant. The dimension factor (when combined with gender) was also a significant predictor of the intelligence variable.

One problem with computing so many correlations (e.g., 70 correlations between personality and handwriting in each study) is that the likelihood of getting a significant correlation by chance is increased. Comparing across the two studies is one way to assess the reliability of the correlations to be sure that significant correlations are not happening by accident. There were five significant correlations with personality in the first study and eight in the second study. Only one was significant in both: Openness to experience correlated with writing width. None of the significant correlations with gender and intelligence were repeated across both studies. In other words, one personality feature may be related to one handwriting feature, but the average correlation between the two studies was .24.

The conclusion reached by Furnham et al. (2003) regarding handwriting and personality is one that is already familiar to us from our review of graphology research: "… the two are essentially unrelated" (p. 92). The projects section will allow you to explore graphology research for yourself, including addressing some unanswered questions raised by Furnham et al.

INFOTRAC® COLLEGE EDITION EXERCISES

You can use the InfoTrac College Edition to read about additional studies using correlational methodologies. This was discussed in Chapter 4. You can also use the InfoTrac College Edition to learn more about the relationship between graphology and personality. For example, when I typed in "graphology and personality" I got back 21 citations. Many of these were related to employee selection. One that was particularly interesting was written by Tripician (2000). He was a former graphologist who became disillusioned and described his personal journey. His article is a good source of ideas for research projects.

IMPLEMENTING THE DESIGN

Materials

To replicate Furnham et al. (2003) you will need a variety of materials. The NEO PI-R and the NEO-FFI (a shorter version of the test) are both copyrighted and must be purchased. However, a number of personality tests are available in the public domain. Typing "free five factor personality test" into Google provided me with a variety of resources, including a website from the open directory project (http://www.dmoz.org/Science/Social_Sciences/ Psychology/Personality/ Five-Factor_Model/Tests/) that contained a number of online personality tests. If you choose to substitute one of these tests, you should search for information about their reliability and validity first, and try to choose the best instrument possible. Alternatively, you can search for a scale using a psychology research database. A number of scales are available, and many of these have been extensively evaluated for reliability and validity. For example, Donnellan, Oswald, Baird, and Lucas (2006) presented a 20-item scale for measuring the big-five personality factors, along with reliability and validity studies.

For a full replication you will also need measures of intelligence. The Baddeley (1968) test used by Furnham et al. (2003) is available. Their mental rotation test is not readily available. The Wonderlic Personnel Test used in their Study 2 is also not readily available. However, there are versions of it available online (e.g., http://www.angelfire.com/fl3/existence/wonderlic.html). Again, if you use an online resource, it is best if you have some idea of the reliability and validity of the test. A search of psychology databases should also produce various measures of intelligence.

Finally, you will need a handwriting analysis tool. The criteria used by Furnham et al. (2003) are available. However, there are also other resources available. Given the variability in graphological systems and the interpretations of handwriting features, you will need to check carefully that your system matches onto theirs in a reliable way. There are also web-based tools available (e.g., http://hwa.org/). However, the reliability of these tools is a function of the training of the person making the judgments, so you might want to evaluate interjudge reliability if you use these tools.

Suggested Projects

1. You could replicate the Furnham et al. (2003) study. Given the concerns about graphology research noted in Science Note 6.1, it would be a good idea to compare their results to other graphology systems or handwriting features. As noted in the Materials section, personality measures and handwriting systems are readily available. Is there a set of handwriting features that can reliably predict aspects of personality?

    a. Furnham et al. (2003) also suggested that there may be some variables that are related to handwriting (e.g., age or education). Ben-Shakhar et al. (1986) noted that gender can be detected from handwriting at better than chance levels. One project would be to investigate the extent to which these types of variables can be predicted from handwriting.

    b. Furnham et al. (2003) also pointed out that a criticism of their study is that the handwriting samples came from exams. People taking exams are under pressure that they are not under in other circumstances. Perhaps a replication of their study with handwriting samples collected from a less stressful situation would allow you to address this criticism.

    c. Furnham et al. (2003) made an effort to have samples that did not suffer from impression management issues (participants could not be trying to look good for the examiner since they did not know about the personality portion of the test). Would it matter if participants were writing samples while they were aware that their personality would be evaluated?

    d. Furnham et al. (2003) noted that their intelligence measures suffered from a restricted range (all of the participants were college students). You might branch out into different populations to increase the range in intelligence scores.

2. Rafaeli and Drory (1988) proposed a number of methodological issues that could contaminate research into the relationship between graphology analysis and personnel selection. Evaluating the effects of these variables suggests a number of projects (I will focus on two that lend themselves nicely to research methods projects, but they suggest many more potential variables):

    a. Rafaeli and Drory (1988) noted that characteristics of the writer can have effects on the reliability of graphology as they have on the reliability of other tests. For example, sex, age, and race have been shown to affect performance on personality tests. A project could control for these variables and examine the relationship between handwriting and personality within these groups. They suggested other variables that might also affect the reliability and validity of handwriting variables: handedness, locus of control, introversion, and social desirability.

    b. Rafaeli and Drory (1988) also noted that characteristics of the graphologist can matter. Galbraith and Wilson (1964) found that experience could matter. Other variables that might matter are the gender of the graphologist and the number of graphologists used in a study.

3. Furnham et al. (2003) suggested something that we could call the "gap problem" as an interesting research direction: Why do people believe in graphology in the face of evidence that it does not work? A number of ideas have been proposed:

    a. *The use of Barnum statements* (that are vague enough to be generally true of anyone) has been noted by a number of critics. For example, Greasley (2000) in discussing a report that a person being analyzed is "sensitive, broad-minded and curious" notes that "most people like to think they are sensitive to some extent, rather than insensitive, and broad-, rather than narrow-, minded" (p. 49). Perhaps graphological assessments appear to be successful because they would apply to anyone.

        i. Boyce and Geller (2002) suggested using graphology as a teaching aid for psychology students. In their study, they had students

METHODOLOGY NOTE **6.2**

The projects in section 3a are not strictly correlational. However, the importance of addressing the question has led me to include them in this chapter. You can learn about the experimental methodology used in these projects in Chapter 7.

rate the extent to which graphology was a science and provided a personality statement supposedly derived from graphology that was actually adapted from Forer (1949; Forer was the first to investigate the Barnum effect). All students actually received the same profile. After rating the accuracy of graphology again, students were told the true nature of the study. They rated graphology as a science one final time. The results were that receiving the profiles significantly increased students' belief in graphology as a science. Finding out that everyone got the same profile decreased it.

ii. McKelvie (1990) conducted a similar project, but in his study a control group did not receive a personality profile. At the end of the study, participants receiving a personality profile increased their belief in graphology relative to the control group. Again, an explanation for why graphology seems credible is that Barnum statements lead to a feeling that the graphologist has uncovered facts about a person's personality, even though those facts could apply to anyone. Additional projects related to the Barnum effect are presented in Chapter 3.

b. *Illusory correlation* occurs when things that seem like they ought to be related (but are not) are seen as related. This can occur even when valid relationships exist in a set of data (Chapman & Chapman, 1969), either because two things are strongly associated in the mind of the observer or because of a bias towards confirmation when looking at the data. For example, Chapman and Chapman found that Rorschach signs that validly detected homosexuality were very unlikely to be reported by clinicians in response to a survey about the signs associated with homosexuality, but invalid signs with strong verbal associations to homosexuality were likely to be reported. With respect to graphology, Greasley (2000) noted that angular lines are often associated with "unfriendly" and curves with "friendly" in and out of the context of a graphological analysis. Perhaps graphological reports look accurate to people because they confirm a pre-existing illusory correlation. I will say at the outset that this type of project will be difficult. King and Koehler (2000) created a set of materials (handwriting samples and "analyses" of the samples) such that there was no systematic relationship between any handwriting feature and the personality descriptions in the analysis. They had participants review the handwriting samples and analyses and report the degree to which they thought the handwriting features and personality traits were related. The correct answer was essentially zero. However, King and Koehler found that participants did perceive relationships in the data (based on semantic association) and that those relationships were the same as the ones identified by graphologists. This suggests two projects:

i. Replicate some features of the King and Koehler (2000) study. You can try to locate their materials or create some of your own. There are numerous potential semantically or metaphorically

METHODOLOGY NOTE **6.3**

King and Koehler (2000) were concerned about **demand characteristics** (where some aspect of the situation "tells" participants how to respond and could affect the data). In their case, since participants were rating 84 relationships, they probably felt that answering "zero" to all of them was inappropriate (the situation suggests that at least *some* of the variables should be related). In the absence of any actual relationships, but with a demand characteristic that caused participants to feel that they had to rate something as related, they may have fallen back on illusory correlations. To correct this, King and Koehler conducted a second experiment in which there were relationships for participants to find. The main result was replicated; naïve participants made their judgments on the basis of the degree of semantic association.

related handwriting feature–personality trait pairings available in the literature beyond the ones chosen by King and Koehler.

ii. Generate a list of graphology signs and have participants match those signs to personality traits. You can evaluate the extent to which participants (naïve to the theory underlying graphology) uncover the same relationships as graphologists. This would support Greasley's (2000) contention that most of what graphologists "find" is based on metaphor and analogy.

4. Is there something in the content of handwriting written by specific populations or under specific circumstances that makes it distinguishable? Frederick (1968) noted that a graphologist was not able to pick out samples produced by a hospitalized psychotic, but in his study, graphologists were better than non-graphologists (police detectives and secretaries) at selecting which of a set of suicide notes was a real note. For a research methods project, you could evaluate whether there is a set of clues in a handwriting sample generated in a particular kind of situation that would make the genuine article detectable (e.g., resignation letters, academic appeals).

5. Meier and Robinson (2004) found that when participants judged the valence of words, they were faster to judge positive words when they appeared at the top of a computer screen and negative words when they appeared at the bottom of a computer screen. This suggests that there may be an empirical foundation for some of the metaphorical relationships graphologists claim to exist in handwriting features (e.g., positive is up). You could identify a set of graphological features that are supported by empirical evidence from the metaphor literature (e.g., upward sloping writing corresponds to a positive personality) and then compare reliability and validity for those features to features not supported by a theoretical framework. Perhaps some of the problems with validity arise from the fact that valid and invalid signs are lumped together in most studies.

REFERENCES

Baddeley, A. D. (1968). A 3 min reasoning test based on grammatical transformation. *Psychonomic Science, 10,* 341–342.

Ben-Shakhar, G., Bar-Hillel, M., Bilu, Y., Ben-Abba, E., & Flug, A. (1986). Can graphology predict occupational success? Two empirical studies and some methodological ruminations. *Journal of Applied Psychology, 71,* 645–653. doi:10.1037/0021-9010.71.4.645

Boyce, T. E., & Geller, E. S. (2002). Using the Barnum effect to teach psychological research methods. *Teaching of Psychology, 29,* 316–318.

Carroll, R. T. (2009). Graphology. *The Skeptic's Dictionary.* Retrieved from http://www.skepdic.com/graphol.html

Chapman, L. J., & Chapman, J. P. (1969). Illusory correlation as an obstacle to the use of valid psychodiagnostic signs. *Journal of Abnormal Psychology, 74,* 271–280. doi:10.1037/h0027592

Dawes, R. M. (1994). *House of cards: Psychology and psychotherapy built on myth.* New York: Free Press.

Donnellan, M. B., Oswald, F. L., Baird, B. M., & Lucas, R. E. (2006). The Mini-IPIP scales: Tiny-yet-effective measures of the big five factors of personality. *Psychological Assessment, 18,* 192–203. doi:10.1037/1040-3590.18.2.192

Fluckinger, F. A., Tripp, C. A., & Weinberg, G. H. (1961). A review of experimental research in graphology: 1933–1960. *Perceptual and Motor Skills, 12,* 67–90.

Forer, B. R. (1949). The fallacy of personal validation: A classroom demonstration of gullibility. *Journal of Abnormal and Social Psychology, 44,* 118–123. doi:10.1037/h0059240

Frederick, C. J. (1968). An investigation of handwriting of suicide persons through suicide notes. *Journal of Abnormal Psychology, 73,* 263–267. doi:10.1037/h0025871

Furnham, A., Chamorro-Premuzic, T., & Callahan, I. (2003). Does graphology predict personality and intelligence? *Individual Differences Research, 1,* 78–94.

Furnham, A., & Gunter, B. (1987). Graphology and personality: Another failure to validate graphological analysis. *Personality and Individual Differences, 8,* 433–435. doi:10.1016/0191-8869(87)90045-6

Galbraith, D., & Wilson, W. (1964). Reliability of the Graphoanalytic approach to handwriting analysis. *Perceptual and Motor Skills, 19,* 615–618.

Goodwin, C. (2009). Retrieved from http://www.toughcases.net/graphology.html

Grapho-Guides. (2009). Retrieved from http://graphologist_1944.tripod.com/

Greasley, P. (2000). Handwriting analysis and personality assessment: The creative use of analogy, symbolism, and metaphor. *European Psychologist, 5,* 44–51. doi:10.1027//1016-9040.5.1.44

Handwriting Research Corporation. (2009). Retrieved from http://www.handwriting.com/facts/history.html

King, R. N., & Koehler, D. J. (2000). Illusory correlation in graphological inference. *Journal of Experimental Psychology: Applied, 6,* 336–348. doi:10.1037/1076-898X.6.4.336

Klimoski, R. J., & Rafaeli, A. (1983). Inferring personal qualities through handwriting analysis. *Journal of Occupational Psychology, 56,* 191–202.

Lilienfeld, S. O., & Landfield, K. (2008). Science and pseudoscience in law enforcement: A user-friendly primer. *Criminal Justice and Behavior, 35,* 1215–1230. doi:10.1177/0093854808321526

McKelvie, S. J. (1990). Student acceptance of a generalized personality description: Forer's graphologist revisited. *Journal of Social Behavior and Personality, 5,* 91–95.

Meier, B. P., & Robinson, M. D. (2004). Why the sunny side is up: Associations between affect and vertical position. *Psychological Science, 15,* 243–247.

Neter, E., & Ben-Shakhar, G. (1989). The predictive validity of graphological inferences: A meta-analytic approach. *Personality and Individual Differences, 10,* 737–745. doi:10.1016/0191-8869(89)90120-7

Rafaeli, A., & Drory, A. (1988). Graphological assessments for personnel selection: Concerns and suggestions for research. *Perceptual and Motor Skills, 66,* 743–759.

Rafaeli, A., & Klimoski, R. J. (1983). Predicting sales success through handwriting analysis: An evaluation of the effects of training and handwriting sample content. *Journal of Applied Psychology, 68,* 212–217. doi:10.1037/0021-9010.68.2.212

Simner, M. L., & Goffin, R. D. (2003). A position statement by the International Graphonomics Society on the Use of Graphology in Personnel Selection Testing. *International Journal of Testing, 3*, 353–364.

Tett, R. P., & Palmer, C. A. (1997). The validity of handwriting elements in relation to self-report personality trait measures. *Personality and Individual Differences, 22*, 11–18. doi:10.1016/S0191- 8869 (96)00183-3

Thomas, S. L., & Vaught, S. (2001). The write stuff: What the evidence says about using handwriting analysis in hiring. *SAM Advanced Management Journal, 66*, 31–35.

Tripician, R. J. (2000). Confessions of a (former) graphologist. *Skeptical Inquirer, 24*, 44–47.

Experimental Designs

The research techniques in Part 2 all involve manipulating some aspect of the situation to determine its effect on behavior. The experimental designs start with the simplest possible situation (two groups) and move to more complex designs (factorial designs). Field experiments are basically the same experimental techniques applied in a real world setting.

CHAPTER 7

Two Group Experiments

I'll believe it if you see it

Abstract

Psychology: Social forces have been shown to influence people's behavior in a variety of ways (e.g., the number of bystanders can affect helping behavior). Could social forces be partially responsible for people's belief in the paranormal?

Skeptic/Pseudoscience: The impact of others on belief could provide an additional explanation for how beliefs come about in the absence of empirical evidence to support those beliefs.

INTRODUCTION: WHAT IS AN EXPERIMENT?

Until now, the methods we have used have allowed us only to describe relationships that exist between two variables. For example, we could observe that there is a relationship between defendence and belief in the paranormal (Auton, Pope, & Seeger, 2003; Chapter 5). We have not been able to say that one variable caused a change in another variable. To do that, we need to do an experiment, and that is the topic of this chapter.

There are three components of an experiment:

1. Manipulate something.
2. Measure something (this component is present for all designs, but the specific variable measured should be influenced by the variable being manipulated).
3. Random assignment.

Let's consider each in turn. Unlike the designs in Part 1, we will actually choose some variable to manipulate and control its presentation. As an example, the Forer/Barnum effect (see Chapter 3) is that people believe that a report prepared especially for them and presenting generally positive information does, in fact, describe them, even when the information in the report is generic and not actually about that person. Forer (1949) did not manipulate any variables in his study; he merely measured students' willingness to accept a personality sketch. However, we could think of a number of variables to manipulate. For example, Forer found that people were willing to endorse vaguely positive information. What would happen if the information were highly critical of the person being evaluated? Will the kind of information influence the magnitude of the Forer effect? Choosing what to manipulate can be difficult. Careful work with observation, survey, or correlation designs can reduce the burden by suggesting which variables are related.

You are already familiar with measurement from the designs in Part 1. Let's introduce some new terminology. The variable that we manipulate is called the **independent variable**. It is independent because we can choose to manipulate anything and the specific values of that variable are also unrestricted. The variable we measure will be the **dependent variable**. It is dependent because its value depends on the value of the independent variable that we have presented. As an example, consider the Forer effect manipulation discussed above. Kind of information would be the independent variable (for this example, we would manipulate whether the information was positive or negative). How well the profile described the participant would be the dependent variable. The profile evaluation depends upon the kind of information included in the profile (e.g., people should be less likely to endorse a negative evaluation).

A useful metaphor for thinking about independent variables is to treat the variable as the name of a dimension. For example, if we were going to turn the Forer effect study into an experiment, the independent variable would be kind of information. Once the dimension has been identified, you can select values of that dimension to present to participants (you will need at least two values to conduct an experiment). The simplest thing to do is to choose values at the extremes of the dimension. For example, for kind of information we could choose "positive" or "negative."

What we are discussing is the two-group experiment. Usually, one group is called a **treatment group** because it receives some treatment (e.g., negative information). The other group is called the **control group** because it receives no treatment (e.g., positive information). If the experiment is well conducted, the only difference between the treatment and control groups is that one got a treatment and one did not. If you compare scores on the dependent variable for the two groups and the scores are different, then you can conclude that the treatment caused the difference.

Once you have identified the treatment and control groups, you need to come up with a good **operational definition**. This is a definition of the treatment in terms of the operations required to produce it. An operational definition creates a very concrete description of the conditions of an experiment. For example, an operational definition for the control group in our Forer effect study might be that participants will read Forer's (1949) original personality sketch using his original procedure.

Random assignment is probably the most important component of an experiment. It ensures that each participant in the experiment has an equal

METHODOLOGY NOTE **7.1**

In the Forer effect example, the assignment of treatment and control groups might seem somewhat arbitrary, but the control group is the group that is closest to the normal situation. Assuming that personality and astrology profiles are generally positive would make a positive profile the control group and a negative profile the treatment group. As is usually the case, some time in the library researching the phenomenon can help with making the distinction between treatment and control groups.

METHODOLOGY NOTE **7.2**

When choosing a control group, a special concern is something called a **placebo effect**. People might be affected by their knowledge of how the independent variable is supposed to affect them and not by the independent variable itself. For example, people know how they are supposed to behave after consuming alcohol, so they may behave that way even if the alcohol itself is not producing the behavior. To prevent this, we should make both groups think they are receiving the same treatment. After the experiment, we will know that any differences are due to the treatment and not placebo effects.

chance of being in either group. For a two-group experiment, one way to do random assignment would be to flip a coin as each person arrives to participate; heads would be group 1, tails would be group 2.

Why is random assignment so important? We need to be certain that the groups in an experiment are equal before we begin. We could try to match them to make sure they are equal, but people differ from one another in an infinite number of ways. No matter how carefully we match, there would always be the possibility that some systematic difference exists. By using random assignment, we reduce any systematic biases that may exist. (Random assignment will not guarantee equal groups; it just guarantees that the selection process itself is unbiased.)

One of the main differences between experiments and the designs in Part 1 of the book is that experiments allow a researcher to make a causal conclusion. This is possible due to the greater control over the situation researchers typically have in experiments, and to the logic of the experiment itself. For example, we can overcome the interpretive ambiguity problem in correlation research because we know (due to manipulation of an independent variable) the causal direction of the relationship.

Experiments are designed to control a variety of potential confounds. A confound is something that covaries with the independent variable and could account for the changes seen in the dependent variable. "Covaries" means that the confound changes as the independent variable changes. For example, if we

METHODOLOGY NOTE **7.3**

When we do research we are concerned with two sorts of validity. Internal validity has to do with the quality of the study. An experiment high in **internal validity** allows us to draw strong conclusions about the relationship between the independent and dependent variables. **External validity** has to do with whether or not the results will generalize. Usually we have to make trade-offs to maximize these validities. For example, to increase internal validity we have to increase control over the situation. This control makes the research less natural, and harms generalizability. To make the experiment more natural requires us to relinquish control, which opens the door for problems with internal validity. Wooffitt (2007b) examined these issues in the context of mediums performing psychic readings. Wooffitt called for more reliance on evaluations based on ecologically valid (naturalistic) settings in which psychic readings take place, and less reliance on controlled experiments, partially on the assumption that the artificial nature of experiments was negatively affecting the results. For experimental designs you will usually see a bias of maximizing internal validity and worrying about generalizability after an effect is found. However, as you design your own studies it is a good idea to make an effort to attend to both internal and external validity.

measured the effect of amount of study on exam performance, but we tested one study time group in the morning and the other study time group in the afternoon, time of day would be a confound. One group had a particular amount of study time, but was also tested in the morning, the group with the other amount of study time was tested in the afternoon. If time of day could explain differences in exam performance, then we have reintroduced the problem of interpretive ambiguity. Did the independent variable cause changes in the dependent variable, or did the confound do it?

Campbell and Stanley (1963) listed seven confounds that are particularly threatening to internal validity. As a researcher, you want to exercise appropriate control and make good design decisions to correct for these confounds. For example, the **history confound** occurs when something happens during a study besides the manipulation of the independent variable. It is important to exercise sufficient control over the situation to ensure that the treatment and control groups both have the same experiences during the experiment (except that the treatment group gets the treatment). Another confound is **statistical regression**. The basic concept is that extreme scores tend to get less extreme over repeated measurements. One way we correct for this is to use random assignment. Rather than putting participants into groups based on how extreme their scores are (opening the door to regression), random assignment creates unbiased groups that should be roughly equal at the start of the study. Having a control group also helps with regression. If the only effect operating in an experiment is regression, then the treatment and control groups will change the same amount, and no difference will be found. To the extent that the treatment has an effect beyond regression, this will show up in the results.

Other threats to internal validity are experimenter effects and demand characteristics. Experimenter effects arise from (usually unconscious) things the experimenter does that affect the outcome (e.g., Rosenthal & Fode, 1963). The best way to prevent experimenter effects is to run your studies double-blind. In a **double-blind** study, neither the participant nor the experimenter knows the condition to which the participant has been assigned. Ideally, the experimenter would also be blind to the hypothesis of the study as well. In this case, it is difficult for overt or unconscious behavior from the experimenter to influence the outcome of the experiment.

Demand characteristics are harder to deal with. These arise from the fact that participants are not passive responders (Orne, 1962). Rather, they are actively engaged in an exchange with the experimenter and are trying to understand what is happening. In part, if participants view the research project as advancing the cause of science, they may want to help (what Orne called the "good subject"). Any clues to the hypothesis will influence the good subject to try to make the experiment "work out." Obviously, this can contaminate the data. Even in the absence of clues, participants will often infer a purpose. For example, Orne had participants complete 2,000 sheets of math problems to see when they would give up. They did not. In a related study, after each sheet was completed participants tore it into 32 pieces. Again, they kept going even though it was clear the "data" were useless. However, at the end of the study they reported that they saw it as a test of endurance. In other words, they complied because they inferred a hypothesis and wanted to do well.

As a researcher you must be sensitive to these kinds of effects and try to minimize them. However, this can only be done with a thorough understanding of the research area and a review of previous research. For example, Wooffitt (2007a) studied transcripts of ESP experiments in an attempt to understand how demand characteristics might produce experimenter effects in ESP research (some experimenters are more likely to find evidence of ESP

METHODOLOGY NOTE **7.4**

As a check on your comprehension, think about ways to convert the following design from a correlation study to an experiment. Wood, Perunovic, & Lee (2009) found in their Study 1 that people reporting low self-esteem also reported that positive self-statements (e.g., "I will win!") sometimes made them feel worse. People with high self-esteem reported that positive self-statements were helpful. If you wanted to do an experiment to understand the effect of positive self-statements on people with high and low self-esteem, what would you manipulate? What would the treatment group be? What would the control group be? What are some potential problems for your design? Are there ethical issues involved? Once you have answered the questions, you can consult Wood et al. as their Study 2 was an experimental manipulation.

than others). Woofitt's data suggested that minor variations in the interactions between researchers and participants could influence the results by communicating to participants what was expected.

Let's examine the properties of an experiment by looking at research investigating social influences on the perception of a paranormal phenomenon.

TARGET ARTICLE: SOCIAL ENHANCEMENT OF PYRAMID POWER

(Be sure to look at Appendix D to assist you in evaluating the sources cited in this chapter. Be especially aware of the guidelines for evaluating Internet and other non-peer reviewed sources.)

Asch (1951) presented his participants with a difficult dilemma. In a "perception" task (judging which of three lines matched the length of a standard line), participants would find themselves in a "minority of one." One by one, seven people announced that the wrong answer was the one that they chose. And, the incorrect choice was the most extreme wrong answer available. Asch set up the situation so that it was unambiguous, there was no way for the participant to believe that the group's responses were somehow correct. The evidence from their senses told them that the group was wrong, but the group was unanimous in its opinion. In this situation, some people managed to hold out and give the correct answer every time ($N = 13$). Many others produced at least one incorrect response ($N = 37$). In the control group (who wrote down their answers rather than calling them out), only 2 participants made an error, 35 managed to get them all correct. The results indicated that people will conform to group opinions when they find themselves in a minority of one and they have to announce their opinion publicly (even when their conforming answers are clearly wrong). (See Bond & Smith, 1996 for a more recent meta-analysis of studies using this task.)

Something like this could partially explain the gap problem explored throughout this book: In the absence of good evidence in favor of a paranormal phenomenon, why do people believe in it? Perhaps social pressures are leading them to conform to group opinion. The social situation surrounding the experience of paranormal phenomena could contribute at least as much to people's belief as the internal variables explored in other chapters (e.g., personality and reasoning ability). Auton et al. (2003) found evidence to support this idea. In their study, personality variables did not distinguish between believers and non-believers, but social factors did (friends' beliefs, watching paranormal television programs, and reading paranormal books).

In our target article for this chapter, Markovsky and Thye (2001) investigated social influences on people's belief in pyramid power. Pyramids are supposed to concentrate energies in such a way that things that are stored in them are preserved relative to things stored outside of pyramids. For example, a piece of fruit kept in a pyramid should stay fresh longer than a similar piece of fruit stored outside of a pyramid.

Markovsky and Thye (2001) took pairs of bananas that were rated by 5 judges as being identical, and placed them under a pyramid or a box (the bananas were switched for each participant to control for the fact that a slightly fresher looking banana might have accidentally been placed under the pyramid). Participants were given a cover story about the preservative power of pyramids (e.g., how pharaohs' mummies were so well preserved). Participants were told that these bananas had been placed under their respective containers a week ago, and they judged the freshness of the bananas.

METHODOLOGY NOTE **7.5**

Markovsky and Thye (2001) were unable to find any empirical studies evaluating whether or not pyramids actually did have preservative powers. So, they collected their own data. Markovsky and Thye (2002) compared bananas stored in the open to bananas stored in a box or a pyramid. The box and pyramid bananas appeared to be equally fresh, and both were better than the banana stored in the open. Even though this design had three levels of the independent variable (storage condition with the levels open, box, and pyramid), it highlights the importance of choosing control groups carefully. If only two conditions had been chosen, pyramid and open air, the conclusion would have been that pyramids do have preservative power. A second control group helped Markovsky and Thye (2002) uncover the true relationship. Based on this research, we can confidently say that pyramid power for preserving bananas (compared to a box) is non-existent, so that cannot account for any of the results of Markovsky and Thye (2001).

ETHICS NOTE **7.1**

Markovsky and Thye's (2001) study involved mild deception. Participants were led to believe that they were evaluating pyramid power when they were, in fact, in a study of social influence. When using deception in research you need to be sensitive to the ethical issues involved. The issues raised by Merow (2008) are not all directly relevant to the current project, but there is some overlap in the situation. Merow claimed that some deception is necessary to evaluate most paranormal claims because they are otherwise unavailable for study. Merow makes the case that people who hold themselves out as having a particular skill (e.g., psychics) somehow have a limited right to complain if they are deceived by a researcher posing as a client because of the potential greater good (protecting the public from fraudulent claimants). As an exercise in ethics, you might evaluate the extent to which that position is acceptable. Would it be OK to visit a group activity oriented toward believers to study social influence in transmitting paranormal beliefs? How does this relate to individuals recruited as research participants who make no claims to paranormal powers? Are the rules different for them?

In the social influence condition, a confederate of the experimenters also made ratings of the bananas. There were five features judged: preserved-unpreserved, fresh-rotten, hard-soft, light-dark, and new-old. The first three dimensions were the critical ones. For these judgments, the confederate made the first response and the participant made the second response. The confederate rated the pyramid banana as fresher. If the participant was influenced by the confederate, then their freshness ratings for the pyramid banana should be higher than for control participants.

Markovsky and Thye (2001) made five two-group comparisons to test various aspects of social impact theory. The first comparison was to see if their situation had a social impact. The hypothesis was that having a confederate present would move participants' ratings closer to the "fresh" end of the scales. This hypothesis was supported. Participants rated the pyramid banana as significantly fresher when there was a confederate than when there was not a confederate.

Social impact theory is that the social source's number (how many), strength (roughly prestige or validity), and immediacy (how close the source is in space and time) can all have positive influences on social impact, and that impediments (e.g., "a preconceived notion that the claim being made is less than fully legitimate," Markovsky & Thye, 2002, p. 37) can diminish impact. Markovsky and Thye (2001) designed the second comparison to evaluate whether the paranormal nature of pyramid power would be an impediment to social impact. They compared a normal claim (that a plastic container would work better to preserve bananas than a cardboard container) to a paranormal claim (pyramid power). In the normal condition (better preservation under plastic than cardboard), there was an even larger effect of the confederate than in the pyramid condition. Markovsky and Thye (2001) interpreted their results to mean that people can be affected by social forces to increase belief in a paranormal phenomenon, but that, simultaneously, the paranormal nature of the claim can be an impediment to the social impact.

Markovsky and Thye (2001) were also concerned that participants' ratings of the bananas' freshness were a function of the public nature of their responses (they had to call out their ratings after the confederate had already reported their rating). To evaluate this, they also had participants make a private rating of the bananas' freshness. Participants' private ratings also reflected a social influence. The banana under the pyramid was reported to be fresher than the banana under the box (paranormal), and plastic was reported to be a better preserver than cardboard (normal). Again, the normal comparison produced a larger result, suggesting that the paranormal nature of pyramid power is an impediment to social impact.

At this point, we have discussed Markovsky and Thye's (2001) research enough to establish that paranormal beliefs can be transmitted by social influences. We will explore more aspects of their research and other ways in which social forces can influence belief in the paranormal in the projects section.

INFOTRAC® COLLEGE EDITION EXERCISES

You can use the InfoTrac College Edition to read about additional studies using an experimental methodology. For example, typing in "psychology experiment" with the box for "in entire article content" checked, and checking the box for "to refereed publications" gave me a list of 24 articles. Many of these were not two group experiments like the ones in this chapter, so you will have to read through the list if you want to restrict your search to just two group designs. Also, you can vary the search options to broaden the list if you would like to look at more articles. One of the articles that I found was Johnson (2008) investigating how the wording of a refusal affects perceived politeness. Johnson found that including modals in the refusal ("I really don't think I want to do that") was seen as more polite than the same refusal without a modal ("I don't want to do that"). In addition to exploring how the experimental design can be applied to a variety of interesting topics, you can learn a lot of methodological information from reading other people's research. Spend some time with InfoTrac College Edition reading method sections from a variety of articles using experimental designs before tackling your own project.

You can also learn more about social influences using the InfoTrac College Edition. When I typed in "social impact theory" with the "in title, citation, abstract" and "to refereed publications" boxes checked, I found one article (Stahelski & Patch, 1993) using social impact theory to evaluate two persuasion techniques. Using different search terms will allow you to find additional information. For example, "conformity" produced a list of 244 articles. You can also study the power of suggestion on the interpretation of potentially paranormal phenomena. When I typed in "paranormal social" with the same boxes checked, I found a list of 15 articles. Again, using a variety of search terms will help you to locate more sources useful to your research.

IMPLEMENTING THE DESIGN

Suggested Projects

1. Markovsky and Thye's (2001) research inspires a variety of projects.
   a. You could replicate the basic research design. Will the presence of a confederate lead to higher freshness ratings for a piece of fruit kept in a pyramid compared to a control group without a confederate? You could also change the kind of paranormal belief in the experiment to generalize their results.
   b. Markovsky and Thye (2001) investigated different aspects of social impact theory.
      i. You could explore the notion of impediments to impact with additional experiments. You could compare more outlandish paranormal claims to more reasonable claims (either by manipulating the claim or the justification for it).

      ii.   You could vary the status of the source (related to the strength factor in social impact theory). Markovsky and Thye (2001) had a professor as the confederate or a student of equal status to the participant. They found a status effect in the public ratings, but not the private ratings, suggesting that within the realm of the paranormal, higher status may lead to public conformity, but may not change private beliefs.

      iii.   You could also vary the immediacy factor in social impact theory. Markovsky and Thye (2001) manipulated this by having the confederate present or by reading the ratings of someone who had done the task earlier. This manipulation had no effect, but you might be able to vary immediacy in other ways to see if it makes a difference in this context.

      iv.   Markovsky and Thye (2001) did not manipulate the number aspect of social impact theory. However, Asch (1951) found that the effect on conformity increased up to three confederates and leveled off after that (up to groups of 16). Will you find an effect comparing one confederate to three confederates?

    c.   Markovsky and Thye (2001) found (to their surprise) that prior belief did not influence people's performance. They suggested that specific types of belief might be related to the impact that social influences can have. For example, will people be more influenced by social support to believe something less related to their current paranormal beliefs or something more related to their current paranormal beliefs? Markovsky and Thye (2001) proposed that there might be greater resistance to "wilder" beliefs until social support is present.

2.   Social impact can come from a variety of sources. Sparks and colleagues have investigated media effects in a variety of ways (you could classify

SCIENCE NOTE **7.1**

Markovsky and Thye (2001) were unable to find support for all aspects of social impact theory in their studies. They pointed out that this might be a problem with the theory. They claim that terms like "strength" and "immediacy" have definitions that are too imprecise. The problem this presents is how to interpret null results. For example, Markovsky and Thye (2001) found no effect of immediacy when it was defined as a present or absent confederate. One implication is that immediacy is not relevant to the social impact of paranormal beliefs. However, given problems with the definition of immediacy, perhaps Markovsky and Thye (2001) simply failed to manipulate it correctly, or needed more powerful measures. The projects suggest that you try different ways to manipulate the variables, but one possibility is that these aspects of the theory do not apply to this situation. From a broader perspective, in order for theories to be testable, precise definitions of terms are required.

their manipulations as being related to the strength factor in social impact theory, with the media as the source). Note that the dependent variable in many of these studies is belief in the paranormal. You will need to consult each article to replicate the measures used.

    a.   Sparks, Hansen, and Shah (1994) manipulated the disclaimer that appeared before an episode of a popular paranormal television program (their study actually had five levels of the independent variable, but you can easily limit your research to two levels). They found that participants viewing the program with no disclaimer increased their paranormal beliefs after viewing it, and that this effect lasted for three weeks. Participants viewing the program with a disclaimer that the events depicted were impossible decreased their paranormal belief after viewing it, and this effect also lasted for three weeks. You could design an experiment to investigate the effect of prior information on social influences on belief. This study could also be extended beyond the realm of media. For example, if you included disclaimers about the source of a personal anecdote about the paranormal, that might show a similar effect.

    b.   Sparks and Pellechia (1997) manipulated news stories about a UFO abduction. In one story a scientist was cited as supporting the idea that UFO abductions are possible, in a different story a scientist supported the idea UFO abductions were unlikely (there were additional conditions, but again you can limit your study to two). They found that a scientist affirming UFO abductions increased belief, but a scientist disconfirming them had no effect. You could vary the credibility of a news report to see how that would affect social impact. A couple of ways to do this might be to change the source of the story or to change the kind of scientist in the story (e.g., are physicists seen as more credible in the realm of UFOs than psychologists?).

    c.   Sparks, Pellechia, and Irvine (1998) used televised reports that were one-sided or two-sided with respect to UFOs and found an effect of the kind of report on belief. That might be another variable that affects the strength of a source.

3.   In his research program, Asch (1951) manipulated a variety of variables (Bond & Smith, 1996 reviewed many of these). For example, a unanimous majority was more powerful than a majority with even one dissenter. Will the presence of a skeptic affect the social impact of other confederates supporting paranormal belief? Asch manipulated the majority in a variety of ways. In the "true partner" condition, one confederate always gave the correct answer, supporting the participant in responding correctly. Asch also had a true partner condition in which the confederate stopped being a true partner part way through and joined the majority, and a true partner condition in which one of the confederates started giving correct answers part way through. Will these manipulations affect social impact in a paranormal context?

4.   Wiseman and Greening (2005) looked at the effect of suggestion in a videotape of a person supposedly bending a key with the power of their

mind. For half of the participants, they heard the person who bent the key say that the key was still bending after placing it on the table. Control participants did not hear the statement. Participants who heard the statement were more likely to believe that the key continued to bend than participants who did not hear the statement. You could manipulate various aspects of this experiment to replicate Markovsky and Thye's (2001) test of social impact theory. For example, you could manipulate immediacy by having a fellow student in the room deliver the "it's still bending" statement as opposed to an equivalent person in the videotape. You could manipulate the strength of the source by varying who delivers the message.

5. Wiseman, Watt, Stevens, Greening, and O'Keeffe (2003) evaluated which features of a supposedly haunted environment might be associated with perceptions of haunting (e.g., lighting and temperature). You could evaluate the influence of social suggestion on haunting sensations. Will the variables that affect social impact in the pyramid power situation generalize to a "haunted" environment? As an example, you could see if haunting reports increase if a confederate suggests feeling something unusual. Or, you could vary the number of confederates, their immediacy (as in "many people have reported in the past that this place is haunted"), or their strength (the credibility of the source).

REFERENCES

Asch, S. E. (1951). Effects of group pressure upon the modification and distortion of judgments. In H. Guetzkow (Ed.) *Groups, Leadership and Men* (pp. 177–190). Pittsburgh, PA: Carnegie Press.

Auton, H. R., Pope, J., & Seeger, G. (2003). It isn't that strange: Paranormal belief and personality traits. *Social Behavior and Personality, 31*, 711–720. doi: 10.2224/sbp.2003.31.7.711

Bond, R., & Smith, P. B. (1996). Culture and conformity: A meta-analysis of studies using Asch's (1952b, 1956) line judgment task. *Psychological Bulletin, 119*, 111–137. doi: 10.1037/0033-2909.119.1.111

Campbell, D. T., & Stanley, J. C. (1963). *Experimental and Quasi-Experimental Designs for Research.* Chicago: Rand McNally.

Forer, B. R. (1949). The fallacy of personal validation: A classroom demonstration of gullibility. *The Journal of Abnormal and Social Psychology, 44*, 118–123. doi:10.1037/h0059240

Johnson, D. I. (2008). Modal expressions in refusals of friends' interpersonal requests: Politeness and effectiveness. *Communication Studies, 59*, 148–163. doi:10.1080/10510970802062477

Markovsky, B., & Thye, S. R. (2001). Social influence on paranormal beliefs. *Sociological Perspectives, 44*, 21–44. doi:10.1525/sop.2001.44.1.21

Markovsky, B., & Thye, S. R. (2002). Social influence and the power of the pyramid. *Skeptic, 9*, 36–41.

Merow, K. (2008). But you deceived me! The necessity of deception in investigation of the paranormal. *Skeptical Inquirer, 32*, 44–47.

Orne, M. T. (1962). On the social psychology of the psychological experiment: With particular reference to demand characteristics and their implications. *American Psychologist, 17*, 776–783. doi: 10.1037/h0043424

Rosenthal, R., & Fode, K. L. (1963). Psychology of the scientist: V. Three experiments in experimenter bias. *Psychological Reports, 12*, 491–511. Retrieved from http://www.ammonsscientific.com/AmSci/

Sparks, G. G., Hansen, T., & Shah, R. (1994). Do televised depictions of paranormal events influence viewers' beliefs? *Skeptical Inquirer, 18*, 386–395.

Sparks, G. G., & Pellechia, M. (1997). The effect of news stories about UFOs on readers' UFO beliefs: The role of confirming or disconfirming testimony from a scientist. *Communication Reports, 10,* 165–172. Retrieved from http://www.westcomm. org/publications/comm_reports.asp

Sparks, G. G., Pellechia, M., & Irvine, C. (1998). Does television news about UFOs affect viewers' UFO beliefs?: An experimental investigation. *Communication Quarterly, 46,* 284–294. Retrieved from http://www.tandf.co.uk/journals/titles/01463373 .asp

Stahelski, A., & Patch, M. E. (1993). The effect of compliance strategy choice upon perception of power. *The Journal of Social Psychology, 133,* 693–698. Retrieved from http://www.heldref.org/ pubs/soc/about.html

Wiseman, R., & Greening, E. (2005). 'It's still bending': Verbal suggestion and alleged psychokinetic ability. *British Journal of Psychology, 96,* 115–127. doi:10.1348/000712604X15428

Wiseman, R., Watt, C., Stevens, P., Greening, E., & O'Keeffe, C. (2003). An investigation into alleged 'hauntings'. *British Journal of Psychology, 94,* 195–211. doi:10.1348/000712603321661886

Wood, J. V., Perunovic, W. Q. E., & Lee, J. W. (2009). Positive self-statements: Power for some, peril for others. *Psychological Science, 20,* 860–866.

Wooffitt, R. (2007a). Communication and laboratory performance in parapsychology experiments: Demand characteristics and the social organization of interaction. *British Journal of Social Psychology, 46,* 477–498. doi:10.1348/014466606X152667

Wooffitt, R. (2007b). Epistemic authority and neutrality in the discourse of psychic practitioners: Toward a naturalistic parapsychology. *Journal of Parapsychology, 71,* 69–104. Retrieved from http://www.rhine.org/journal.shtml

CHAPTER 8

One-Way Designs
I remember reading this chapter before

Abstract

Psychology: The unreliability of memory is an important psychological phenomenon. Psychology research provides evidence for a variety of ways that memory can be unreliable.

Skeptic/Pseudoscience: If possible paranormal events occur in conditions that have been shown to be conducive to false memory formation, it is possible that a sincere memory of a "paranormal" event cannot be taken as evidence for the reality of that event. This is a particularly troubling problem for research into paranormal events for which the only evidence is eyewitness reports.

INTRODUCTION: EXPERIMENTS WITH MORE THAN TWO GROUPS AND ONE INDEPENDENT VARIABLE

Sometimes you will want to include more than two groups in your experimental design. Designs with more than two groups, but only one independent variable are called **one-way designs**. (In Chapters 9 and 10, we will consider designs with more than one independent variable.) There are two reasons you might need more than two levels of an independent variable. First, you may want to cover the entire range of an independent variable, and two levels may not be enough. Second, you may want to include additional control groups to evaluate various hypotheses about the phenomenon you are studying. We will consider an example of each as we discuss one-way designs.

In Chapter 7, we discussed how we could make Forer's (1949) study of the Barnum effect into an experiment by manipulating the kind of information in a person's horoscope. This would allow us to tell if people are willing to accept vaguely worded negative information to the same extent that they accept vaguely worded positive information. However, valence is a continuous dimension, and two values might not cover the entire range. Instead, we could have multiple values of valence: extremely negative, negative, neutral, positive, and extremely positive. The independent variable is the valence of the horoscope, and the values line up along that dimension, making this a one-way design.

If we see an orderly change in people's acceptance of the profiles as the content moves from extremely negative to extremely positive that would suggest that the Barnum effect is influenced by the kind of feedback. Other patterns would also be meaningful. For example, if people accepted the mildly positive, neutral, and mildly negative feedback, but not extreme feedback, that would suggest that in addition to using generalities that could apply to anyone, these generalities also need to be relatively neutral to produce a Barnum effect. Having multiple levels of the independent variable would allow us to uncover more information about the basic effect than would be available with just two levels.

Stroop (1935) presented a classic psychology experiment that can be used to illustrate what can be learned from multiple control groups. He showed participants color words written in ink colors that did not match the words (e.g., the word red in blue ink). When participants had to name the color of the ink, it took longer for them to do that in the mismatching words condition than in a control condition (boxes printed in different colors). Some have interpreted this as evidence for reading being automatic. Even though they were supposed to name the color, participants could not help but read the word, and that produced response competition between the color and the word, slowing them down.

Let's consider an additional question about this response competition. Is it the fact that the words are color words that makes people slower, or will people slow down for *any* word, no matter what it names? To answer this question, we need a third kind of stimulus (and a third group in the experiment). These stimuli need to be noncolor words written in the same colors as the color words. For instance, we could use the number words *one, two, three,* and *four* written in red, green, yellow, and blue. If we have people name the colors of these noncolor words, we can find out if simply looking at a word produces the interference or if it is the fact that the words name colors that produces the interference.

One thing to note about our new design with three groups is that all three still comprise the levels (or conditions) of one independent variable. You can tell this because they all line up on a single dimension. In this case, the dimension would be something like "amount of response competition." At one end are the color words, in the middle are the number words, and at the other end are the boxes. As you move from one end to the other, the thing that changes is the extent to which the item produces response competition. In other words, this is a one-way design.

As we discussed in Chapter 7, coming up with the appropriate control group can be difficult. Think about the Stroop experiment again. Each of the following control groups could be used to understand some aspect of the interference that causes people to slow down when they name the colors of color words.

a. Colored rectangles.
b. Number words.

c. Pseudoword homophones (letter strings that are not words but sound like color words, such as *bloo*).

d. Color words written in the color that they name (like *red* in red).

We have already discussed the first two. Pseudowords could tell us whether it is the visual appearance of the word that interferes or if it is the sound of the word (because they all sound like color words but do not look like color words). Color words written in the color named could tell us whether the interference comes from simultaneously processing two sorts of information (words and colors) or if it is due to response competition (trying to choose between two types of responses). If it is the former, people should be slow even when the words match the color. If it is response competition, people should be fast in this condition. We could do four separate two-group experiments to answer these questions, but that would waste time, and it would also rule out certain comparisons (like number words versus pseudo-words). Instead, we would do one big experiment with five kinds of stimuli.

Our target articles for this chapter used one-way designs. We will look at what happens to people's memory after various manipulations.

TARGET ARTICLE: MISREMEMBERING THE PARANORMAL

(Be sure to look at Appendix D to assist you in evaluating the sources cited in this chapter. Be especially aware of the guidelines for evaluating Internet and other non-peer reviewed sources.)

French (2003) provided a comprehensive review of the potential relationship between false memories and paranormal phenomena. The basic question is this: in the absence of conscious fraud, how reliable are sincere memories of paranormal phenomena? As French puts it, "sincerity is no guarantee of accuracy" (p. 154). This presents a problem for researchers trying to understand

METHODOLOGY NOTE **8.1**

As a check on your comprehension, think about ways to generalize the following designs to more than two groups. Heatherton and Sargent (2009) found that high exposure to smoking in movies was associated with more smoking than low exposure to smoking in movies. If this had been an experiment (you would not actually want to manipulate smoking exposure if you thought it might increase smoking), the variable would have been exposure with two levels: high and low. Would there be any reason to include more levels? What would they be? How would it be beneficial to expand the independent variable? Bosson, Vandello, Burnaford, Weaver, and Wasti (2009) presented men with a task to perform that threatened their manhood (hair dressing) or a neutral task (braiding a rope to reinforce it), and measured which follow-up activity they would choose, hitting a punching bag or doing puzzles. Men whose manhood had been threatened by their primary task were more likely to choose the aggressive follow-up task. If you were to include more levels of the independent variable, what would they be? What could you learn from them?

paranormal phenomena. If the only evidence for an event is eyewitness testimony, and there is a chance that that testimony is reporting a distorted memory, then how can a researcher attempt to explain what happened? This is a problem both for researchers who believe in paranormal phenomena and for skeptics.

Before we get into the research in this area, I want to highlight a guiding principle of this book. The main goal is to apply psychology research methods to an interesting real world problem: In the absence of good evidence to support belief in paranormal phenomena, why do so many people believe? To the extent that this book is about belief itself, a subsidiary goal is to understand belief in the paranormal by applying what we know about psychology. Whereas I am generally skeptical about paranormal phenomena, I do not believe it is appropriate to dismiss people's belief out of hand. Instead, our goal is to understand how that belief may have arisen, and, hopefully, help people to evaluate their own and others' experiences.

The topic for this chapter presents conflicts for that position. French (2003) says "A listener may decide that a particular account must be inaccurate simply because the account contradicts that person's understanding of what is and what is not possible. Is it reasonable that such a person, without any claim whatsoever to first-hand knowledge of the events in question, should feel justified in adopting this skeptical position?" (p. 170). French's answer is "yes." What decision should we make when the only evidence in favor of something that appears to be impossible is someone's testimony? Given that we have ample evidence that people's memory can be distorted, the more parsimonious explanation is that that person is misremembering than that the impossible happened. We will apply a principle called Occam's razor in this chapter: Given two possible explanations, choose the simpler. Rather than believe the impossible, we will side with French and assume that the person's testimony is wrong. As Newman and Baumeister (1996) put it with respect to alien abductions "The project of this article has been to take UFO abduction accounts seriously, but not literally" (p. 122).

SCIENCE NOTE **8.1**

French says that testimony that seems too incredible to be true can be dismissed as a possible memory distortion. Not everyone agrees with this conclusion. In response to an article explaining alien abduction experiences (in part) as memory distortions (Newman & Baumeister, 1996), McLeod, Corbisier, and Mack (1996) take issue with the observer's assumption about what is and is not possible. As they say "If such technologically advanced, nonhuman beings were to exist, how would we know whether they can or cannot move through walls?" (p. 157). Later, they say (because physical proof of alien abductions is lacking) "In focusing attention on obtaining physical proof of alien contact, it might be that substantial evidence is being overlooked" (p. 160). This evidence is "the substantial number of

(continues)

Science Note **8.1** (continued)

individuals who are reporting abduction experiences" (p. 160). They also note that some abduction experiences "seem more like out-of-body experiences or even encounters with strange forms of light, sound, vibratory, or other energies capable of creating strong tactile sensations but without the occurrence of anything that could be called an abduction in any literal sense" (p. 157). And, "In clinical psychology, the reality of what happened is less important than the whole constellation of behaviors associated with the abuse" (p. 158). I would argue that this puts the alien abduction experience outside of the realm of science. The aliens can do anything, we are powerless to understand their motives or capabilities, we must simply accept people's reports of their behavior at face value. And, actual reality is not what matters. In science, we need testable predictions, confirmable by evidence, with data repeatable by others. Trying to draw a line between what is and is not science is difficult and controversial. However, we could take as one principle the notion of **risky prediction** (Popper, 1962). It is necessary that something could happen to prove our hypotheses false. If we throw out the notion that testimony that violates physical laws must be false, and instead accept an "aliens could be capable of anything" mindset unconcerned with actual reality and physical evidence, what could possibly falsify the hypothesis that aliens are abducting people?

In fact, McLeod et al.'s (1996) description of alien abduction experiences fits Popper's (1962) profile of pseudoscience quite nicely (p. 36). They seek confirmations of abduction experiences rather than trying to disconfirm them, they fail to make risky predictions, their theory does not forbid anything (as in walking through walls or violating other physical laws), the theory is irrefutable (no evidence could prove it wrong), their research is not designed to refute (so it is not really a test), evidence is counted that is not the result of a risky prediction, and explanations are allowed to prop up the theory when it looks like it might be proven false (e.g., aliens can do anything, how can we be expected to understand them with our limited intelligence?).

McLeod et al. (1996) were concerned about the mystery of abduction experiences, but they seem to want to preserve the sense of mystery rather than accept explanations that are more ordinary. In a way, deciding *a priori* that alien abductions cannot be taking place may not be as exciting as believing in them without evidence. But, that seems to be missing the really interesting aspect of reports of alien abduction experiences. As Clark and Loftus (1996) put it in that same exchange, "...we argue that these are the kinds of questions to be asking with regard to space alien abduction memories—questions about the workings of the mind. This is where we will find the pay dirt in alien abduction stories" (p. 143).

Our target articles for this chapter will allow us to circumvent some of the thornier philosophical issues in trying to determine whether people's reports represent memory distortions or real experiences. We will consider research into memory distortions in which researchers presented people with an event, manipulated some aspect of the experience, and then collected participants' reports of what they saw. The target articles for this chapter are not concerned with paranormal experiences. Instead, we will learn about how memory can be distorted and apply that research to the paranormal.

Our first target article is Loftus and Palmer (1974). Their basic question had to do with how the wording of a question asked after an event could influence memory for that event. They presented participants with films of traffic accidents, and then asked participants for their memories of those films. One question asked how fast the cars were going when the accident happened. The frame for this question was "About how fast were the cars going when they * each other?" In place of the "*" were the words "contacted," "hit," "bumped," "collided," or "smashed." Note that this was a one-way design. The independent variable was the word used, and the values were arranged along a continuum from more extreme to less extreme.

Loftus and Palmer (1974) were interested in the effect of the word used on people's speed estimates. As expected, the word mattered. For "smashed" people guessed 40.8 miles per hour, whereas for "contacted" people guessed 31.8 miles per hour. These results suggested that how a question was worded could influence people's report of an event. However, will the question wording affect people's memory for the event?

METHODOLOGY NOTE **8.2**

When we do research we are concerned with two sorts of validity. **Internal validity** has to do with the quality of the study. An experiment high in internal validity allows us to draw strong conclusions about the relationship between the independent and dependent variables. **External validity** has to do with whether or not the results will generalize. Usually we have to make trade-offs to maximize these validities. For example, to increase internal validity we have to increase control over the situation. This control makes the research less natural, and harms generalizability. To make the experiment more natural requires us to relinquish control, which opens the door for problems with internal validity. The tension between internal and external validity will be especially relevant for this chapter. By controlling people's experiences, we will be able to make clear cause-and-effect statements about the effect of various manipulations on people's memory. However, some would argue that these results will not generalize to real paranormal experiences. Since the methodology for this chapter is experimental, we will follow the experiment bias of maximizing internal validity and worrying about generalizability after we find an effect. A more complete understanding of these issues would require converging evidence from multiple research design types.

Loftus and Palmer's (1974) Experiment 2 addressed the memory question. They used a one-way design with three levels of the independent variable. After watching a film of an accident, participants were asked to estimate the speed with the word "smashed," the word "hit," or no question about speed was asked. In a way, the variable was amount of distortion: high speed implied, medium speed implied, or no speed implication. A week later, participants were asked to remember the accident again, and the critical question was "Did you see any broken glass?" More participants who were asked the "smashed" question remembered broken glass than participants who were asked the "hit" question or no question. In other words, the kind of question asked immediately after an event influenced people's memory for that event.

A similar result was presented by Loftus and Zanni (1975). When a new item is introduced into a discourse, an indefinite article is used. For example, "Sally read a book." When something has already been introduced, a definite article is used. For example, "Sally did not like the book." Contrast the question "Would you like *a* drink?" with "Would you like *the* drink?" In the second, you would be expected to already know about some drink that had previously been introduced into the conversation. If someone asked you "Would you like the drink?" out of the blue, you would probably respond "What drink?" On the other hand, "Would you like a drink?" would get a yes or no response. To sum up, "the" implies that something exists for sure, and has already been introduced into the discourse.

Loftus and Zanni (1975) took advantage of this distinction between articles. After viewing an accident film, questions were asked with either "a" or "the." The research question was whether or not people would falsely recognize more objects that had not been seen if the question used "the" rather than "a." The results were that they did. In other words, something as simple as the article used in a question can affect people's memory. (Note that even though there were only two levels of the independent variable, this was still a one-way design.)

Loftus, Miller, and Burns (1978) investigated whether a presupposition in a question could introduce a memory distortion. Imagine that you said to someone "I sure am gaining weight" and that person said "Have you stopped exercising?" This question presupposes that you have been exercising. On the other hand, you would probably feel insulted if the person asked "Have you tried exercising?" Presuppositions operate during routine discourse, can they affect memory?

In Loftus et al.'s (1978) Experiment 2, participants saw a series of slides. Some participants saw a car at a yield sign, some saw the car at a stop sign. Later, participants were asked if another car passed the car they saw while it was at the yield sign, stop sign, or intersection. In other words, participants were given consistent presuppositions, inconsistent presuppositions, or no presuppositions (making it a one-way design). After the initial test there was a 20 minute delay, and then participants had a recognition test (they chose which of two slides they had seen before). Participants given misleading presuppositions made more mistakes.

We can take a break at this point to see how this research on the effect of suggestions could apply to memory in a paranormal context. Wiseman, Greening, and Smith (2003) created a paranormal experience in the controlled environment of a séance that they conducted. This allowed them to investigate memory for paranormal events when they knew, for a fact, that no paranormal event took place. In addition to freeing us from worrying whether participants' reports of paranormal phenomena are real or memory distortions, by manipulating the "paranormal" events, Wiseman, Greening, et al. will be able to make causal conclusions about the relationship between what happens during an event and how people remember it.

Wiseman, Greening, et al. (2003) manipulated what happened to various objects during a séance whose ostensible purpose was to move objects with the power of participants' minds (participants were told that the researchers felt it would be unethical to try to contact departed spirits for research purposes). During the séance, two objects (a maraca and a ball) moved (an assistant manipulated them with a pole while the room was dark), one object (a table) did not move, but the medium suggested that the table levitated, and one object (a bell) did not move and no movement suggestion was made. Therefore the manipulated independent variable was kind of movement with three levels: actual movement, suggested movement, and no movement. Participants reported whether the bell or table moved using a 7-point scale, and their responses were classified as yes (it moved), uncertain, or no. Wiseman, Greening, et al. found that suggestion did affect memory. For the table, which did not move, but which was suggested to be moving, 31% reported that it moved. For the bell, which did not move and no movement suggestion was made, only 10% reported that it moved (unfortunately, Wiseman, Greening, et al. did not report results for the actual movement condition, which would have been an interesting control group). In other words, a verbal suggestion given during a séance affected participants' memory.

The research reviewed so far provides a variety of mechanisms for memory distortions to be introduced into reports of paranormal phenomena. Something as simple as asking "did you hear *the* voice?" as opposed to "did you hear *a* voice?" could influence people's reports. Other subtle differences in the wording of questions could also matter. And, things said during an event can affect people's memory for that event. None of these influences require any conscious fraud or intent to mislead. Rather, ordinary questions

METHODOLOGY NOTE **8.3**

There is a problem with the assignment of Wiseman, Greening, et al. (2003) to the one-way design for this chapter. In their Experiment 1, they had one manipulated variable and one measured variable. In a sense, this was a factorial design because they were looking at how two variables combined. However, our focus here is on how suggestions affect memory, so we will ignore their variable classifying participants on belief in the paranormal.

and recountings of events can contaminate memory, enhancing memories for paranormal events.

A related question has to do with whether memories can be created for events that never happened (as opposed to distortions of memories for things that did happen). One way this can happen is to use hypnosis to probe people's memories. Newman and Baumeister (1996) provided a comprehensive review of the problems with using hypnosis as a memory tool in paranormal investigations (alien abductions). However, our concern here is with laboratory techniques for creating memories for things that never happened.

One laboratory technique that has received an incredible amount of attention is the Deese-Roediger-McDermott (DRM) paradigm (Deese, 1959; Roediger & McDermott, 1995). In their Experiment 1, Roediger and McDermott presented lists of words that were associated with some critical word (e.g., they presented *bed, rest, awake, dream,* and *snooze*), then asked participants to recall the lists. The results were that the probability of recalling the critical, non-presented item (*sleep* in our example) was .40. The recognition test from their first experiment more closely illustrated the one-way design methodology. They had four kinds of items on the recognition test: items that had been presented (e.g., *dream*), the critical items that they expected participants to recognize incorrectly due to their association with the items presented (e.g., *sleep*), items that were weakly associated with the items presented, and items that were unrelated to the items presented. The rate of recognizing a word that had been presented was 86%, for the critical items the rate was 84%, for the weakly related items the rate was 21%, and for the unrelated items the rate was 2%. These results imply that an easily administered laboratory task can reliably lead to false memories.

There is a problem with applying the DRM paradigm directly to paranormal experiences. The ecological (external) validity of a list learning task is quite low when considering paranormal experiences (e.g., hauntings). One could make the case that when multiple elements of a ghost encounter are present that people can "recall" a non-existent ghost based on the same mechanism as the DRM paradigm. As an example, Wiseman, Watt, Stevens, Greening, and O'Keeffe (2003) measured a variety of physical variables in a place that was supposed to be haunted (magnetic fields, temperature, air movement, and lighting). Their hypothesis was that "haunted" places (where a lot of reported haunting activities have taken place) would be identified by their participants as haunted, but that these paranormal experiences would be correlated with differences in physical variables. In their Experiment 2, their participants reported 172 unusual experiences, with five of those being rated as at least probably a ghost, 58 uncertain, and 87 probably not a ghost. The likelihood of an unusual experience was correlated with some of their physical variables (e.g., height of the space). Perhaps certain environmental triggers could converge in memory on the schema for a haunted place and cause participants to remember unusual sensations as true paranormal experiences over time. French, Haque, Bunton-Stasyshyn, and Davis (2009) attempted to build a haunted room in a laboratory setting by manipulating electromagnetic fields and infrasound, and were unable to find a relationship between environmental variables and unusual experiences, suggesting that whatever is being combined into a haunting experience might require the mediation of an overall "spooky" atmosphere.

The more common use of the DRM paradigm in the paranormal research literature is as a measure of individual differences in susceptibility to false memories. Clancy, McNally, Schacter, Lenzenweger, and Pitman (2002) compared susceptibility to DRM effects in three groups: people who had recovered memories of alien abductions, people who thought they had been abducted, but could not remember the experience, and a control group of people who did not believe that they had been abducted. (Note that I am classifying this as a one-way design because of the three levels of experience, but this was not a manipulated independent variable.) Clancy et al. found that their recovered memory group had the most false memory (both recognition and recall), followed by the group that thought they had been abducted, followed by the control group. (Clancy et al. also found a number of other differences between their groups, such as magical ideation; these kinds of differences were the subject of Chapter 5.) French, Santomauro, Hamilton, Fox, and Thalbourne (2008) compared DRM susceptibility in a group of people with alien contact experiences (ranging from seeing UFOs to device implantations) to that of a group with no alien contact experience, and failed to replicate the findings of Clancy et al. that the groups differ on susceptibility to false memories. However, there were differences in the participant populations that might partially explain the different results of the two studies.

Meyersburg, Bogdan, Gallo, and McNally (2009) investigated susceptibility to DRM effects in a group of people reporting past lives. The past-life group reported memories of a previous life (as opposed to just a feeling that they might have lived before). The control group had no memories of a past life. The past-life group had significantly more false memory in the DRM task than the control group. One possible explanation for the different results between Clancy et al. (2002), French et al. (2008), and Meyersburg et al. is the lists used. Meyersburg et al. used only 15-item lists, the ones that produced larger numbers of false memories and the largest differences between groups in all three studies. The situation may be similar to that discussed by Bressan (2002) with respect to the likelihood of reasoning errors in believers and non-believers: The effect will be present when there is room for variability, but it is possible that floor effects (everyone is generally poor at these tasks) mask those differences when the overall effect is small.

Crombag, Wagenaar, and van Koppen (1996) presented a "crashing memories" technique for creating false memories. They asked their participants whether or not they had seen film footage of a plane crash. However, there was no actual film of the crash. In their Study 2, 66% of the participants reported that they had seen the film, and many of those participants were willing to provide details of what they had seen in the film. Crombag et al. interpreted this as a failure of source monitoring. Hearing about the crash, seeing news footage of the crash's aftermath, and common sense filled in gaps in participants' knowledge, and led them to remember film they never saw. Note that people's false memories in this study were for a dramatic event that dominated news coverage. Apparently a combination of real world memory processes plus a small suggestion from a researcher was able to produce a false memory in a majority of the participants.

This kind of situation is closer to the real-life event of having a paranormal experience than the DRM paradigm. The event "recalled" was dramatic, and probably perceived as important by the participants. Like the DRM paradigm, the crashing memories effect has been used to investigate differences in false memory susceptibility in believers and non-believers. Wilson and French (2006) presented participants with four events, three of which had film footage and one of which did not. They classified their participants into believers in the paranormal or non-believers using the Australian Sheep-Goat Scale (sheep are believers and goats are skeptics) and the Anomalous Experiences Inventory measuring belief, paranormal experiences, and ability. Believers reported more false memories than non-believers.

A final laboratory technique for inducing false memories is to implant a false memory for an entire episode that never happened, without the use of hypnosis. There are a variety of ways to accomplish this (see Loftus, 2004 for a review). For example, Hyman, Husband, and Billings (1995) sent their participants' parents a questionnaire asking about six possible childhood events: "(1) getting lost; (2) going to the hospital; (3) an eventful birthday; (4) loss of a pet; (5) a family vacation; and (6) interaction with a prominent or famous person" (p. 184). They also created stories about two events, one positive (a birthday with a clown) and one negative (a trip to the hospital for an ear infection). Participants were interviewed and asked to recall between two and five real events, and one of the false events. After this initial interview, they were asked to think about and try to remember more details from the events. Between one and seven days later, participants were interviewed again. In both interviews, the interviewer was supportive of the effort to remember. For the 74 true events that participants were asked about, they recalled 62 at the first interview, and 65 at the second interview. For the 20 false events, none were recalled at the first interview; four participants recalled a false event at the second interview. Three of these participants were unable to identify which was the false event. Whereas four people recalling a false event may not seem like many, that is 20% of the total. Within the social environment of the interview and the pressure to remember, plus a suggestion that something may have happened to them, participants created a memory of something that they never experienced. In other words, just being asked to remember made them create a false memory.

In their second study, Hyman et al. (1995) used three possible false events (spilling a punch bowl at a wedding, evacuating a store when the sprinklers went off, and releasing the parking break in a car, causing a crash). They had three interviews, with stronger pressure to improve memory between each interview. Hyman et al. found that participants ultimately recalled 195 out of 205 true events, and 13 out of 51 false events. Again, the effort to remember actually created memories. Other research has investigated various aspects of this task. For example, Heaps and Nash (2001) investigated differences between real and false memories. Laney, Fowler, Nelson, Bernstein, and Loftus (2008) investigated the duration of false memories.

With respect to the paranormal, this is another way that false memories of paranormal events could be created. Repeated interviews with the suggestion that something is there to be remembered can create memories in some participants. Rose and Blackmore (2001) used a false memory creation technique to investigate differences in susceptibility between believers and non-believers. Participants viewed slides of some objects and imagined others over repeated testing. Eventually, some participants recalled seeing pictures of objects that they only imagined. Rose and Blackmore found no difference in susceptibility to false memories between believers and non-believers in any of their studies. Rose and Blackmore also had the opportunity to see if this paradigm would increase ESP for the items participants were falsely recalling. There was no evidence of a psi effect. The memory and ESP results were replicated by Roe (2003).

At this point we have seen evidence that subtle influences can change memories for events that have happened, and that memories can be created for events that never took place. Each of these false memory phenomena has implications for reports of paranormal activity. In the projects section, you will have an opportunity to investigate the link between false memory and paranormal experiences.

INFOTRAC® COLLEGE EDITION EXERCISES

You can use the InfoTrac College Edition to read about additional studies using an experimental methodology. For example, typing in "psychology experiment" with the box for "in entire article content" checked, and checking the box for "to refereed publications" gave me a list of 24 articles. Many of these were not one-way experiments like the ones in this chapter, so you will have to read through the list if you want to restrict your search to just one-way designs. Also, you can vary the search options to broaden the list if you would like to look at more studies. As an example of a one-way design, Casali, Robinson, Dabney, and Gauger (2004) investigated the extent to which ear protection would interfere with important workplace sounds. In particular, they investigated how backup alarms on vehicles would be affected with active noise reduction hearing protection devices, standard hearing protection devices, or no ear protection (a one-way design with three levels). They found that hearing protection devices actually resulted in better detection compared to the no protection condition, suggesting that concerns about interference with important warning signals is not a good excuse for not wearing ear protection.

My basic search also turned up a couple of articles with content relevant for this chapter. Paddock, Terranova, Kwok, and Halpern (2000) investigated source monitoring errors in autobiographical memories. They had participants recall three kinds of memories: know (they have heard other people talking about an event they do not personally remember), remember (they have a personal memory of the event), and unsure (a mix of both types).

Participants then completed a guided visualization task. Paddock et al. found that the guided visualization task shifted participants' know and unsure memories towards the remember end of their scale. French and Richards (1993) were interested in the effects of schemas on perception (another possible influence on memories of paranormal events). Participants looked at a clock with roman numerals and attempted to draw it in three conditions: when the memory test was a surprise, when the memory test was announced, and when the clock was still present for the memory test. Participants who did not have the clock present were more likely to report the four as "IV" than as "IIII" (clocks use "IIII" as the roman number for four). In other words, knowledge of the standard roman numeral for four influenced participants' memory for a clock face, even when they were warned of a memory test.

In addition to exploring how the experimental design can be applied to a variety of interesting topics, you can learn a lot of methodological information from reading other people's research. Spend some time with InfoTrac College Edition reading method sections from a variety of articles using experimental designs before tackling your own project.

You can also learn more about the malleability of memory using the InfoTrac College Edition. The search "false memory" with the same boxes checked as before produced 148 results, with a wide variety of topics. For example, Levinson (2007) discussed false memory and memory distortions related to race in judicial decisions. When I typed in "paranormal experiment" with the same search parameters I only got one result, Rose and Blackmore (2001). It would probably be useful to generate additional search terms to locate more focused articles. You can use InfoTrac to find a lot more information about memory and the paranormal before beginning your project.

IMPLEMENTING THE DESIGN

Materials

For projects investigating the creation of false memories of paranormal phenomena in the laboratory, you will need to consult the original articles and replicate their materials.

For projects investigating differences in false memories between different types of participants, you might want to classify participants based on belief in the paranormal. The two most common scales to measure belief in the paranormal are the Australian Sheep-Goat Scale (Thalbourne & Delin, 1993) and the Paranormal Belief Scale (Tobacyk & Milford, 1983). The Anomalous Experiences Inventory (Gallagher, Kumar, & Pekala, 1994) can be used to identify participants' paranormal experiences, beliefs, and abilities. (For ethical reasons, you should probably delete the items comprising the drug-use scale for research methods projects.) Other measures of paranormal experiences can be located based on the project (for example, Meyersburg et al., 2009 described their procedure for classifying participants as having recovered memories of a past life).

The lists used by Roediger and McDermott (1995) were included with their original article. Specific instructions for how those lists were modified

METHODOLOGY NOTE 8.4

> Some of the projects in this section will require repeated testing of the participants. It might be possible to modify these designs to fit into one research session. If you decide to have multiple testing sessions, keep in mind how that will impact planning for your project.

for particular research projects are presented in the relevant articles (e.g., Clancy et al. 2002).

Suggested Projects

1. You can manipulate various aspects of a memory task to evaluate whether or not false memories for paranormal experiences can be created.
   a. Many of the target articles revealed the power of suggestion on memory distortion. You could replicate Wiseman, Greening, et al. (2003) by making a suggestion during an event (e.g., a séance), or you could mirror some of the studies cited in the chapter (e.g., Loftus & Palmer, 1974) by changing the wording of critical questions or embedding presuppositions in questions. Can you create false memories of paranormal experiences through suggestion? Does the timing of the suggestion matter?
      i. Wiseman, Greening, et al. (2003) were concerned that the population in their séances might have affected the results (attendees at a paranormal convention). You could replicate their séance to see how likely people are to accept a suggestion based on population variables. For example, measure suggestibility of skeptics, people who are unsure, and believers.
      ii. Wiseman, Greening, et al. (2003) were also concerned about demand characteristics. Perhaps participants knew that the table did not move, but said it did to please the researchers. You could design a study to investigate the extent to which demand characteristics influence the results. For example, you could have three levels of experimenter instructions (expressing skeptical, unsure, or pro-paranormal positions) and see how the instructions affect memory for the suggested movement.
      iii. French (2003) noted that the conditions under which paranormal events are witnessed overlap with situations in eyewitness testimony research (e.g., poor viewing conditions, p. 157). You could manipulate these variables in a paranormal context and see how the results relate to the eyewitness testimony literature.
   b. Wiseman and Morris (1995) requested different sorts of information from their participants after showing them a videotape of a magician performing tricks. In their Experiment 2, they asked three types of questions. Important questions were related to how a particular trick

worked. For example, in their key-bending trick, the key went out of sight for a moment when it was switched for a bent key. The important question asked whether the key went out of sight. Pseudo-important questions allowed participants to reveal a skeptical mind-set because they were relevant for one of the tricks, but not the trick they were answering questions about (e.g., the critical event in the fork bending demonstration was the magician touching the forks, so touching the pile of keys was the pseudo-important question for the key-bending demonstration). Unimportant questions did not relate to how the trick was done. Wiseman and Morris were interested in whether or not being a skeptic would affect how people would attend to information. This was actually a factorial design (see Chapter 9), but you could replicate their results with just a population of skeptics or believers if you wanted to keep it to a one-way design. For projects, you could vary the extent to which questions were important to the method of the trick with more levels, or you could vary the kind of trick. When something is obviously a magic trick, will that cause participants to be more observant than when something appears to be paranormal?

c. It will be harder to incorporate the DRM paradigm (Roediger & McDermott, 1995) into an experiment creating false memories of the paranormal. However, one suggestion would be to play off of the "haunted places" research of Wiseman, Watt, et al. (2003). Identify as many features of a haunted place as you can from their research, and then manipulate as many of those features as you are able. The independent variable would be the number of features present. You can do this experiment without expensive equipment since height of the room and lighting proved to be two of the more important variables in Wiseman, Watt, et al. Will "longer lists" lead to false recall of paranormal events suggested by the items on those "lists"?

d. In their investigation of false memories using the "crashing memories" technique, Wilson and French (2006) embedded one false event into a set of four real events (footage existed for four of the events). They proposed that placing the false event into a context containing real events might have increased the likelihood that people would be willing to provide details about their memory. This proposal could be tested empirically by varying the number of real events combined with a false event. This research could also be extended to false memories of the paranormal. For example, in a controlled séance (as in Wiseman, Greening, et al., 2003) you could have several actual events to use in a crashing memories questionnaire asking about memory for an event that did not happen. Crombag et al. (1996) proposed that hearing about a plane crash, seeing footage of its aftermath, and common sense helped people to create a memory that they then reported. Your project could be to explicitly manipulate one of these variables. For example, for some participants the item being probed for a false memory could make more sense in the context of the séance, and for others it could make less sense.

e. Garry, Manning, Loftus, and Sherman (1996) used an imagination inflation technique to increase participants' confidence that an event took place. First, participants completed a life events inventory. Eight items on the inventory were unlikely to have happened to participants (e.g., "got in trouble for calling 911"). For four of these events participants completed an imagination exercise in which they imagined themselves as the event happened to them. Participants then completed a second life events inventory. The two groups of critical items were events that did not happen but were imagined and events that did not happen and were not imagined. For the imagined events, participants' confidence increased that those events had happened. Using a different methodology, Thomas and Loftus (2002) found that imagining can also increase false memories for performing bizarre actions. You could incorporate a paranormal experience into this research. Augment the life events inventory with paranormal events (e.g., "you saw a UFO"). Ideas for these could come from scales of paranormal belief and experience (e.g., the Anomalous Experiences Inventory, Gallagher et al., 1994). You could also manipulate the bizarreness of the paranormal experiences to see how that would affect the results. Will you find an imagination inflation effect for paranormal experiences? If so, is it of the same magnitude as the one found by Garry et al.?

f. Bernstein, Laney, Morris, and Loftus (2005) gave participants false feedback after they completed a food preference survey. The false feedback told participants that they became sick after eating dill pickles or hard-boiled eggs as children. A control group received no false feedback. The pickle group was more confident on a later memory test that they had become sick from eating a pickle, and were less likely to choose a pickle to eat on a survey about food choices at a barbecue (but the difference in preference was not significant). In a follow-up study, Bernstein, et al. did find an effect of false feedback on food choices. You could extend this research to a paranormal setting. For example, ask people about experiences in various potentially haunted places, provide false feedback of a paranormal experience, and see if that affects their confidence that it happened or their choice of which places to visit again. Can false feedback in a personally prepared report lead to increased confidence that a paranormal experience happened and affect future behavior?

2. A second line of research has investigated individual differences in susceptibility to false memories.

a. We have considered a variety of techniques to manipulate memory. For each of them, a project could be to see if there is a difference between believers in the paranormal and non-believers for susceptibility to false memory. You could break believers into three groups to cover the full range of belief (believers, unsure, and skeptics).

b. You could do a project similar to 2a, except break the groups on the basis of experience. For example, Clancy et al. (2002) compared alien abductees with memories, people who thought they had been abducted but did not remember, and people who had not been abducted using a DRM paradigm task. French et al. (2008) had two groups of alien contactees, but they lumped a variety of different experiences into their contact group. If people reporting alien contact experiences are difficult to come by, an alternative would be to group participants on the experiences and abilities scales of the Anomalous Experiences Inventory (Gallagher et al., 1994). Are experiencers and non-experiencers different in susceptibility to false memories?

c. Russell and Jones (1980) found that when presented with information that disconfirmed their belief, believers in the paranormal were more likely to misremember that information compared to when the information supported their belief. (Russell and Jones also included non-believers in a factorial design, but you can work with just believers in a one-way design.) You could replicate their design and include more values of "confrontational" evidence: supportive, mixed, disconfirming, and unrelated. How strongly do believers' memory errors "work" to preserve belief?

REFERENCES

Bernstein, D. M., Laney, C., Morris, E. K., & Loftus, E. F. (2005). False memories about food can lead to food avoidance. *Social Cognition, 23,* 11–34. doi: 10.1521/soco.23.1.11.59195

Bosson, J. K., Vandello, J. A., Burnaford, R. M., Weaver, J. R., & Wasti, S. A. (2009). Precarious manhood and displays of physical aggression. *Personality and Social Psychology Bulletin, 35,* 623–634. doi:10.1177/0146167208331161

Bressan, P. (2002). The connection between random sequences, everyday coincidences, and belief in the paranormal. *Applied Cognitive Psychology, 16,* 17–34. doi:10.1002/acp.754

Casali, J. G., Robinson, G. S., Dabney, E. C., & Gauger, D. (2004). Effect of electronic ANR and conventional hearing protectors on vehicle backup alarm detection in noise. *Human Factors, 46,* 1–10. doi:10.1518/hfes.46.1.1.30387

Clancy, S. A., McNally, R. J., Schacter, D. L., Lenzenweger, M. F., & Pitman, R. K. (2002). Memory distortion in people reporting abduction by aliens. *Journal of Abnormal Psychology, 111,* 455–461. doi:10.1037//0021-843X.111.3.455

Clark, S. E., & Loftus, E. F. (1996). The construction of space alien abduction memories. *Psychological*

Inquiry, 7, 140–143. doi:10.1207/ s15327965pli0702_5

Crombag, H. F. M., Wagenaar, W. A., & van Koppen, P. J. (1996). Crashing memories and the problem of 'source monitoring.' *Applied Cognitive Psychology, 10,* 95–104. doi:10.1002/ (SICI)1099-0720(199604)10:2<95::AID-ACP366>3.0.CO;2-#

Deese, J. (1959). On the prediction of occurrence of particular verbal intrusions in immediate recall. *Journal of Experimental Psychology, 58,* 17–22. doi:10.1037/h0046671

Forer, B. R. (1949). The fallacy of personal validation: A classroom demonstration of gullibility. *The Journal of Abnormal and Social Psychology, 44,* 118–123. doi:10.1037/h0059240

French, C. C. (2003). Fantastic memories: The relevance of research into eyewitness testimony and false memories for reports of anomalous experiences. *Journal of Consciousness Studies, 10,* 153–174.

French, C. C., Haque, U., Bunton-Stasyshyn, R., & Davis, R. (2009). The "haunt" project: An attempt to build a "haunted" room by manipulating complex electromagnetic fields and infrasound. *Cortex, 45,* 619–629. doi:10.1016/j.cortex.2007.10.011

French, C. C., & Richards, A. (1993). Clock this! An everyday example of a schema-driven error in memory. *British Journal of Psychology, 84,* 249–253.

French, C. C., Santomauro, J., Hamilton, V., Fox, R., & Thalbourne, M. A. (2008). Psychological aspects of the alien contact experience. *Cortex, 44,* 1387–1395. doi:10.1016/j.cortex.2007.11.011

Gallagher, C., Kumar, V. K., & Pekala, R. J. (1994). The anomalous experiences inventory: Reliability and validity. *The Journal of Parapsychology, 58,* 402–428. Retrieved from http://www.rhine.org/journal.shtml

Garry, M., Manning, C. G., Loftus, E. F., & Sherman, S. J. (1996). Imagination inflation: Imagining a childhood event inflates confidence that it occurred. *Psychonomic Bulletin and Review, 3,* 208–214.

Heaps, C. M., & Nash, M. (2001). Comparing recollective experience in true and false autobiographical memories. *Journal of Experimental Psychology: Learning, Memory, and Cognition, 27,* 920–930. doi:10.1037//0278-7393.27.4.920

Heatherton, T. F., & Sargent, J. D. (2009). Does watching smoking in movies promote teenage smoking? *Current Directions in Psychological Science, 18,* 63–67.

Hyman, I. E., Jr., Husband, T. H., & Billings, F. J. (1995). False memories of childhood experiences. *Applied Cognitive Psychology, 9,* 181–197. doi: 10.1002/acp.2350090302

Laney, C., Fowler, N. B., Nelson, K. J., Bernstein, D. M., & Loftus, E. F. (2008). The persistence of false beliefs. *Acta Psycholigica, 129,* 190–197. doi: 10.1016/j.actpsy.2008.05.010

Levinson, J. D. (2007). Forgotten racial equality: Implicit bias, decision making, and misremembering. *Duke Law Journal, 57,* 345–424.

Loftus, E. F. (2004). Memories of things unseen. *Current Directions in Psychological Science, 13,* 145–147.

Loftus, E. F., & Palmer, J. C. (1974). Reconstruction of automobile destruction: An example of the interaction between language and memory. *Journal of Verbal Learning and Verbal Behavior, 13,* 585–589. doi:10.1016/S0022-5371(74)80011-3

Loftus, E. F., & Zanni, G. (1975). Eyewitness testimony: The influence of the wording of a question. *Bulletin of the Psychonomic Society, 5,* 86–88. Retrieved from http://www.psychonomic.org/psp/publications-resources.html

Loftus, E. F., Miller, D. G., & Burns, H. J. (1978). Semantic integration of verbal information into a visual memory. *Journal of Experimental Psychology: Human Learning and Memory, 4,* 19–31. doi:10.1037/0278-7393.4.1.19

McLeod, C. C., Corbisier, B., & Mack, J. E. (1996). A more parsimonious explanation for UFO abduction. *Psychological Inquiry, 7,* 156–168. doi:10.1207/s15327965pli0702_9

Meyersburg, C. A., Bogdan, R., Gallo, D. A., & McNally, R. J. (2009). False memory propensity in people reporting recovered memories of past lives. *Journal of Abnormal Psychology, 118,* 399–404. doi:10.1037/a0015371

Newman, L. S., & Baumeister, R. F. (1996). Toward an explanation of the UFO abduction phenomenon: Hypnotic elaboration, extraterrestrial sadomasochism, and spurious memories. *Psychological Inquiry, 7,* 99–126. doi:10.1207/s15327965pli0702_1

Paddock, J. R., Terranova, S., Kwok, R., & Halpern, D. V. (2000). When knowing becomes remembering: Individual differences in susceptibility to suggestion. *The Journal of Genetic Psychology, 161,* 453–468. Retrieved from http://www.heldref.org/pubs/gnt/about.html

Popper, K. R. (1962). *Conjectures and refutations: The growth of scientific knowledge.* New York: Basic Books.

Rose, N., & Blackmore, S. (2001). Are false memories psi-conducive? *The Journal of Parapsychology, 65,* 125–144. Retrieved from http://www.rhine.org/journal.shtml

Roe, C. A. (2003). Revisiting false memories as a vehicle for psi. *Journal of the Society for Psychical Research, 67,* 281–295. Retrieved from http://www.spr.ac.uk/expcms/index.php?section=41

Roediger, H. L., III, & McDermott, K. B. (1995). Creating false memories: Remembering words not presented in lists. *Journal of Experimental Psychology: Learning, Memory, and Cognition, 21,* 803–814. doi:10.1037/0278-7393.21.4.803

Russell, D., & Jones, W. H. (1980). When superstition fails: Reactions to disconfirmation of paranormal beliefs. *Personality and Social Psychology Bulletin, 6,* 83–88. doi:10.1177/014616728061012

Stroop, J. R. (1935). Studies of interference in serial verbal reactions. *Journal of Experimental Psychology, 18,* 643–662. doi:10.1037/h0054651

Thalbourne, M. A., & Delin, P. S. (1993). A new instrument for measuring the sheep-goat variable: Its psychometric properties and factor structure. *Journal of the Society for Psychical Research, 59,* 172–186. Retrieved from http://www.spr.ac.uk/expcms/index.php?section=41

Thomas, A. K., & Loftus, E. F. (2002). Creating bizarre memories through imagination. *Memory and Cognition, 30,* 423–431. Retrieved from http://www.psychonomic.org/psp/publications-resources.html

Tobacyk, J., & Milford, G. (1983). Belief in paranormal phenomena: Assessment instrument development and implications for personality functioning. *Journal of Personality and Social Psychology, 44,* 1029–1037. doi:10.1037/0022-3514.44.5.1029

Wilson, K., & French, C. C. (2006). The relationship between susceptibility to false memories, dissociativity, and paranormal belief and experience. *Personality and Individual Differences, 41,* 1493–1502. doi:10.1016/j.paid.2006.06.008

Wiseman, R., Greening, E., & Smith, M. (2003). Belief in the paranormal and suggestion in the séance room. *British Journal of Psychology, 94,* 285–297. doi:10.1348/000712603767876235

Wiseman, R., & Morris, R. L. (1995). Recalling pseudo-psychic demonstrations. *British Journal of Psychology, 86,* 113–125.

Wiseman, R., Watt, C., Stevens, P., Greening, E., & O'Keeffe, C. (2003). An investigation into alleged 'hauntings.' *British Journal of Psychology, 94,* 195–211. doi:10.1348/000712603321661886

CHAPTER **9**

Factorial Designs 1

?siht daer uoy naC

Abstract

Psychology: The ability to detect lying is an interesting psychological question, and it poses significant methodological challenges. The development of a highly reliable and valid method for lie detection would be a major achievement. If this tool could also be used to improve communication and therapeutic effectiveness, that would increase its value even more.

Skeptic/Pseudoscience: Some pseudoscientific techniques rely on "wishful listening" phenomena. People increase their estimates of a technique's validity without realizing that its "success" is superimposed on the data from their own expectations.

INTRODUCTION: EXPERIMENTS WITH TWO OR MORE INDEPENDENT VARIABLES

In the experiments discussed in the last two chapters, we have manipulated only one independent variable. Sometimes it is necessary to manipulate more than one independent variable in order to fully understand what causes a behavior. The general term for any design with more than one independent variable is **factorial design**.

We have been considering ways to generalize Forer's (1949) exploration of the Barnum effect in previous chapters. We can continue that here by considering how additional variables might be useful. Our proposal to make the Forer study into an experiment was to manipulate the kind of information in people's horoscopes (e.g., positive or negative). Will people accept negative information to the same extent that they will accept positive information? Another interesting question would be to evaluate how different types of people would react to different types of information. For example, true believers in astrology might accept any kind of information, whereas skeptics might only be swayed by positive information (Glick, Gottesman, & Jolton, 1989). This would require adding another variable, belief in astrology, with two levels: believe or do not believe. Belief would be a non-manipulated variable, but this could still be considered a factorial design. Alternatively, we could try to manipulate belief by presenting material before the study that is either highly supportive of the accuracy of astrology or highly critical. To understand how belief influences the acceptance of positive and negative information would require a design with two independent variables.

Song and Schwarz (2009) conducted an experiment using a factorial design. Their initial studies were conducted to see how people would interpret food additive names that were easy to pronounce (e.g., Magnalroxate) versus names that were difficult to pronounce (e.g., Hnegripitrom). The basic hypothesis was that since ease of processing is interpreted by people as reflecting familiarity, and familiarity is interpreted by people as being safer, names that are easier to pronounce should seem less risky than names that are difficult to pronounce. In fact, in their first two studies, Song and Schwarz found that harder-to-pronounce food additive names were rated as more harmful.

In their Study 3, Song and Schwarz (2009) used a factorial design to evaluate whether the elevated risk perception associated with hard to pronounce names would extend to desirable as well as undesirable risk. To evaluate this, they had two independent variables. The first independent variable was the names used for roller coasters. This variable had two levels, easy to pronounce (e.g., Tihkoosue) and difficult to pronounce (e.g., Tsiischili). The second independent variable was the kind of risk rated, with two levels: desirable risk (e.g., adventurous) and undesirable risk (e.g., likely to make you sick). One possibility is that the elevated risk perception is only for negative aspects (as in Studies 1 and 2 with harmfulness). Alternatively, difficult to pronounce names could elevate all types of risk perception.

Crossing two levels of pronunciation difficulty with two types of risk produced a 2 x 2 factorial design. The first number in the name refers to the number of levels of the first independent variable. The second number is the number of levels of the second independent variable. The multiplication sign is read "by." There is a lot of information in this notation. With Song and Schwarz's (2009) design (2 x 2) you would know:

1. *That there were two independent variables.* Each number represents one independent variable.
2. *That there were two levels of the first variable and two levels of the second.* Each number represents a number of levels.
3. *That there are four conditions in the experiment.* Treat the name as a multiplication problem, and you get four conditions in the experiment.

How do you know what will happen in each condition? The best way is to make a chart, as in Figure 9.1.

A person in condition 1 will be given an easy to pronounce name and evaluate desirable risk (adventurousness). A person in condition 4 will be given a difficult to pronounce name and evaluate undesirable risk (getting sick).

Pronunciation Difficulty

	Easy	Difficult
Desirable Risk	Easy (Tihkoosue) Desirable Risk (Adventurous) 1	Difficult (Tsiischili) Desirable Risk (Adventurous) 2
Undesirable Risk	Easy (Tihkoosue) Undesirable Risk (Getting Sick) 3	Difficult (Tsiischili) Undesirable Risk (Getting Sick) 4

*(Left axis label: **Risk Type**)*

FIGURE **9.1** The Design of the Song and Schwarz (2009) Experiment.

For two-group experiments, we flipped a coin to randomly assign people to conditions. For a complex design like this, we would have to use a random number table. Start at a random location in the random number table, and write down the first four numbers between one and four in the order you encounter them. Then, assign your first four participants to conditions using these numbers. For example, in my random number table, 3 was the first number I encountered. So, my first participant would get an easy to pronounce name and evaluate undesirable risk. Repeat in multiples of four until everyone has been run. Alternatively, you can use a website like random.org to generate a list of random digits. Using the "Sequence Generator" option, and entering "1" as the smallest and "4" as the largest, I received the order "4, 3, 1, 2."

As in one-way designs, you can run a factorial design between participants or within participants. For between-participants designs, every person would be in one and only one condition. For within-participants designs, every person would be in every condition. With factorial designs, you have another option in addition to between- and within- participants; you can run a **mixed design**. In a mixed design, you have at least one between-participants variable and at least one within-participants variable. This allows you to take advantage of some of the benefits of within-participants designs even if you cannot run all of the independent variables within participants.

We have already considered one reason to use factorial designs. Basically, in the real world, multiple variables operate to produce a behavior. If you do not include them all in your design, you are not going to understand the full relationship. For Song and Schwarz (2009), the concern is that the type of risk may combine with ease of pronunciation to affect the ratings. There are two other good reasons to do factorial designs, efficiency and information:

1. *Efficiency.* By combining multiple simple experiments into one large experiment, you can gather more information in less time. This is especially true if you use a within-participants or mixed design.

METHODOLOGY NOTE **9.1**

In general terms, within-participants designs are desirable. As the researcher, you need to run fewer participants in your study, you are better able to equate the groups since the same people are in all conditions, and you have more statistical power. However, if the treatment effect from one level of an independent variable will carry over to subsequent levels, then you cannot use a within-participants design. For example, if I wanted to know how participants' memory would be affected if I told them the title of an ambiguous passage before they read it versus not telling them, I would not be able to undo participants' knowledge of the title to let them go back and read the passage without the title (I cannot run the order title-no title in my study). If I only ran one order (no title-title) I would open myself up to an order confound (better memory with the title could come from practice with the task and not the manipulation). Consider this issue for Song and Schwarz (2009). Could they run risk type within participants? In other words, could the same participant rate both desirable and undesirable risk for the same name? Could they run ease of pronunciation within participants (could the same participant rate both an easy to pronounce name and a hard to pronounce name)?

2. *Information*. There are two sorts of information available after you conduct a factorial design. The first sort of information is about **main effects**. These are the effects of a single variable. Looking at a main effect is similar to looking at the results of a one-way design with just that variable in it. The question you can address is: What effect does this variable have? You will have one main effect for each independent variable in your design. The real gain from doing factorial research is to look at interactions. An **interaction** is the combined effect of two or more variables. These combined effects can only be investigated with a factorial design.

Let's consider the information available from Song and Schwarz' (2009) study. There were two main effects: ease of pronunciation and risk type. What were the results for the two main effects? For ease of pronunciation, participants rated easy to pronounce names as less risky than difficult to pronounce names, and this effect was significant. With respect to kind of risk, the means were close together and the main effect was not significant. In other words, ease of pronunciation had an effect, but type of risk did not.

How do we determine if there was an interaction in Song and Schwarz' (2009) study, and what would it mean if there were? A graph of their data is presented in Figure 9.2.

First, the technical definition of an interaction is "the effect of one independent variable is different at different levels of the other independent variable." So, what we are looking to see is whether the effect of ease of pronunciation is different for the two kinds of risk. One way this might happen is if undesirable risk was affected by ease of pronunciation, but desirable risk

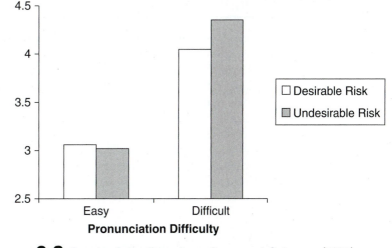

FIGURE **9.2** Graph of the Data from Song and Schwarz (2009).

was not; for example, if familiarity activated people's "safeness" schema when they were evaluating undesirable risk, but it did not activate the "safeness" schema when evaluating desirable risk. On the other hand, if there were no interaction, that would mean that regardless of the kind of risk (desirable or undesirable), participants rated easier to pronounce names as less risky.

A careful examination of Figure 9.2 will reveal that there was no interaction in Song and Schwarz' (2009) data. There is a large difference in the height of the bars when comparing across ease of pronunciation (the bars for the easier names are both lower). However, the means for kind of risk are virtually the same within each level of risk. In other words, the difference between desirable and undesirable risk is not different at different levels of ease of pronunciation.

What implications could we draw from these results? Song and Schwarz (2009) suggested that people making up product names should take ease of pronunciation into account to avoid negative perceptions of their product. On the other hand, we might also infer that a harder to pronounce name might be more desirable for something like a roller coaster for which a higher perceived desirable risk will increase people's urge to ride it.

The results of an interaction between message content and message direction will be important for our target article for this chapter. Basically, we will test the theory that it is possible to perceive the content of reverse speech (secret messages embedded in forward speech that your mind detects by reversing speech as you listen).

TARGET ARTICLE: HEARING BACKWARDS MESSAGES

(Be sure to look at Appendix D to assist you in evaluating the sources cited in this chapter. Be especially aware of the guidelines for evaluating Internet and other non-peer reviewed sources.)

METHODOLOGY NOTE **9.2**

As a check on your comprehension, let's consider a study in which there was an interaction. Sebanz and Shiffrar (2009) were interested in how well people could detect bodily deception (in particular, whether a basketball player was throwing a fake pass or a real pass). They had two independent variables in their Experiment 1. The first was the kind of information. Participants viewed moving displays or a static picture of the pass. The second variable was experience. Some participants were novice basketball players and some were experienced (this was not a manipulated independent variable, but it does not undermine the logic of the factorial design). The dependent variable was accuracy at determining whether passes were real or fake. Can you describe the design and diagram it? How many groups will there be and what will happen in each group? Based on a review of the literature, Sebanz and Shiffrar (2009) were not sure if experts would do better than novices (some data have shown that they do not), and they were not sure whether or not the kind of information would matter. Work out a prediction each way. What would the data look like if there was no difference between experts and novices and kind of information did not matter? Is an interaction expected in that case? On the other hand, what would the data look like if experts were better than novices, but only for moving stimuli? Is an interaction expected in that case? After you have had a chance to work out these issues, you can consult the original article and find out what happened.

The topic of lie detection has generated an extraordinary amount of research attention and an extraordinary amount of controversy. Even a cursory review of the literature on lie detection reveals a wide variety of reasons why accurate lie detection techniques would be useful to have. For example, recent research has investigated identifying members of terrorist cells (Liu & Rosenfeld, 2009), applications to police work (Iacono, 2008), evaluating postconviction sex offenders (Grubin, 2008), evaluating claims of memory failures (Lee et al., 2009), and employment screening (Walczyk, Mahoney, Doverspike, & Griffith-Ross, 2009). A "proactive" lie detection technique could help voters understand politicians' true motivations, help law enforcement in evaluating suspects, and assist in espionage efforts (Oates, 1996).

Given the importance of lie detection, it is not surprising that a variety of lie detection techniques have been proposed. What follows is just a sample of some of the more recent attempts to detect lying. We will begin with the technique that comes to mind when people hear about lie detecting: the polygraph. In these tests, examinees are measured on a variety of physiological variables (e.g., skin conductance, respiration, and heart rate, Iacono, 2008). The basic premise is that items of importance to a person will create physiological arousal. By comparing questions about a specific incident (e.g., a crime) to questions about something else, examiners can look for a difference in physiological reactions that might be associated with guilt. For example, in the relevant–irrelevant technique, questions related to a crime are paired with questions that are not relevant (e.g., "Is today Tuesday?" Iacono, 2008). Guilty people should show increased physiological reaction when confronted with questions about their crime. Iacono pointed out a problem with this technique: people who are innocent might still have a physiological reaction to an accusatory question. A fundamental problem is that people who are afraid of being found guilty by mistake might show the same physiological arousal as a person who actually is guilty (Iacono, 2008).

One way around this is to use a technique called the comparison question test. The examiner and the examinee work out a list of control questions that should cause increased arousal in the examinee (they are personally relevant, and there is reason to expect that the person will experience anxiety about answering them, Iacono, 2008). An innocent person will have a strong physiological reaction to the control questions but not much reaction to questions about the crime (since they have no personal importance attached to them). A guilty person should show more arousal to the crime-related questions. Again, a difference in physiological arousal will be taken as an indicator of guilt.

Iacono (2008) listed a number of problems with polygraph tests using the comparison question test. First, the procedure is not standardized. The set of control questions has to be created for each examinee, and it takes a skilled examiner to create a good set of questions. Second, there are problems with the theoretical underpinnings of the technique that would affect both innocent people (e.g., they might not be lying to the control question) and guilty people (e.g., they might have a strong response to a control question). Iacono also points out that studies evaluating the accuracy of polygraph tests suffer from a fatal methodological flaw that guarantees high accuracy rates (see for example Mangan, Armitage, & Adams, 2008, and a critique of their study by Verschuere, Meijer, & Merckelbach, 2008). Also, countermeasures are available that would allow a guilty person to defeat the test. Finally, independent scientific evaluations of the comparison question test have been consistently negative. For example, discussing these reviews Iacono said "they have concluded that the accuracy claims of the polygraph profession are exaggerated and indefensible" (p. 1302).

One final point from Iacono's (2008) review of lie detection: Why do people continue to use the comparison question test if the evidence for its effectiveness is not very good? One reason is that it works. After a person has failed the test, it is possible to use that as leverage to get a confession. Also, there is something called the "bogus pipeline" effect (Meijer, Verschuere, Merckelbach, & Crombez, 2008). The idea is that once someone is hooked up to a machine that he or she believes can detect lying, he or she is more likely to tell the truth. In fact, Grubin (2008) argues that this effect can be useful in increasing disclosures made by postconviction sex offenders that can be used to improve their treatment plans and reduce recidivism (this was part of Meijer et al.'s critique of using polygraphs with postconviction sex offenders).

Other approaches to physiological measures have been proposed. For example, Vandenbosch, Verschuere, Crombez, and De Clercq (2009) evaluated

SCIENCE NOTE **9.1**

As part of his review of polygraph testing, Iacono (2008) said that independent evaluations were routinely negative. "That these negative conclusions are based on review of the same literature that proponents rely on indicates that the standards for what constitutes adequate science are considerably relaxed for those whose livelihood depends on the legitimacy of the CQT as a lie detector" (p. 1302; the CQT is the comparison question test). This raises the question of what the standards of adequate science should be. In part, that is the topic for Appendix E. However, as part of his review, Iacono summarized a list of scientific standards relevant to lie detection. His criticism (derived from a report evaluating polygraphy): "the field (a) is devoid of meaningful theory, (b) has failed to accumulate knowledge, (c) relies on studies of poor quality, (d) ignores evidence that contradicts the likely effectiveness of the technique, (e) continues to make claims that are unsubstantiated, and (f) makes claims that are difficult to believe given what we know about human psychophysiology" (p. 1303). It might be profitable to compare this list to some of the suggestions made in Appendix E. More important, it is always a good idea to evaluate research against these sorts of criteria. It is sometimes difficult to discriminate science from pseudoscience (and lie detection is a really good test of that effort), but you can find some consensus about what constitutes science.

the validity of a new physiological measure used in a task called the concealed information test. In this procedure, stimuli are presented to participants, and some of these are relevant to secret knowledge the participant possesses (e.g., in the Vandenbosch et al. study it was the item stolen in a mock crime). The hypothesis is that a guilty person will have an orienting response to something related to his or her concealed knowledge, but an

METHODOLOGY NOTE **9.3**

Meijer et al. (2008) highlighted an important problem with validity. Laboratory studies of lie detection allow careful control over the research environment and certain knowledge of who is and is not lying. These studies have high **internal validity**. However, they lack **external validity**. The stakes in a laboratory study of lie detection are not as high as in the real world (e.g., prison time). On the other hand, field studies have high external validity, but they lack the researcher control that is necessary to draw firm conclusions (e.g., it is difficult to measure actual guilt with a high degree of certainty to compare against predictions from lie detection techniques). As in all psychology research, trying to find a balance between these two kinds of validity can be very difficult.

innocent person would have the same reaction to all test items since they will all be neutral. If several critical (guilty knowledge) items are used, and the pattern of responding suggests familiarity with all of them, the hypothesis is that this would be strong evidence of guilty knowledge. According to Iacono (2008), this procedure has better validity than the comparison question test.

Lie detection by paying attention to nonverbal cues has also been proposed (see, for example, Porter & ten Brinke, 2008, for a recent study of nonverbal cues to deceptive facial expressions). Vrij (2008) reviewed research on nonverbal cues (primarily in an effort to encourage less reliance on them). Some cues people pay attention to are perceived enthusiasm, blushing, an inappropriate emotional response (e.g., not showing enough emotion when given bad news), tone of voice, narrowing of the lips, speech rate, failing to make eye contact, and fidgeting. Vrij provided a variety of reasons for attention to nonverbal behavior over what people are saying. One is the assumption that people can control their speech content when they are lying but that their nonverbal behavior will let the truth slip out. In fact, this assumption will underlie our target article for this chapter. Vrij also presented a comprehensive overview of techniques to evaluate the content of speech and contrasted these with nonverbal cues. His conclusion was that attending to the content of speech leads to more accurate lie detection than attending to nonverbal cues.

Simpson (2008) reviewed research suggesting that functional Magnetic Resonance Imaging (fMRI) could be used to detect lying. The basic idea is to look at differences in blood flow in the brain when someone is telling the truth and when someone is lying. Telling a lie is hypothesized to involve suppression of the true information and construction of a new story. The hypothesis is that trying to suppress the truth will lead to a particular pattern of blood flow that will distinguish lies from true responses. For example, Spence, Kaylor-Hughes, Brook, Lankappa, and Wilkinson (2008) compared blood flow in a woman who had been convicted of poisoning her child, but claimed to be innocent. When she was endorsing statements that she was guilty, she had a different blood flow pattern than when she was endorsing her own version of events. Lee et al. (2009) used fMRI to discriminate between responses that were incorrect, but unintentionally so, and responses that were intentionally incorrect.

Although Simpson (2008) held out hope for neuroimaging techniques for lie detection, he did list some potential problems. For example, people routinely hold back information when they are being interrogated, even if they are not guilty of a crime (e.g., expressions of anger at the process). How could this normal effort at impression management be distinguished from deception? Merikangas (2008) took a more skeptical view of fMRI lie detection overall and highlighted a problem, raised by Meijer et al. (2008), related to sex offenders. If someone does not believe that something is a lie (e.g., sex offenders are able to justify their behavior and believe that they did not do anything wrong), how will fMRI or any other method detect it?

A final set of lie detection techniques could be labeled cognitive techniques. The idea is to measure some aspect of cognitive functioning and use that to assess truthfulness. For example, Walczyk et al. (2009) used reaction time to discriminate true responses from lies. They were motivated to find an effective method of employee screening. They found a difference between lies and true responses for some items, especially for yes/no questions, and that there were still some reaction time differences for rehearsed lies (the kind most likely to be told in employment screenings). There were some limitations to their findings. The two areas that produced the largest differences were the two with which the participants were most familiar. Questions about the previous Saturday night did not show an effect. If real world lies are closer to last Saturday night in importance, then their technique would not be effective for screening. Also, they noted the validity problem common to this type of research. In the controlled environment of a laboratory study, participants had far less incentive to "sell" their lies than someone in an employment situation.

Another technique using reaction time is the autobiographical implicit association test (aIAT). The implicit association test (IAT) was introduced by Greenwald, McGhee, and Schwartz (1998). The IAT provides an implicit way to measure how strongly concepts are associated in a person's memory. One of its main advantages is that it is less susceptible to conscious motivations than more direct tests (e.g., lying to look good). For example, Greenwald et al. in their Experiment 3 found that White participants who reported no negative racial stereotypes on explicit measures did show a preference for associating white with positive and black with negative when using an IAT procedure. Greenwald et al. interpreted this to mean that the participants still held negative racial attitudes, at least implicitly.

There are several steps in administering the IAT. For Greenwald et al.'s (1998) Experiment 3, the first step was to distinguish stereotypically African American names (e.g., Tashika) from stereotypically White names (e.g., Betsy). To be sure that the names were strongly associated with each group, the names were classified into the two groups by a different set of participants prior to the study. The next step was to classify words as pleasant (e.g., lucky) or unpleasant (e.g., poison). The third step was to respond to words that were African American names or pleasant with one key and words that were White names or unpleasant with a different key. The fourth step was to reverse the response keys for African American and White names to allow for the fifth step. The fifth step was to answer with one key for African American names or unpleasant words and a different key for White names or pleasant words. The basic logic is this: If White-pleasant and African American-unpleasant are more strongly associated than White-unpleasant and African American-pleasant for the participants, then the White-pleasant and African American-unpleasant response times will be faster than the White-unpleasant and African American-pleasant response times (e.g., step 5 will be faster than step 3). This would indicate an unconscious bias in the participants.

Sartori, Agosta, Zogmaister, Ferrara, and Castiello (2008) introduced the aIAT to detect lying. The main change from the IAT was to expand from single words to sentences (e.g., "I'm in a little room with a computer"). The main comparison was between true-innocent with false-guilty pairings and true-guilty with false-innocent pairings. The idea was that innocent people would be faster for true-innocent/false-guilty and guilty people would be faster for true-guilty/false-innocent. Sartori et al. found this result. However, Verschuere, Prati, and De Houwer (2009) were able to show that the aIAT can be easily beaten with an instruction sheet telling participants to slow down on the true-innocent block (Experiment 1), or experience with Greenwald et al.'s (1998) flower-insect IAT (Experiment 2), and that this can happen even if the test has a response deadline to foil intentionally slower responses (Experiment 3).

Vrij et al. (2008) noted that lying should increase cognitive load (it takes more effort to simultaneously conceal the truth and come up with a new story than to simply report the facts). They proposed that techniques that actively enlarge the difference between liars and truthful participants by increasing load even further might increase discrimination between them. To do this, they had participants report events in reverse order. This did lead to better detection of liars, both in the experiment and in a group of police officers who watched videotaped participants.

This brief review of lie detection reveals two things. First, there has been a large amount of research attention devoted to detecting liars and, second, most of the ideas that have been tried have significant problems. However, the need to detect truthful responses from lies is still very real, ranging from identifying terrorists (Verschuere et al., 2009) to potentially saving businesses billions of dollars each year (Walczyk et al. 2009).

Another candidate technique promising to separate lies from the truth is reverse speech (Oates, 1996; www.reversespeech.com). This technique will be evaluated by our target articles for this chapter. The topic of reverse speech is interesting for two reasons. First, translating the idea of reverse speech into testable hypotheses is challenging and provides insight into the scientific process. Second, the phenomenon that explains how reverse speech works has applications to a number of domains in the paranormal and pseudoscience fields.

The basic idea behind reverse speech is that forward speech is accompanied by a secondary speech channel. The secondary channel is spoken in reverse and can be uncovered by taping a person speaking and then playing the tape backwards. This secondary channel is inserted by the unconscious and contains the truth. According to Oates (1996) this truth can be an explicit contradiction to the forward speech as in a lie detection situation, it can elaborate on the content of the forward speech (e.g., help a person uncover their true motives or feelings about something), or it can provide answers to "big" questions (e.g., reversals can uncover facts about the evolution of consciousness).

A review of the case studies in Oates' (1996) book reveals that reverse speech can be applied to many of the lie detection problems outlined above (e.g., guilty knowledge of suspects in a murder investigation), plus additional situations not considered in the lie detection literature (e.g., improving the therapy process by uncovering what is in a person's unconscious). Can it work as promised? Byrne and Normand (2000) presented the first skeptical

SCIENCE NOTE **9.2**

It might seem strange that authors like Byrne and Normand (2000) claimed that there is no evidence to support reverse speech when Oates' book and website are full of examples. The problem can be summed up in the phrase "the plural of anecdote is not data." Oates' examples have been chosen because they fit the hypothesis. What percentage of speech examples would not contain reversals? How reliable are people's reports of what they hear in reversals (without being told in advance what to listen for)? Evidence comes from controlled studies in which the people making important judgments are blind to the conditions. For example, if a reverse speech analyst chose 20 speech segments that did not contain a reversal and 20 that did, and an independent sample of reverse speech analysts was able to tell them apart at better than chance levels, that would suggest that whatever reverse speech analysts are looking for can be reliably detected. Whether or not what they hear is truly connected to what they think it means would be a subject for additional research. For example, Byrne and Normand suggested having a group of participants include some lies and some true statements in a brief interview. Could a reverse speech analyst distinguish one from the other?

review of reverse speech. They pointed out that not only is there no empirical evidence to support Oates' claims, many of the claims actually contradict what is known. For example, Oates' claim that the right hemisphere is responsible for reverse speech and the left hemisphere is responsible for forward speech is inconsistent with research on hemispheric specialization.

Begg, Needham, and Bookbinder (1993) presented data suggesting that reverse speech cannot work (their research was not specifically directed at the reverse speech hypothesis). Begg et al. presented participants with statements recorded either forward or backwards. Participants then rated the truth of these statements. Participants who heard the statements forward showed an illusory truth effect (participants thought that statements they had heard previously were more true). Participants who heard the statements backwards did not show an illusory truth effect. In other words, the meaning of backwards statements did not seem to be perceived.

Our first target article for this chapter is Kreiner, Altis, and Voss (2003). They reasoned that if Oates' claims that people can be influenced by what they hear in reverse speech were correct, then words presented in reverse speech should show repetition priming. Repetition priming occurs when someone is faster to respond to a stimulus the second time they see it. Kreiner et al. used a lexical decision task. Participants saw strings of letters and had to decide if they were a word (e.g., lie) or a pseudoword (e.g., libe). The words were preceded by an auditory prime. This prime could be the same word or a different word. Based on repetition priming, participants should be faster to respond "real word" when the word had been presented previously than when the word had not been presented previously. Kreiner et al. also manipulated the direction in which the priming word was played. Some priming words were played forward and some were played in reverse. All of the words used were taken from examples from the reverse speech website to ensure that they were the kinds of materials covered by the theory.

The Kreiner et al. (2003) study used a factorial design. The first independent variable was priming, and the levels were primed and unprimed. The second independent variable was prime direction with the levels forward and backward. This was a 2 x 2 design. One possible outcome of this design could be dubbed the "reverse speech works" hypothesis. If this hypothesis were true, then primed words should lead to faster response times than unprimed words, and the direction should not matter. In other words, we should see a main effect of priming, no effect for direction, and no interaction. The alternative hypothesis could be called the "reverse speech does not work" hypothesis. In this case, there should be a main effect of priming (with primed words generating faster response times) and a main effect of direction (with forward primes generating faster response times). However, these main effects would be qualified by an interaction between priming and direction. Priming effects would only be seen when the primes were presented forward. When the primes were presented backwards, they would not be understood, so there would be no priming.

Kreiner et al.'s (2003) data clearly supported the "reverse speech does not work" hypothesis. When the prime was presented forward there was a significant effect of priming. When the prime was presented backward there was no effect of priming. This demonstrated that one critical claim made by reverse speech proponents (that people can detect and respond to the content of reverse speech) is not supported.

Our second target article for this chapter is Langston and Anderson (2000). The approach taken by Langston and Anderson was similar to that taken by Kreiner at al. (2003): Can we find evidence for an effect of reverse speech on listeners? Langston and Anderson based their study on Oates' (1996) claim that reverse speech may be responsible for that vague feeling that someone is not being truthful, or ESP-type effects in which a person suddenly understands something about someone else's motivations without being told them. It might be possible that explicit information contained in reverse speech is not understood, but the emotional content of reverse speech can be detected.

To evaluate whether or not emotional information in reverse speech could be detected, Langston and Anderson (2000) manipulated the extent to which messages would be anxiety provoking. In their first experiment they presented lists of words that were arousing (e.g., infected, polio, mutilated) or neutral (e.g., depicted, agency, cable). These lists were presented either forward or reversed. This was also a 2 x 2 factorial design. The independent variables were list type (arousing or neutral) and direction (forward or backward). Again, it is possible to identify two hypotheses. The "reverse speech works" hypothesis is that arousing information should produce arousal regardless of the direction in which it is presented (a main effect for list type with no main effect for direction and no interaction). The "reverse speech does not work" hypothesis would be that arousing information would only be effective when the lists were played forward. In other words, there would be an interaction between list type and direction. For forward there would be a difference between arousing and neutral words, for backwards there would be no effect.

Langston and Anderson's (2000) results supported the hypothesis that reverse speech does not work. Arousing words played forward produced significantly more arousal than neutral words played forward. Arousing words played backwards produced the same amount of arousal as neutral words played backwards. One potential problem with this study was that the stimuli were lists of isolated words. In a follow-up study, Langston and Anderson presented an arousing text passage or a neutral text passage. The arousing passage came from a book describing a person suffering from the Ebola virus and included a graphic description of a person vomiting into an airsickness bag (along with a variety of other terrible effects of Ebola). The neutral passage came from the same book and described a trip into the mountains. This experiment was also a 2 x 2 factorial, with the variables passage type (arousing or neutral) and direction (forward or backwards). The hypotheses and predictions were the same as in the first experiment, as were the results. Arousing information played forward produced arousal. Arousing information played backwards did not.

We are now ready to turn our attention to the other interesting feature of the reverse speech phenomenon. Given that its theoretical basis is contrary to known facts (Byrne & Normand, 2000), and empirical tests of a key assumption show that it is not supported, why do people believe in it? One possible explanation is "wishful listening" (a kind of *pareidolia*, Carroll, 2009). After listening to the examples provided on the website, it is hard not to hear what is supposed to be there. However, if you listen to the examples before you know what you are supposed to hear, you might get a better sense of how strong (or weak) the phenomenon is.

A number of studies have examined the effect of listener expectations on perception. Vokey and Read (1985) recorded Jabberwocky and the 23rd psalm backwards. They then listened for messages and wrote down all that they were able to hear. They then played the backwards passages to participants and asked them to listen for statements that they had detected in the passages or statements that should not be there. Participants were able to distinguish between statements that were "in" the backwards passages and statements that were not. They then had participants listen for a new statement in the backwards passages. Even though it was as much "in" the passage as the other statements, participants were unlikely to have detected it until they were asked to listen for it. In other words, what is "there" in the passage is a function of what the listener expects as much as a function of the passage itself. This effect translates nicely to the situation in which a reverse speech practitioner tells an audience what to listen for and then plays a tape. Once the expectation has been set up, people hear what they expect. Enough examples like this can lead to belief in the validity of the phenomenon.

Thorne and Himelstein (1984) also showed an effect of wishful listening. They played backwards music to three groups of participants. One group was told to listen to the music and record their reactions, a second group was told to write down words they might hear, and a third group was told to find satanic messages. Participants listening for satanic messages reported the most satanic content in the recordings. In this case, there were no messages; all of the messages participants reported came from their expectation. This might explain how a reverse speech analyst might locate messages in the first place. A simple mind set (e.g., this person has concerns about a business decision) would allow them to project messages on a meaningless stream of backwards speech (Benoit & Thomas, 1992, showed that being a true believer would also influence performance in this kind of task).

At this point, we have a proposed lie detection technique and a fair amount of evidence to suggest that it will not work. You will have the opportunity to explore these issues further in the projects section.

INFOTRAC® COLLEGE EDITION EXERCISES

You can use the InfoTrac College Edition to read about additional studies using a factorial design. Typing in "factorial design" with the boxes for "in citation, title, abstract" and "to refereed publications" checked gave me a list of 85 articles. Many of these articles dealt with the same methodological issues discussed in this chapter. For example, Gier, Kreiner, and Natz-Gonzalez (2009) investigated the effect of inappropriate highlighting of texts on comprehension. They expected an effect of the highlighting variable (none, appropriate, or inappropriate). However, they thought it was worth considering whether there would be an interaction between highlighting and difficulty (low or high). As it turned out, there was an interaction, but the inappropriate highlighting did impact both more and less difficult texts. You might consider this as you choose a used textbook to buy. It is important that the person who highlighted it knew what they were doing. Before beginning your study, you should read additional examples of factorial designs.

You can also find more information about the effect of expectation on perception using the InfoTrac College Edition. For example, when I typed in "subliminal perception" with the boxes for "in citation, title, abstract" and "to refereed publications" checked, I found 14 articles, including Byrne and Normand (2000). I also found a discussion of subliminal messages in rock music by Moore (1996). The search string "reverse speech" located Kreiner et al. (2003). You should try additional search strings and read a variety of articles to see what you can learn about reverse speech, subliminal perception, and wishful listening before beginning your project.

IMPLEMENTING THE DESIGN

Materials

You will need a way to produce reverse speech. One useful tool is Audacity (http://audacity.sourceforge.net/). The software is free and runs in most operating systems. You will also need stimuli. The target articles contain sufficient information to recreate their materials.

For Kreiner et al. (2003) you will need a way to collect reaction times. There are a variety of products available for presenting psychology experiments, and there is a chance that you already have access to one. If not, you can try the free DMDX Display Software (http://www.u.arizona.edu/~kforster/dmdx/dmdx.htm). If you do not already know how to use experiment presentation software, this might be difficult to use. A search of the Internet might turn up additional free software for controlling psychology experiments.

Suggested Projects

1. You could replicate one of the target articles for your project.
   a. For Kreiner et al. (2003), the list of materials and instructions for producing them are included in their article. You will need to create experiment scripts to replicate their lexical decision task. As an alternative, you could try to use a dependent variable that does not depend on reaction time. For example, Begg et al. (1993) used the illusory truth effect as a dependent variable (you would probably need to use statements instead of words as the stimuli). Do statements presented forward produce an illusory truth effect compared to statements presented backwards?
   b. Langston and Anderson (2000) used a paper and pencil measure of arousal as the dependent variable (from Mackay, Cox, Burrows, & Lazzerini, 1978). To replicate their study, you will need to record the word lists and play them for participants, then measure arousal using the arousal scale.
2. Two questions that are relevant for any measurement instrument are: Is it reliable? and Is it valid? In this case, will reverse speech analyses be consistent between different raters, and do reverse speech analyses validly detect what they claim to be detecting? Both of these questions would make interesting projects.
   a. Byrne and Normand (2000, p. 49) suggested a reliability project. Have participants listen to various samples of reverse speech and report what they hear. Then, see how well they agree. One potential problem for this project is that Oates (1996) claims that it takes extensive training to hear reversals accurately. Given that it will probably be difficult for you to find a sample of reverse speech analysts to participate in your study, you could try to get around this problem by manipulating the clarity of the materials and participants' knowledge in a factorial design. For example, you could have a 2 x 2 design with knowledge (know the topic of the message in backwards speech or not) and clarity (very clear message or less clear message) as factors. An effect of knowledge would speak to listener expectancies on the effect. If there is no knowledge effect, then that would suggest that the reports are driven by the messages themselves. If there is an effect of knowledge, then that would suggest that the

reports are a result of expectation. An effect of clarity might speak to the training issue. If listeners detect more of the clear messages, then Oates may be right that training is required to get accurate perceptions. What would an interaction between knowledge and clarity indicate?

b. You could test reliability by providing participants with practice. Give some participants many examples and train them on how to identify messages. Give a second group no training. Again, cross that with message clarity in a 2 x 2 factorial. If training has no effect, and participants are accurate at detecting messages, then that would suggest that detecting reversals can be done reliably by anyone. A training effect would support Oates' (1996) contention that it takes practice to detect reversals. What might an interaction mean in this design?

c. Assessing validity will be a little more challenging. One way was suggested by Byrne and Normand (2000, p. 49). Have some participants lie about critical information, and have other participants tell the truth. Can listeners tell true from false statements? Again, this basic study is complicated by claims from Oates (1996). To detect reversals requires extensive training, and there may only be a reversal every 15 seconds or so. In other words, not every lie will have an accompanying reversal. One solution to this problem would be to have participants make a more gestalt rating. For example, Oates claimed that emotional speech produced more frequent reversals than casual conversation. You could manipulate the type of speech and then play it forward or backwards (another 2 x 2 factorial). Have participants evaluate the emotionality of the speech. They may not be good at detecting specific reversals, but the increased rate of reversals in the emotional speech should allow them to be able to tell that it is more emotional whether it is played forward or backward. What would an interaction mean in this study?

3. Research on reverse speech could be dichotomized in a different way. One issue is whether reversals are present in the material in the first place, and a second issue has to do with whether or not reversals have an effect. The target articles for this chapter dealt with the second issue. It will be harder to determine if the reversals Oates (1996) claimed to find are really "in" the recording or come from the mind of the listener. However, Vokey and Read (1985) suggested a way to attack this problem. Select a sample of messages from reverse speech websites that have multiple words. Have participants listen for particular words, ask them if they heard other words, then have them listen again for these new words. For example, if a reversed message was "evil lips are hammering it," you could have participants look for "evil lips" the first time, ask them if they heard "hammering," and then have them listen again for "hammering." The dependent variable would be confidence that the word was present. If participants report low confidence that "hammering" was in the passage before listening for it, and high confidence after listening for it,

then that would indicate that what was heard was more "wishful listening" than "in" the message. You could manipulate other independent variables along with expectation to answer specific questions about reverse speech. For example, will being exposed to the forward message have an effect (the two levels would be heard the forward speech or did not hear it)? Or, how many times can a participant listen to a passage before they hear a word they are not listening for (number of exposures would be the independent variable)? Is there a number of presentations that, if exceeded, would lead to hearing all of the words?

4. It is not directly related to reverse speech, but you could replicate some of the research inspired by the satanic messages in rock music controversy.

   a. Vokey and Read (1985) asked: What can be detected in backward speech? They found that people could discriminate male from female voices, changes of speaker, and the language of the forward speech (if they had categories to sort the languages into). They could not separate statements from questions, tell if statements had the same or different meaning, or tell if statements made sense. You could extend this research by manipulating aspects of the forward message and seeing if people could detect those differences in backwards speech. For example, you could manipulate similarity of content in multiple ways and see if the cues combine. One independent variable would be the sentence form. Active and passive sentences using the same words have very similar meanings (e.g., "Mary ate the apple/The apple was eaten by Mary"). The second independent variable could be degree of rewording (e.g., "Mary ate the apple/Mary ate the fruit"). Will participants be more accurate at rating the similarity in meaning for active–passive pairs versus reworded pairs?

   b. Thorne and Himelstein (1984) gave participants three task sets (record impressions, listen for messages, and listen for satanic messages). What would be the effect of other independent variables on the relationship between task set and hearing things? For example, you could give a presentation on the extent to which satanic messages are present in rock music, with a bias towards these messages being very common, and a different presentation saying that the messages did not exist. Or, you could tell participants they were listening to heavy metal music versus Christian heavy metal music. Does the kind of music they think they are hearing backwards affect their ratings?

REFERENCES

Begg, I. M., Needham, D. R., & Bookbinder, M. (1993). Do backward messages unconsciously affect listeners? No. *Canadian Journal of Experimental Psychology, 47,* 1–14. doi: 10.1037/h0078772

Benoit, S. C., & Thomas, R. L. (1992). The influence of expectancy in subliminal perception experiments. *The Journal of General Psychology, 119,* 335–341.

Byrne, T., & Normand, M. (2000). The demon-haunted sentence: A skeptical analysis of reverse speech. *Skeptical Inquirer, 24,* 46–49.

Carroll, R. T. (2009). Pareidolia. *The Skeptic's Dictionary.* Retrieved from http://skepdic.com/pareidol.html

Forer, B. R. (1949). The fallacy of personal validation: A classroom demonstration of gullibility. *The Journal of Abnormal and Social Psychology, 44,* 118–123. doi:10.1037/h0059240

Gier, V. S., Kreiner, D. S., & Natz-Gonzalez, A. (2009). Harmful effects of preexisting inappropriate highlighting on reading comprehension and metacognitive accuracy. *The Journal of General Psychology, 136,* 287–300.

Glick, P., Gottesman, D., & Jolton, J. (1989). The fault is not in the stars: Susceptibility of skeptics and believers in astrology to the Barnum effect. *Personality and Social Psychology Bulletin, 15,* 572–583. doi:10.1177/0146167289154010

Greenwald, A. G., McGhee, D. E., & Schwartz, J. L. K. (1998). Measuring individual differences in implicit cognition: The implicit association test. *Journal of Personality and Social Psychology, 74,* 1464–1480. doi:10.1037/0022-3514.74.6.1464

Grubin, D. (2008). The case for polygraph testing of sex offenders. *Legal and Criminological Psychology, 13,* 177–189. doi:10.1348/135532508X295165

Iacono, W. G. (2008). Effective policing: Understanding how polygraph tests work and are used. *Criminal Justice and Behavior, 35,* 1295–1308. doi:10.1177/0093854808321529

Kreiner, D. S., Altis, N. A., & Voss, C. W. (2003). A test of the effect of reverse speech on priming. *The Journal of Psychology, 137,* 224–232.

Langston, W., & Anderson, J. C. (2000). Talking Back (wards): A test of the Reverse Speech hypothesis: Are listeners able to detect the emotional content of backward speech? *Skeptic, 8,* 30–35.

Lee, T. M. C., Au, R. K. C., Liu, H.-L., Ting, K. H., Huang, C. M., & Chan, C. C. H. (2009). Are errors differentiable from deceptive responses when feigning memory impairment? An fMRI study. *Brain and Cognition, 69,* 406–412. doi:10.1016/j.bandc.2008.09.002

Liu, M., & Rosenfeld, J. P. (2009). The application of subliminal priming in lie detection: Scenario for identification of members of a terrorist ring. *Psychophysiology, 46,* 889–903. Abstract retrieved from http://www.wiley.com/bw/journal.asp?ref=0048-5772

Mackay, C., Cox, T., Burrows, G., & Lazzarini, T. (1978). An inventory for the measurement of self-reported stress and arousal. *British Journal of Social and Clinical Psychology, 17,* 283–284.

Mangan, D. J., Armitage, T. E., & Adams, G. C. (2008). A field study on the validity of the Quadri-Track Zone Comparison technique. *Physiology & Behavior, 95,* 17–23. doi:10.1016/j.physbeh.2008.03.001

Meijer, E. H., Verschuere, B., Merckelbach, H. L. G. J., & Crombez, G. (2008). Sex offender management using the polygraph: A critical review. *International Journal of Law and Psychiatry, 31,* 423–429. doi:10.1016/j.ijlp.2008.08.007

Merikangas, J. R. (2008). Commentary: Functional MRI lie detection. *Journal of the American Academy of Psychiatry and the Law, 36,* 499–501. Retrieved from http://www.jaapl.org/

Moore, T. E. (1996). Scientific consensus and expert testimony: Lessons from the Judas Priest trial. *Skeptical Inquirer, 20,* 32–38, 60.

Oates, D. J. (1996). *Reverse Speech: Voices from the unconscious.* San Diego, CA: ProMotion Publishing.

Porter, S., & ten Brinke, L. (2008). Reading between the lies: Identifying concealed and falsified emotions in universal facial expressions. *Psychological Science, 19,* 508–514.

Sartori, G., Agosta, S., Zogmaister, C., Ferrara, S. D., & Castiello, U. (2008). How to accurately detect autobiographical events. *Psychological Science, 19,* 772–780.

Sebanz, N., & Shiffrar, M. (2009). Detecting deception in a bluffing body: The role of expertise. *Psychonomic Bulletin and Review, 16,* 170–175.

Simpson, J. R. (2008). Functional MRI lie detection: Too good to be true? *Journal of the American Academy of Psychiatry and the Law, 36,* 491–498. Retrieved from http://www.jaapl.org/

Song, H., & Schwarz, N. (2009). If it's difficult to pronounce, it must be risky: Fluency, familiarity, and risk perception. *Psychological Science, 20,* 135–138.

Spence, S. A., Kaylor-Hughes, C. J., Brook, M. L., Lankappa, S. T., & Wilkinson, I. D. (2008). 'Munchausen's syndrome by proxy' or a 'miscarriage of justice'? An initial application of functional neuroimaging to the question of guilt versus innocence. *European Psychiatry, 23,* 309–314. doi:10.1016/j.eurpsy.2007.09.001

Thorne, S. B., & Himelstein, P. (1984). The role of suggestion in the perception of satanic messages in rock-and-roll recordings. *The Journal of Psychology, 116,* 245–248.

Vandenbosch, K., Verschuere, B., Crombez, G., & De Clercq, A. (2009). The validity of finger pulse line length for the detection of concealed information. *International Journal of Psychophysiology, 71,* 118–123. doi:10.1016/j.ijpsycho.2008.07.015

Verscheure, B., Meijer, E., & Merckelbach, H. (2008). The quadri-track zone comparison technique: It's just not science. A critique to Mangan, Armitage, and Adams (2008). *Physiology and Behavior, 95,* 27–28. doi:10.1016/j.physbeh. 2008.06.002

Verschuere, B., Prati, V., & De Houwer, J. (2009). Cheating the lie detector: Faking in the autobiographical implicit association test. *Psychological Science, 20,* 410–413.

Vokey, J. R., & Read, J. D. (1985). Subliminal messages: Between the devil and the media. *American Psychologist, 40,* 1231–1239. doi:10.1037/0003-066X.40.11.1231

Vrij, A. (2008). Nonverbal dominance versus verbal accuracy in lie detection: A plea to change police practice. *Criminal Justice and Behavior, 35,* 1323–1336. doi:10.1177/0093854808321530

Vrij, A., Mann, S. A., Fisher, R. P., Leal, S., Milne, R., & Bull, R. (2008). Increasing cognitive load to facilitate lie detection: The benefit of recalling an event in reverse order. *Law and Human Behavior, 32,* 253–265. doi:10.1007/s10979-007-9103-y

Walczyk, J. J., Mahoney, K. T., Doverspike, D., & Griffith-Ross, D. A. (2009). Cognitive lie detection: Response time and consistency of answers as cues to deception. *Journal of Business and Psychology, 24,* 33–49. doi:10.1007/s10869-009-9090-8

CHAPTER 10

Factorial Designs 2

It gets sticky when I rub it

Abstract

Psychology: The ideomotor effect is pervasive in psychology and is applicable to a variety of research areas.

Skeptic/Pseudoscience: The ideomotor effect underlies pseudoscientific phenomena like dowsing and Ouija boards. It also provides the reason why personal experience is poor evidence to support a paranormal or pseudoscientific phenomenon.

INTRODUCTION: EXPERIMENTS WITH TWO OR MORE INDEPENDENT VARIABLES

The target article for this chapter uses a factorial design. Factorial designs were discussed at length in the opening section of Chapter 9. If you have not already done so, you may want to read that section before continuing with this chapter.

TARGET ARTICLE: THE IDEOMOTOR EFFECT

(Be sure to look at Appendix D to assist you in evaluating the sources cited in this chapter. Be especially aware of the guidelines for evaluating Internet and other non-peer-reviewed sources.)

Before reading this chapter, I would like you to try a demonstration. You will need to gather a few materials first. You will need a piece of thread about two feet long, a key (any kind of metal will work, but try to avoid keys with plastic or other materials on them), a piece of fruit, and some processed sugar. To set up for the exercise, place the fruit and sugar on separate plates, at least a foot apart. Then, put the thread through the key to make a pendulum. Holding the two ends of the thread between the forefinger and thumb of your dominant hand, allow the key to dangle over the sugar. You should find that for refined sugar, the key will slowly start to turn in a circle. Next, hold the key over the piece of fruit. Due to the natural sugars in fruit, the key will swing back and forth in a straight line. Try the demonstration before reading any further.

If you were able to get the demonstration to work, you have experienced an ideomotor effect. *The Skeptic's Dictionary* defines the ideomotor effect as "the influence of suggestion or expectation on involuntary and unconscious motor behavior" (Carroll, 2009, para. 1). In the case of the demonstration, I suggested to you how the pendulum should move, and you experienced it moving that way. An important component of the definition has to do with the unconscious aspect of the movement. The sensation is that the movement is coming from outside the body and that it is not under the control of the person making it. It is this aspect of ideomotor movements that leads to belief in paranormal phenomena. The experience of ideomotor effects is so compelling (because the movement is really there) that it can have a powerful effect on belief (Hyman, 1999, provided examples of how even skeptics can be fooled by ideomotor effects).

This aspect of ideomotor action, in which an idea can induce an unconscious and undetectable movement on the part of the person receiving the suggestion, is just one part of a much larger phenomenon. In a review of the history of ideomotor action, Stock and Stock (2004) described three ways in which ideomotor actions can be triggered: direct stimulation, sensory information, and ideas. They presented this in the context of Laycock's work with people with rabies who had hydrophobia (fear of water). Laycock found that he could elicit a physical reaction from people with hydrophobia by touching them with water, showing them water, or suggesting to them that they might drink some water. One of the earliest applications of ideomotor effects to paranormal phenomena was when Carpenter (1852, as cited in Stock & Stock) used it to explain spiritualist phenomena such as table turning at séances. The expectation that some physical manifestation of spirit presences should occur at a séance caused ideomotor actions on the part of the participants and led to those things taking place.

The idea of ideomotor action induced from perception has been explored in a variety of ways. For example, Berger (1962) investigated how one person's emotional response could lead to a similar emotional response in an observer. Berger's example was that a mother could have an emotional response to seeing her child fall (without waiting to see how the child responded), hearing her child cry out (without seeing what happened or an emotional reaction), or seeing her child's emotional reaction. Berger showed that a performer's emotional response can enhance ideomotor responding, but the performer's movements also caused ideomotor responses.

Bavelas, Black, Lemery, and Mullett (1986) induced ideomotor responses by simulating an injury to one of the experimenters and recorded participants' facial responses. Twenty-six of 32 participants showed some ideomotor-induced facial expression as a result of witnessing the injury. Bavelas et al. also found that part of the response was socially determined (there was more response when the person being injured was making eye contact with participants).

Brass, Bekkering, and Prinz (2001) investigated how perceptual information would affect movements. Participants watched a video clip of a person's finger lifting up or tapping, and they either lifted up or tapped their finger. When the directions of the movement matched, responding was faster, suggesting that seeing the finger in the video triggered an ideomotor movement in the participant. Knuf, Aschersleben, and Prinz (2001) found that participants made ideomotor movements to attempt to control a ball after it was too late for their movements to influence its performance. De Maeght and Prinz (2004) extended these findings by showing that people also made ideomotor movements to control a ball even when they were observing someone else play. They interpreted these findings to explain why people move around when watching important parts of sporting events or why people stomp an imaginary brake when riding in a car with a bad driver.

It is when we turn our attention to ideomotor actions derived from ideas that we encounter a possible explanation for the paranormal and pseudosciences. For example, dowsing is supposed to work to detect underground or hidden resources (usually water, Randi, 1999). There are a variety of techniques, but the basic idea is that something held in the dowser's hands (e.g., a forked stick) will react in the presence of the thing being sought (e.g., point down suddenly when it crosses water). Randi has tested many dowsers, and none has ever been able to succeed under controlled conditions. Whittaker (n.d.) presented an overview of grave dowsing in Iowa and found that it does not work and recommended that cemetery caretakers stop using it.

Randi (1999) pointed out the power of ideomotor effects. In spite of the evidence of their failure during testing, dowsers continued to believe. Because the ideomotor effect is not under conscious control, it really does feel like the dowsing rod is moving of its own accord, and the power of this personal experience is too strong to overcome. Hyman (1999) reported a similar phenomenon when a chiropractor, after failing a test, complained that the testing procedure does not work. The power of personal experience is so strong that it is hard to believe in a procedure that shows that it is wrong.

Our target article for this chapter is an essay on the ideomotor effect by Hyman (1999). Hyman chose the title "the mischief-making of ideomotor action," which is an excellent description of what ideomotor action does: it makes mischief. Hyman described tests of ideomotor action as an explanation for spiritualist phenomena. For example, he described a study by Faraday that demonstrated conclusively that when tables move in séances, it is the sitters moving the table and not the table moving itself.

Hyman also described how the ideomotor effect can explain some findings in psychology, such as facilitated communication. The idea behind facilitated communication was that a person (the facilitator) could gently guide the hand of a person with a communicative disorder (e.g., autism) and allow that person to spell out messages. The facilitator was not supposed to be producing the messages, simply allowing the person being facilitated to communicate. Burgess et al. (1998) evaluated facilitated communication in a laboratory task. Participants were trained in facilitation by watching a videotape, and then attempted to facilitate a question-answering session with a confederate of the experimenter. Each facilitator was told information about the confederate that was unknown to the confederate and then facilitated that information (e.g., the name of the confederate's brother). All facilitators answered at least one question; the average number of questions answered was three and a half out of six. The facilitators were confident that the information had come from the confederate and not themselves, even though this was impossible. Interestingly, this effect was not influenced by showing participants a report skeptical of facilitated communication prior to their participation. The ideomotor effect was so strong that it overwhelmed Burgess et al.'s skepticism manipulation.

Hyman's (1999) main concern was with how the ideomotor effect could explain certain kinds of alternative medicine procedures. For example, in applied kinesiology, a person is asked to resist the efforts of a practitioner to move their arm as they hold it out. Then, various substances are applied to their body. If the person is supposed to be allergic to a substance, then their arm will suddenly become very easy to move. This could be the result of an ideomotor effect if the person knows how they are supposed to react to various substances. In fact, Hyman's double-blind testing showed that the effect only works if the practitioner and the participant know which substances are being administered.

Hyman (1999) also described a study evaluating procedures for detecting illness that rely on rubbing on a plastic plate. For example, in one procedure a lens is moved across a person's body as the practitioner rubs on a plastic surface. As the lens is moved over diseased areas, the plastic surface will suddenly become stickier. Hyman's hypothesis was that ideomotor effects accounted for the increased stickiness of the plastic plate.

METHODOLOGY NOTE **10.1**

Hyman's (1999) essay demonstrated the importance of **double-blind testing** in which the researcher and participant are unaware of the condition being tested and do not know the expected outcome. With something like ideomotor action, it is impossible to avoid being susceptible to the effect. Therefore, a proper test can only be conducted if the participants are unaware of the condition being tested. For example, in Hyman's test of applied kinesiology, chiropractors were trying to detect a difference in reaction between glucose (a "bad" sugar) and fructose (a "good" sugar). When the chiropractor and participant knew which sugar had been administered, participants could resist the chiropractor's pressure when fructose had been administered, but not when glucose had been administered. In a second testing session, nobody in the room knew which kind of sugar was being administered. In this case, the results were random. Participants' and chiropractors' knowledge of the expected outcome of the test determined the results. Again, the power of the ideomotor effect is that it does not require an effort at conscious cheating. Any time you are trying to evaluate something, double-blind testing is a good idea, but it is especially important when unconscious influences on the results are so likely.

To demonstrate this, Hyman (1999) told one group of participants that red playing cards reflect a different kind of light than black playing cards and that this difference can be detected by rubbing on a plastic surface. In one condition, he told participants that holding their hands over red cards would make the surface feel stickier. In another condition, he told the participants that black cards would make the surface stickier. Participants then held their hands over the different cards and rated the stickiness. Note that this was a 2 x 2 factorial design. One independent variable was the cover story (red sticky or black sticky), and the second independent variable was the card color being rated (red or black). Hyman expected an interaction. For the red sticky cover story, red cards should lead to higher stickiness ratings than black cards. For the black sticky cover story, black cards should lead to higher stickiness ratings.

Hyman (1999) reported finding the expected interaction, but he did not report statistical results. However, this experiment is easy to replicate, and the effect is quite powerful. As an example, I conducted a study with a student (George Leigh) in which we told participants that either green or red paper would make a plastic surface stickier and then had them rate stickiness on a 5-point scale with 5 indicating very sticky. When participants expected red paper to be stickier, the average rating for red paper was 3.26 and the average rating for green paper was 1.87. When they expected green paper to be stickier, the average rating for red paper was 2.19 and the average rating for green paper was 3.31. The interaction between cover story and paper color rated was significant, $F(1, 37) = 70.79$, $MSE = 0.42$, $p < .01$. As another indicator of the power of the effect, 31 out of 39 participants showed the effect, 7 tied, and 1 showed a reversed effect.

Hyman's (1999) demonstration illustrated another possible method for evaluating fantastic claims (in addition to double-blind testing). If we truly expected red paper to be more arousing than green, and then tested only that possibility, we would have been convinced of the accuracy of the hypothesis. However, also telling people that green paper should be stickier provided a stronger test. If participants could overcome the power of suggestion and still rate red paper as stickier when they thought green paper would be stickier, that would be good evidence that the effect is coming from the paper color and not the participants' expectation.

Hyman's (1999) interpretation of his demonstration was that the effects people find using stickiness ratings to diagnose illness are a result of ideomotor action. You will have an opportunity to experiment with ideomotor action for yourself in the projects section.

INFOTRAC® COLLEGE EDITION EXERCISES

You can use the InfoTrac College Edition to read about additional studies using a factorial design. This issue was discussed in Chapter 9.

You can also use the InfoTrac College Edition to find more information about the ideomotor effect. Using the search term "ideomotor" with the box for "in entire article content" checked, I found 44 articles. Most of these were applications of the ideomotor effect to neurological problems. You might need to think of additional search terms to expand the list, possibly by looking for terms in the articles in the reference section. You can use the InfoTrac College Edition to seek additional information about the ideomotor effect before beginning your project.

IMPLEMENTING THE DESIGN

Suggested Projects

1. You could replicate projects suggested in Hyman's (1999) review.
    a. You could replicate Hyman's (1999) playing card study. Hyman's cover story and procedure are presented in his article. You will need a scale for participants to use to rate stickiness. It might also be interesting to measure arousal (Hyman reported that some of his participants became very concerned during the demonstration.) An arousal scale was presented by Mackay, Cox, Burrows, and Lazzarini (1978).
    b. One problem with Hyman's (1999) demonstration is that there is not a control group in which an effect is not expected. You could try to create a cover story that is so contrary to facts that the ideomotor effect will not occur. This will demonstrate that ideomotor effects you do find are not simply coming from participants' willingness to give you what you want. For example, you could tell participants that arousing words (e.g., attack, drown) actually produce less arousal than neutral words (e.g., pencil). If participants show an effect for paper color, but not for words, that would suggest that the paper color data are truly an ideomotor effect.
    c. You could also replicate Hyman's (1999) investigation of applied kinesiology. Test various substances on participants and see whether or not they can resist practitioner pressure on their arms based on the cover story provided. This would be a 2 x 2 factorial design. The first independent variable would be cover story (e.g., glucose or fructose is the "bad" sugar) and the second independent variable would be knowledge of the substance being applied (e.g., know or do not know). The dependent variable would be a rating of how hard it was to resist the practitioner's pressure. Hyman's hypothesis would be that there would be an interaction. When participants know which substance they are testing, the results should be consistent with the cover story. When participants do not know the substance being tested, then the results should not be consistent with the cover story. A different way to conceptualize this design would be to use belief in the paranormal as a non-manipulated independent variable. Will believers be more susceptible to ideomotor effects than non-believers?
    d. Hyman (1999) also described a dowsing demonstration. He was able to get participants to locate a hidden water source under the room using dowsing rods, but where they "found" water was a function of where he led them to expect it. The first independent variable would

be location expectation (with the levels location 1 and location 2). In this study you could use a variable suggested by Burgess et al. (1998) as the second independent variable. Tell some participants that dowsing should be successful, and tell others that it should not work. The dependent variable would be confidence that the location they found had water below it. You would expect higher confidence ratings for the expected location, but only for people who thought dowsing should work.

e. Hyman (1999) also described a study by Chevreul. Chevreul was motivated by claims that pendulum movements could be used to detect which kinds of chemical elements were in a sample. In his study, when he knew there was mercury in the sample, the pendulum he held over it moved. When a glass plate was placed over the mercury, the movement was reduced. When Chevreul did not know whether the plate was present (he was blindfolded and an assistant either did or did not put the plate over the sample), Chevreul could not reproduce the effect. You could replicate this design (but use an element like copper that is less dangerous to handle than mercury).

f. Hyman (1999) also described Faraday's research on table moving in séances. Faraday stacked cardboard on the table (Hyman described the procedure in some detail) and predicted that the cardboard sheets would slide one way if the table moved of its own volition, and a different way if the sitter moved the table. Faraday's data were that sitters moved the table. You could turn this into a factorial design by manipulating the instructions provided (e.g., which direction the table should move), characteristics of the participants (e.g., believers or non-believers), or the cover story (e.g., the table should or should not move).

2. You could also go beyond Hyman's (1999) review and investigate other ideomotor effects.

a. Gardner (1996) invoked ideomotor effects to explain egg balancing. On certain days (e.g., the spring equinox), people are supposed to be able to balance an egg on end, but only on those days. However, Gardner noted that there is no physical reason why this should be so, and, in fact, eggs can be balanced on any day. His hypothesis was that ideomotor effects cause it to seem as though eggs can only be balanced on some days and not others. To test this, you could use a factorial design. The first independent variable would be the cover story (either it should or should not be possible to balance eggs), and the second independent variable could be any of the things we have considered so far (e.g., participant population). A different approach would be to vary what is being balanced and claim that one can be balanced and one cannot (similar to Hyman's, 1999, card color task). The trick would be to find something that can be balanced but is as difficult to balance as an egg (perhaps hard-boiled versus raw).

b. One interesting aspect of egg balancing is that the ideomotor action actually works against the desired outcome of balancing the egg.

Wegner, Ansfield, and Pilloff (1998) investigated what they called ironic ideomotor effects. For example, in putting a golf ball, an ironic ideomotor effect would be if an instruction not to make a particular kind of mistake actually increased the likelihood of that mistake. Wegner et al. used a 2 x 2 factorial design. One independent variable was the presence of visual feedback. Previous studies showed that when people are not looking, the ideomotor effect is reduced. So, their participants could either easily see their putter or had a hard time seeing the putter. The second independent variable was mental load. Some participants had to remember a six-digit number while putting and others did not. Load was expected to magnify the ironic ideomotor effect. All participants were instructed not to overshoot (the ironic instruction). Participants with a mental load overshot more, and load interacted with visual feedback. When the putter was visible, participants overshot more with load than without. When they could not see the putter as well, load did not matter. You could use their methodology to further explore how ideomotor effects can work against a desired outcome. Perhaps this is why it seems like people make a mistake right after someone warns them not to.

c. Burgess et al. (1998) proposed that facilitated communication could be a useful laboratory task for investigating ideomotor action. However, their study involved a great deal of deception (presenting the confederate as a person with a number of developmental disabilities), and this deception had some potential to do harm (the participants were anxious about their performance due to their desire to help and were pleased that they were helping, even though it was all a "trick"). When the potential outcome justifies it, it can be acceptable to use deception. Your institution's Institutional Review Board (IRB) will make that determination (see Appendix A). For a research methods project, this level of deception seems inappropriate. However, the facilitated communication situation is very similar to using a Ouija board. You could manipulate whether or not participants know information and then see if they can "uncover" this information with a Ouija board. The best second independent variable for this study would be prior belief. Are believers more susceptible to ideomotor effects when using a Ouija board than non-believers? You could also manipulate aspects of the social situation in this study. Based on social impact theory (see Chapter 7), you could manipulate the number of credulous confederates using the Ouija board, the strength of the information (the cover story could be supportive or not supportive), or the immediacy (e.g., are the others currently present?).

d. Spangenberg, Greenwald, and Sprott (2008) proposed an ideomotor explanation for the question-behavior effect (that asking a question about something increases the likelihood that it will be done). Spangenberg et al. claimed that question-behavior effects have a lot in common with ideomotor tasks (e.g., the effects appear to be automatic). You could design a study to evaluate question-behavior effects in the context of the ideomotor effect. Keep in mind, however, that question-behavior effects have also been found for negative behaviors (Williams, Block, & Fitzsimons, 2006), so you should exercise caution in the kinds of questions you ask.

3. You could also investigate individual differences in susceptibility to the ideomotor effect.

   a. Burgess et al. (1998) measured ideomotor susceptibility with the Chevreul pendulum illusion. Participants held a pendulum over a line and imagined it moving in the direction of the line on one trial (they also imposed a cognitive load on this trial by having participants count backwards). For the prevent trial, participants were to keep the pendulum from moving (a kind of ironic ideomotor effect was expected). The extent to which the pendulum moved in the Chevreul task was correlated with how many answers participants correctly facilitated in the main study. You could use ideomotor susceptibility as a non-manipulated independent variable and look for interactions between that and other variables (e.g., belief in the paranormal).

   b. Platek, Mohamed, and Gallup (2005) investigated contagious yawning. When people read about others yawning (or see others yawning), there is a reasonably high probability that they will yawn as well. Platek et al. cited research that susceptibility to contagious yawning was affected by individual differences (e.g., schizotypy as discussed in Chapter 5). You could use contagious yawning susceptibility as a measure of ideomotor susceptibility and include it in factorial designs looking at other variables. For example, are people more susceptible to contagious yawning more likely to show Hyman's (1999) playing card effects?

4. A slightly different take on the projects would be to investigate how ideomotor effects cause belief. For example, you could expose participants to one of the ideomotor tasks described in Hyman (1999) (with degree of success as the first independent variable) and manipulate the context of the task as the second independent variable (e.g., a supportive or skeptical cover story). The ideomotor effect has been proposed as a source of paranormal and pseudoscientific beliefs. Is it?

REFERENCES

Bavelas, J. B., Black, A., Lemery, C. R., & Mullett, J. (1986). "I show how you feel": Motor mimicry as a communicative act. *Journal of Personality and Social Psychology, 50,* 322–329. doi:10.1037/0022-3514.50.2.322

Berger, S. M. (1962). Conditioning through vicarious instigation. *Psychological Review, 69,* 450–466. doi:10.1037/h0046466

Brass, M., Bekkering, H., & Prinz, W. (2001). Movement observation affects movement execution in a simple response task. *Acta Psychologica, 106,* 3–22. doi:10.1016/S0001-6918(00)00024-X

Burgess, C. A., Kirsch, I., Shane, H., Niederauer, K. L., Graham, S. M., & Bacon, A. (1998). Facilitated communication as an ideomotor response. *Psychological Science, 9,* 71–74. doi: 10.1111/1467-9280.00013

Carroll, R. T. (2009). Ideomotor effect. *The Skeptic's Dictionary.* Retrieved from http://www.skepdic.com/ideomotor.html

De Maeght, S., & Prinz, W. (2004). Action induction through action observation. *Psychological Research, 68,* 97–114. doi: 10.1007/s00426-003-0148-3

Gardner, M. (1996). The great egg-balancing mystery. *Skeptical Inquirer, 20,* 8–10.

Hyman, R. (1999). The mischief-making of ideomotor action. *The Scientific Review of Alternative Medicine, 3,* 34–43.

Knuf, L., Aschersleben, G., & Prinz, W. (2001). An analysis of ideomotor action. *Journal of Experimental Psychology: General, 130,* 779–798. doi:10.1037/0096-3445.130.4.779

Mackay, C., Cox, T., Burrows, G., & Lazzarini, T. (1978). An inventory for the measurement of self-reported stress and arousal. *British Journal of Social and Clinical Psychology, 17,* 283–284.

Platek, S. M., Mohamed, F. B., & Gallup, G. G., Jr. (2005). Contagious yawning and the brain. *Cognitive Brain Research, 23,* 448–452. doi:10.1016/j.cogbrainres.2004.11.011

Randi, J. (1999). *The matter of dowsing.* Retrieved from http://www.randi.org/library/dowsing/

Spangenberg, E. R., Greenwald, A. G., & Sprott, D. E. (2008). Will you read this article's abstract? Theories of the question-behavior effect. *Journal of Consumer Psychology, 18,* 102–106. doi:10.1016/j.jcps.2008.02.002

Stock, A., & Stock, C. (2004). A short history of ideo-motor action. *Psychological Research, 68,* 176–188. doi:10.1007/s00426-003-0154-5

Wegner, D. M., Ansfield, M., & Pilloff, D. (1998). The putt and the pendulum: Ironic effects of the mental control of action. *Psychological Science, 9,* 196–199. doi:10.1111/1467-9280.00037

Whittaker, W. E. (n.d.). *Grave dowsing reconsidered.* Retrieved from http://www.uiowa.edu/~osa/burials/

Williams, P., Block, L. G., & Fitzsimons, G. J. (2006). Simply asking questions about health behaviors increases both healthy and unhealthy behaviors. *Social Influence, 1,* 117–127. doi:10.1080/15534510600630850

CHAPTER 11

Field Experiments

It's almost as good as making the team

Abstract

Psychology: Magical thinking is very common, and may serve an important role in psychological well-being, in addition to explaining a number of beliefs and behaviors of interest to psychology.

Skeptic/Pseudoscience: Magical thinking underlies many pseudoscientific beliefs (such as superstition, idiosyncratic theories of contagion, and belief in "forces" that impact people's lives).

INTRODUCTION: FIELD EXPERIMENTS

A field experiment involves manipulating a variable (as in an experiment) but in a natural setting. What are the benefits of conducting research in a natural setting? First, participants' behavior is more natural. Even though the experimenter may be manipulating a variable, we can still take advantage of the high external validity available with observation designs. We can be reasonably sure that the behavior exhibited in our study is the same as the behavior that would ordinarily be exhibited if we were not observing.

Spangenberg, Greenwald, and Sprott (2008) presented a discussion of the question-behavior effect and proposed that the effect could be explained as a kind of ideomotor effect (the topic of Chapter 10). The question-behavior effect is that asking people about a behavior increases the likelihood that they will do that behavior. For example, asking a consumer about an intended purchase increases the likelihood that they will make that purchase (Morwitz, Johnson, & Schmittlein, 1993). The question-behavior effect seems like an ideal candidate to investigate using field experiments. The implications are reasonably significant (e.g., you can be "tricked" into buying something by someone asking you if you intend to buy it). However, these implications are only meaningful if they generalize to the real world.

Greenwald, Carnot, Beach, and Young (1987) performed a field experiment investigating the question-behavior effect related to voting behavior in the 1984 presidential election. They called students who were not registered to vote and asked them about voter registration. For the treatment group, they asked if the students intended to register to vote. The control group was not asked this question. They also called students who were registered to vote and either did or did not ask them if they intended to vote. The hypothesis was that asking about intent would increase the likelihood of the behavior happening. Greenwald et al. determined whether or not students registered or voted by checking county records and by follow-up telephone calls. Registrations increased for students who were asked if they intended to register, but the increase was not significant. There was a significant increase in actual voting for people asked if they intended to vote. We will revisit the design of this study as we consider the design issues for field experiments.

In a field experiment, because we are manipulating a variable, we can create high internal validity and possibly even make a causal conclusion at the end of the study. However, field experiments will require you to sacrifice some of the control available in the laboratory. In the real world, it is very hard to anticipate all of the unexpected events that could arise during your experiment. As one example, Greenwald et al. (1987) made 550 calls in the registration experiment. Of these, 419 were answered and 66 of those people were eligible. Eventually, Greenwald et al. found that four of the 66 were not actually eligible for the study. Greenwald et al. were able to evaluate eligibility independently of the participants' responses. If they had not been, these participants could have influenced the results. In the voting study, three of the participants could not be reached for a follow-up and were counted as not voting, possibly affecting the results.

A lack of control tops the list of potential problems for field experiments. In order to say conclusively that the variable you manipulated caused the changes in the dependent variable, the only thing that can differ between conditions is the manipulated variable. All of the other random events that occur in the real world (which you cannot reasonably expect to control) will weaken your ability to attribute causality to the manipulated variable (essentially, they could become history confounds). One way to combat confounds is to have a control group. If something happened between the initial interviews and the election in the Greenwald, et al. (1987) study, it would affect both groups equally and not impact the difference in voting rates. Without a control group, it would be impossible to know if voting behavior was affected by the question or by outside events.

Another potential problem for field experiments has to do with naturalness. Even though field experiments are conducted in a natural setting, you may be interfering with what normally takes place in that setting. This interference could have ramifications that you are not aware of. In order to ensure that your situation will seem natural to participants, you should

METHODOLOGY NOTE **11.1**

Whenever you conduct research, you want the results to be valid. Two important kinds of validity are internal and external validity. **Internal validity** has to do with the design of the experiment. If you have conducted a "clean" experiment (free from errors like confounds), then you can make a causal conclusion at the end. **External validity** (also called generalizability) has to do with your ability to extend the findings to a population. No matter how interesting your results are, if they only apply to a tiny subset of people in very specialized circumstances, they will not be very valuable. The two kinds of validity usually compete. To get high internal validity, you need control over the situation. Control makes the situation less natural, lowering external validity. To increase external validity, you give up control, lowering internal validity. Field experiments walk the line where the two kinds of validity intersect. We manipulate the situation, gaining some internal validity, but use a natural setting, preserving external validity.

evaluate data from naturalistic observations first so you are aware of the kinds of events that would ordinarily transpire in the setting. The Greenwald et al. (1987) study had relatively high external validity. The survey that participants completed about their registration or voting intent was not different from the kind of activity that typically takes place before an election.

The target article for this chapter used a field experiment. The researchers were interested in magical thinking. In particular, they wanted to know if people felt that their visualizations before a basketball game affected the outcome of the game.

ETHICS NOTE **11.1**

Field experiment research raises special ethical considerations. For observation studies, you can make the case that you are merely observing public behavior, so you do not need to get people's permission before watching what they do. In a field experiment, however, you are intervening in the situation. When you intervene, you always raise the possibility of doing harm to the participant, and it is unfair to put people at risk without allowing them the opportunity to evaluate the risk for themselves. Most of the time, you can get consent from participants and still collect data in a natural setting. For research methods projects, you should avoid field experiments for which obtaining consent is not possible.

METHODOLOGY NOTE **11.2**

As a check on your comprehension, consider a study by Spangenberg, Obermiller, and Greenwald (1992). They were interested in evaluating the effectiveness of subliminal self-help tapes. Three kinds of tapes were used (weight loss, self-esteem, and memory), and the tapes were labeled with one of those three labels in a full factorial design. For example, one third of the tapes with the weight loss label were weight loss tapes, one third were self-esteem tapes, and one third were memory tapes. The design allowed Spangenberg et al. to tease apart the effects of expectancies (from the labels) and the actual content of the tapes on participants' perceptions. Why is this kind of research best conducted as a field experiment as opposed to a laboratory experiment? What kinds of threats to internal validity are created by the study being conducted in the field? Does the design of the study allow the results to generalize to people using subliminal self-help tapes in the real world? (This is an important question since the results were that the tapes do not work.)

TARGET ARTICLE: MAGICAL THINKING

(Be sure to look at Appendix D to assist you in evaluating the sources cited in this chapter. Be especially aware of the guidelines for evaluating Internet and other non-peer-reviewed sources.)

The Skeptic's Dictionary (Carroll, 2009) lists several features of magical thinking. Magical thinking is responsible for a variety of superstitious rituals, idiosyncratic theories of contagion, the reason why relics of saints are venerated, and a variety of other interesting parapsychological phenomena. Carroll cites Zusne and Jones' (1989) definition of magical thinking as having two components: the idea that things that are similar to one another (or have contacted one another) maintain some kind of connection, and the idea that a person's thoughts can influence physical events.

Magical thinking can be a double-edged sword. Blacher (1997) presented an account of benign magical thinking. Some forms of magical thinking can be comforting and cause no harm. For example, a superstitious ritual can give a person a sense of control over uncontrollable events. As long as that ritual is not harmful, why not perform it? Blacher cites the case of a "hard-scientist" who was relieved when his wife broke her ankle. His reasoning was that two recent misfortunes she had suffered meant that she was "due" for a third, and a broken ankle was not as bad as many of the other things that could have happened. In this case, magical thinking provided a coping mechanism for misfortune.

Magical thinking can also have a dark side. Stevens (2001) presented a discussion of magical thinking in alternative medicine. For example, homeopathy is based on the concept that "like cures like" and that highly diluted solutions of substances can maintain effectiveness due to contact with the original, concentrated substance. Homeopathic treatments are selected because the substances create similar symptoms as the disease they are supposed to treat (the similarity part of magical thinking). These substances are then diluted to the point that a dose may not contain a single molecule of the original substance (the contact part of magical thinking; see, for example, Randi, 2003, on why toxic substances are not dangerous in homeopathic treatments). Stevens cited statistics that more people visit alternative medicine providers than physicians. In cases in which something is really wrong, this can represent an "opportunity cost." The person sought help and received magical thinking solutions that did not help. For the kinds of diseases that cannot be cured by placebo effects alone, forgoing treatment in favor of something like homeopathy can be very dangerous.

Rozin and colleagues have investigated the contact aspect of magical thinking. For example, Rozin, Millman, and Nemeroff (1986) investigated a number of aspects of sympathetic magic. To investigate negative contagion, they asked participants how much they would like a sip of juice, dropped a dead, sterilized roach into the juice and stirred it for five seconds before removing it, then asked people to rate again how much they would like a sip. There was a substantial decline in desire to have a sip of "roached juice." To investigate negative similarity, Rozin et al. (1986) asked participants to throw darts at a picture of Adolf Hitler (expecting increased accuracy), to eat sugar from a chemical bottle labeled "Sodium Cyanide," or to eat fudge shaped like dog feces. There were large effects of the law of similarity in most cases. For example, even when participants saw the sugar placed into the jars and put the labels on the jars themselves, they did not want to eat sugar from a jar labeled "Sodium Cyanide." There were also some effects of positive contagion (e.g., willing to wear a blouse worn by someone they liked) and positive similarity (e.g., a decrease in dart throwing accuracy when the target was a picture of U.S. President John Kennedy). However, positive effects were weaker than negative effects. Taken together, the results supported the hypothesis that sympathetic magic could affect the choices made by participants.

METHODOLOGY NOTE **11.3**

Rozin et al. (1986) were concerned about possible demand characteristics in their study. Demand characteristics arise from a participant's perceptions of what the desired outcome of a study might be. In this case, it would be obvious to participants that they should not want to drink "roached juice" and so they would know that a lower rating for that juice was expected. Rozin et al. addressed the problem of demand characteristics by pointing out that participants showed violations of magical thinking (if it was all demand characteristics, then all of the variables would have shown similar effects). Also, participants were embarrassed to be admitting to magical thinking, working against doing it for the benefit of the experimenter. If possible, you should minimize demand characteristics in your studies. If you cannot, then you should attempt to measure their effect. It is also possible to argue against them on logical grounds, as in Rozin et al.

Rozin, Markwith, and McCauley (1994) extended these results to a more real world situation: Avoiding objects used by people with AIDS. They asked participants how they would feel about wearing a sweater after it had been worn by various people and then cleaned (with or without a photo of the other person), how they would feel about driving a car previously driven by various people, and how they would feel about sleeping in a hotel bed slept in by various people. These ratings measured the contagion by contact aspect of sympathetic magic. Rozin et al. found evidence for aversion to misfortune (a person who lost a leg in an accident that was not their fault contaminated the objects), aversion to infection (people with tuberculosis or AIDS contaminated the objects), and aversion to moral taint (homosexuals contaminated the objects). They also found a general aversion to strangers. For example, a healthy man wearing the sweater contaminated it. These results suggest ways that sympathetic magical thinking could impact people in their daily lives and interactions with others.

Our target article for this chapter investigated the other main aspect of magical thinking: that thoughts can influence physical events. Pronin, Wegner, McCarthy, and Rodriguez (2006) investigated people's perceptions of the power of their thinking in a variety of ways. In their first experiment (a laboratory study), participants were induced to have evil thoughts about a confederate or neutral thoughts about a confederate. To get evil thoughts, the confederate was late for the study and acted like a jerk throughout. Participants were told that the study was investigating psychological aspects of voodoo. To see if voodoo hexes would have an effect, participants and the confederates completed a health survey, and then the participant thought about the confederate for a minute and then stuck pins into a voodoo doll with the confederate's name on it (the law of similarity). The confederate then reported a mild headache. Participants in the evil thoughts condition (the confederate behaved badly) did have more evil thoughts. These participants also felt more responsible for the confederate's headache than participants in the neutral thoughts condition.

In a second study, participants either visualized a blindfolded student taking shots with a basketball as being successful or visualized that student lifting weights. The blindfolded student was a confederate who could actually see what he was doing and attempted to make six out of eight shots. In addition to the person making the visualizations, another person just watched the visualizing and shooting (but knew what the visualizer was thinking). Again, Pronin et al. (2006) found evidence for magical thinking. Spectators who visualized successful shooting felt more responsible. Also, people watching visualizers of successful shooting rated them as more responsible. So, magical thinking extends to believing in the effect that other people's thoughts will have.

The third study was a field experiment. Pronin et al. (2006) went to a Princeton basketball game and asked spectators to participate in the study. Before the game began, some people thought about how key players could contribute to the team's performance. Other people thought about how key players could be picked out in a crowd. During a time-out, participants completed surveys about how much influence they had on the team's performance. People who thought about how players might contribute felt that they had a stronger influence.

The field study replicated the results in the laboratory. Pronin et al. (2006) discussed some of the ways that the natural environment contributed potential sources of error to the study. For example, participants varied in how many games they attended, how strongly they rooted for the team, how familiar they were with the team, and how much attention they were able to pay to the game. Pronin et al. interpreted these difficulties as a positive thing because, in spite of all of the variation in the natural setting, they were still able to replicate their laboratory work. In the real world, variables that had an impact in the laboratory still affected participants' judgments of responsibility.

Pronin et al.'s (2006) final study was a correlation study undertaken in the field. The motivation was to see if negative thoughts would also be perceived as causing an undesired outcome. For example, thinking ill of someone you love immediately before their being affected by a negative event could lead to a perception of the negative thought causing the bad outcome, even though that outcome might not be wanted. Pronin et al. had fans watching the Super Bowl rate how much they had thought about the game and then had them rate their responsibility for the outcome. The more people thought about the game, the more responsible they felt whether their team won (positive causation) or lost (negative causation). In other words, magical thinking operated regardless of the outcome.

In the projects section, you will have an opportunity to investigate magical thinking for yourself.

INFOTRAC® COLLEGE EDITION EXERCISES

You can use the InfoTrac College Edition to read about additional studies using field experiments. Typing in "field experiment" gave me a list of 205 articles. Many of these were literally "field" experiments and were related to agricultural research. However, there were also some interesting psychology-related articles in the list. For example, Breau and Brook (2007) investigated the effect of telling mock jurors that they were on a mock jury on those jurors' deliberations. They specifically discussed the advantages of using a field experiment. Spend some time with InfoTrac College Edition reading method sections from a variety of articles using field experiments before tackling your own project.

You can also use the InfoTrac College Edition to explore research about magical thinking. Typing the search string "magical thinking" with "in citation, title, abstract" and "to refereed publications" checked produced a list of 22 sources. A few of those were directly related to our topic, including Blacher (1997) who presented an interesting take on benign magical thinking. Before tackling your own project, you might want to read about related research to help formulate your ideas.

IMPLEMENTING THE DESIGN

Suggested Projects

1. You can replicate the field experiment of Pronin et al. (2006). Their materials are described in the article. You could also vary their methodology.
   a. You could explicitly incorporate positive and negative thoughts into the design. Ask some participants to visualize how certain players could make mistakes that would harm the outcome of the game (in addition to the positive and neutral thoughts conditions).
   b. You could vary the kind of event that participants are attending. For example, basketball is a team sport. Will thoughts be perceived as affecting sports involving individual effort in the same way as team sports?
   c. You could incorporate aspects of sympathetic magic into the design. For example, if participants were asked to cross out pictures of their team versus players on the other team, would that lead to feelings of responsibility for the outcome?
2. You could try to extend laboratory results related to magical thinking to the field setting.
   a. Risen and Gilovich (2008) investigated people's thoughts about tempting fate. In their first study, participants read about "Jon" applying for graduate school and receiving a Stanford shirt from his mother (Stanford was his top choice school). In the tempting fate condition, Jon wore the shirt the next day. In the not tempting fate condition, Jon put the shirt away. Participants rated Jon as less likely to get into Stanford when he tempted fate. To make this a field experiment, you could ask people to wear a button on their shirt predicting success for their team and evaluate how likely they feel that this will have an adverse effect on the outcome of the game. There are a variety of other fate-tempting behaviors that could be tested in a field experiment.
   b. Athletes are notorious for having superstitious rituals (e.g., Van Raalte, Brewer, Nemeroff, & Linder 1991). College students also have many superstitious beliefs. For example, Lewis and Gallagher (2001) found that almost a third of students would not like to take an exam on Friday the 13th. What would happen if you asked people to suspend their rituals before an important event (either students before an exam or athletes before a game)? Would they believe that the outcome would be worse because the ritual had been suspended? Similarly, would positive or negative thoughts about their own performance before an event lead to the expectation that performance would be enhanced or degraded?
   c. Rudski and Edwards (2007) investigated external forces that led to superstitious behavior. Their hypothesis was that the greater the need for control, the more likely it would be that a superstitious ritual would be used. They manipulated the type of event (e.g., exam or

game), the amount of difficulty, how important the outcome was, and how prepared the students were. All of these factors mattered. You could manipulate these variables in a field experiment to see if situational pressures that lead to increased use of superstition translate from the laboratory to the real world.

d. Keinan (2002) conducted a field experiment to investigate the effect of stress on superstitious behavior. Students were interviewed either a half hour before an exam (high stress) or on a regular day (low stress). Students were asked two kinds of questions. Diversion questions (e.g., "What is your favorite TV program?") were about ordinary things not expected to lead to superstitious behavior. The target questions ("knock wood" questions) were designed to get students to knock on wood (e.g., "Have you ever been involved in a fatal road accident?"). Keinan found that the kind of question had an effect when stress was high. These results imply that people have a stronger need for control under high stress and are more likely to turn to superstition in that situation. You could incorporate stress into your studies in the way that Keinan did, or you could incorporate stress into some of the other designs in this chapter. For example, does the magnitude of the game ("bigger" games should lead to more stress) change spectators' opinions about the importance of their thoughts?

e. You could take some of the manipulations of Rozin et al. (1986) into the field.

i. You could prepare fudge in various shapes, including "dog doo" as in Rozin et al. (1986, p. 705), and have a bake sale on campus. Will the shape of the fudge affect people's willingness to buy it? Will normally shaped fudge suffer by being on the same table as "dog doo" fudge? In other words, if there were competing bake sales side-by-side, would the sale with "dog doo" fudge sell less than the sale without it?

ii. If you staged a dart tournament with pictures of people on the dart boards (e.g., hated professors or administrators at the school versus popular people), would students be less accurate when aiming at popular people's pictures?

iii. You probably would not want to use the Sodium Cyanide label in a study (it seems too obvious). However, if you varied the kind of container that had been emptied and then refilled with lemonade at a lemonade stand, would you see a preference for some containers over others? For example, would an empty liquor bottle full of lemonade be less popular than an empty milk jug full of lemonade? Alternatively, you could vary the target audience for the product in the container or the use of the product in the container. Would people be less interested in buying a brownie out of an empty denture cream carton than an empty cookie carton?

iv. If you staged a rummage sale and labeled the clothing as coming from different sources, would the source of the clothing affect the amount that people would be willing to buy? For example, clothing donated by a hospital that was left behind by the families of people who did not survive their surgery versus clothing donated by ordinary people for charity.

3. You could explicitly design studies that incorporate both a field experiment and laboratory component and evaluate the effect that being in the natural setting has on the results. The concern that motivates field experiments is that laboratory studies might produce results that do not generalize. Is this the case?

REFERENCES

Blacher, R. B. (1997). Benign magical thinking. *Perspectives in Biology and Medicine, 40,* 190–196.

Breau, D. L., & Brook, B. (2007). "Mock" mock juries: A field experiment on the ecological validity of jury simulations. *Law and Psychology Review, 31,* 77–92.

Carroll, R. T. (2009). Magical thinking. *The Skeptic's Dictionary.* Retrieved from http://www.skepdic.com/magicalthinking.html.

Greenwald, A. G., Carnot, C. G., Beach, R., & Young, B. (1987). Increasing voting behavior by asking people if they expect to vote. *Journal of Applied Psychology, 72,* 315–318. doi:10.1037/0021-9010.72.2.315

Keinan, G. (2002). The effects of stress and desire for control on superstitious behavior. *Personality and Social Psychology Bulletin, 28,* 102–108. doi:10.1177/0146167202281009

Lewis, J. M., & Gallagher, T. J. (2001). The salience of Friday the 13th for college students. *College Student Journal, 35,* 216–222.

Morwitz, V. G., Johnson, E., & Schmittlein, D. (1993). Does measuring intent change behavior? *Journal of Consumer Research, 20,* 46–61. doi:10.1086/209332

Pronin, E., Wegner, D. M., McCarthy, K., & Rodriguez, S. (2006). Everyday magical powers: The role of apparent mental causation in the overestimation of personal influence. *Journal of Personality and Social Psychology, 91,* 218–231. doi:10.1037/0022-3514.91.2.218

Randi, J. (2003). 'Twas brillig: Homeopathy, the French, psychic dreams, testing astrology, and numerology. *Skeptic, 10,* 6–8.

Risen, J. L., & Gilovich, T. (2008). Why people are reluctant to tempt fate. *Journal of Personality and Social Psychology, 95,* 293–307. doi:10.1037/0022-3514.95.2.293

Rozin, P., Markwith, M., & McCauley, C. (1994). Sensitivity to indirect contacts with other persons: AIDS aversion as a composite of aversion to strangers, infection, moral taint, and misfortune. *Journal of Abnormal Psychology, 103,* 495–504. doi:10.1037/0021-843X.103.3.495

Rozin, P., Millman, L., & Nemeroff, C. (1986). Operation of the laws of sympathetic magic in disgust and other domains. *Journal of Personality and Social Psychology, 50,* 703–712. doi:10.1037/0022-3514.50.4.703

Rudski, J. M., & Edwards, A. (2007). Malinowski goes to college: Factors influencing students' use of ritual and superstition. *The Journal of General Psychology, 134,* 389–403. doi:10.3200/GENP.134.4.389-404

Spangenberg, E. R., Greenwald, A. G., & Sprott, D. E. (2008). Will you read this article's abstract? Theories of the question-behavior effect. *Journal of Consumer Psychology, 18,* 102–106. doi:10.1016/j.jcps.2008.02.002

Spangenberg, E. R., Obermiller, C., & Greenwald, A. G. (1992). A field test of subliminal self-help audiotapes: The power of expectancies. *Journal of Public Policy and Marketing, 11,* 26–36.

Stevens, P., Jr. (2001). Magical thinking in complimentary and alternative medicine. *Skeptical Inquirer, 25,* 32–37.

Van Raalte, J. L., Brewer, B. W., Nemeroff, C. J., & Linder, D. E. (1991). Chance orientation and superstitious behavior on the putting green. *Journal of Sport Behavior, 14,* 41–50.

Institutional Review Boards

To ensure that research follows ethical guidelines and to protect participants from harm, research projects must be reviewed by an Institutional Review Board (IRB). This appendix describes the questions that will be asked by the IRB, along with some suggestions for appropriate answers.

IRB OVERVIEW

A number of historical events inspired a concern for the protection of human participants in research. The National Institutes of Health (2008) training website for researchers presents a brief timeline of these events. One study that had a large impact on regulations was the Tuskegee Syphilis Study. Starting in the 1930s, 400 African American men with syphilis were deceived into believing that they were receiving medical treatment when, in fact, the purpose of the study was to investigate the long-term effect of untreated syphilis. The study continued even after it was clear that treatment improved the outcome of people with syphilis and even after a reliable treatment (penicillin) became widely available. This study violated most of the ethical guidelines that have been developed to protect human research participants, including voluntary participation, informed consent, and protection from harm.

One of the foundational documents for the new ethical guidelines was the Belmont Report (Department of Health, Education, and Welfare, 1979). This report outlined three basic principles for researchers to follow: respect for persons, beneficence, and justice. These principles can be restated as: respect people's autonomy, do no harm, and distribute the research burdens and benefits equitably (the population that participates in the research should also benefit from it).

Most professional organizations whose members engage in medical or behavioral research also have their own ethics codes. The American Psychological Association (APA) (2002) has adopted a revised set of ethical guidelines to protect participants from harm in behavioral research settings. It is the responsibility of researchers to follow these guidelines. You should familiarize yourself with these rules before beginning your project. The complete set of guidelines is most readily available on the APA website (http://www.apa.org/ethics/code2002.html).

Before collecting data, you will be required to have your project reviewed by an Institutional Review Board (IRB). This board is typically composed of people from a variety of disciplines (some of whom do not do research with human participants) and members of the community. The IRB will carefully review your project to ensure that participants are protected and that your research follows ethical guidelines. However, you should keep in mind that you—the person collecting the data—will ultimately be responsible for ethical conduct. In other words, even if your project is approved by the IRB, if problems develop later, you are still obligated to protect participants from harm. A good guide is to keep the principles from the Belmont Report in mind as you conduct your research.

Some institutions will allow your instructor to serve as the IRB that will review your project. Most will require a more formal procedure. This appendix provides some guidelines for completing IRB forms. The simplest way to get approval is to make sure your project follows the ethical principles. There should be no risk to participants, no potential for harm, and minimal or no deception.

THE QUESTIONS

This section will review some questions that you will be asked to complete for the IRB, along with some suggestions for how to answer them.

Project Description

What is your research question? What will participants do in your experiment? What materials will they see? Remember that the scientific merit of the project will be considered as part of the review. It is your responsibility to provide sufficient information to establish that your project will have merit (and that you will not be wasting participants' time). If your description is unclear, then your proposal will be delayed as the IRB seeks additional information from you.

To help you provide sufficient information, you might address the following points (some IRB forms specifically request this information, but you can still include it even if your form does not require it). These questions have been taken from the expedited/full review form from Middle Tennessee State University.

1. What is the research question/purpose of the project?
2. What research has been done previously, and how does that lead to the project being proposed?

3. What is the study design, what will participants do as part of the study, and how will these procedures allow you to answer your question?
4. How will the data be analyzed? (This is especially important for designs that the IRB might not encounter on a routine basis, e.g., qualitative research.)
5. What are the risks/benefits for the participants? A careful evaluation of both risks and benefits helps the IRB to assign your study to a risk category. Also, an honest evaluation from you will help the IRB to have confidence in your ability to conduct the research ethically.
6. How will participants be debriefed? This is especially true if your project involves deception. However, since education is usually the main benefit for participating in psychological research, it is important that you explain the project to the participants and help them to receive the full benefit. You should attach a written version of your debriefing statement to the IRB application.

Participant Population

Who will participate? Our form at Middle Tennessee State University has check boxes for a variety of populations (adult, minor, prisoner, mentally retarded, mentally ill, physically ill, disabled, and other). If you are using college-age adults who do not fall into any other category, the approval process is simple. Whenever you plan to study a population that may not be able to freely volunteer (e.g., minors or prisoners), there will be extra steps to the permission process. For example, if you want to study children, you will have to explain how they will be contacted, how you will get parental consent, and how you will get assent from your participants. You will also need permission from any institution involved in the data-collection process. In other words, if you plan to contact children through their schools, you will need permission from the schools. Your institution may have additional rules.

The best population to study in research methods laboratory projects is adults. College students usually form the population. My students frequently include this statement for their population: "Adult friends of the experimenters will be asked to volunteer to participate."

If you will have a more elaborate sign-up procedure, the IRB will want to know about it. In order to ensure that your participants are truly volunteers, the IRB will need to know what you plan to say to them, what inducements you are offering (if any), and how you are describing the project to potential participants.

Confidentiality

A special procedural issue is how you plan to keep participants' results confidential. This has two components:

1. How will you ensure anonymity (nobody knows who participated in your study)?
2. How will you keep results confidential?

Some IRBs will ask a question that specifically deals with how you will ensure confidentiality. You should list any potentially identifying information that will be collected and explain how you will control access to that information. You will also be asked to explain your plan for the storage and ultimate disposal of the data.

Consent

How will participants give their consent to participate? There are several things a consent form should include. A checklist for consent forms can be found at the website of the Office for Human Research Protections (OHRP) (http://www.hhs.gov/ohrp/humansubjects/assurance/consentckls.htm). You will need to inform participants that the project involves research and describe the research. You need to include enough information for a person to make an informed decision about whether or not to participate. If there are special risks or if you are asking for sensitive information, make that very clear. Also be sure to explain any potential benefits to the participant. Participants should also be informed of their rights. The main right is their ability to quit the experiment at any time without penalty. They also have the right to ask questions. Make it clear that the results will be confidential. Finally, include contact information in case participants have additional questions (also include this on a debriefing sheet that participants will be allowed to keep). The OHRP website also has tips for creating consent forms with additional guidance (http://www. hhs.gov/ohrp/humansubjects/guidance/ictips.htm). Your institution may also have a consent form template that you will be expected to use.

Special Information

Some projects will require more information. Any project involving deception, special participant populations, or risk to participants will have to be justified. You will be required to explain why successful completion of the project requires these elements. You will have to explain how the potential harm to participants is offset by the value of the knowledge to be gained. You will also have to explain how you have tried to minimize harm, even in these situations, and why other ways of conducting the research will not work.

As a rule of thumb, avoid the use of deception. It has the potential to harm participants, and it can make participants suspicious of research (for more on both of these issues, I suggest reading Epley & Huff, 1998). For your research methods lab projects, there will almost always be another way to carry out your experiment that does not involve deception.

TYPES OF FORMS

There are typically three levels of review: exempt, expedited, and full. Exempt projects are exempt from continuing review by the IRB and can be approved for up to three years. These projects involve minimal risk and fall into select research categories. The list of exempt categories can be found on the OHRP website: http://www.hhs.gov/ohrp/humansubjects/guidance/45cfr46.htm#46 .101(b). This particular list is part of the "to what does this policy apply" section of the regulations, so it can be difficult to find. The good news for research methods students is that survey projects and observations of public behavior are typically exempt. This is helpful because the forms for exempt approval are usually less involved due to the minimal risk of these projects. At most institutions a compliance officer will review exempt applications, and this process can be shorter than an expedited or full review.

Expedited review categories are also posted on the OHRP website: http://www.hhs.gov/ohrp/humansubjects/guidance/expedited98.htm. These projects also involve minimal risk but do not fall into any of the categories for exempt review. Research methods projects will usually fall under category 7 for expedited review (e.g., cognitive projects, survey research). Typically, the form for expedited review is more detailed than the exempt review form, and it will be reviewed by a member of the IRB committee. This process takes a little longer than the exempt process, so you will need to plan accordingly.

Research not exempt and not meeting the criteria for expedited review will receive a full review. Usually this research involves more than minimal risk or will have a special participant population (e.g., prisoners). Often, there is a separate and even more detailed form for full review. Because of the risk that is usually involved in this type of research, it is important to assist the IRB in evaluating the scientific merit of the project and to explain clearly what the risks are and how those risks are being minimized. There is also a special concern about the consent process when there is a more than minimal risk for participants. Full reviews will be evaluated by the IRB committee at their regularly scheduled meeting. The forms will be due at least two weeks before the meeting to allow members time to evaluate the research. Because meetings are usually held monthly, you will need to be especially careful in your planning if your research methods project will require a full review. Because of the somewhat rushed nature of the research methods project, it is probably better for the protection of the participants if you limit yourself to projects that fall under the exempt or expedited categories.

Each institution will have different policies covering full reviews. At Middle Tennessee State University, IRB members are assigned as primary and secondary reviewers for full reviews. These members may contact researchers if they feel that additional information is necessary to evaluate the project. Researchers are also encouraged to attend the meeting at which their application will be discussed. They are not allowed to be in the room during discussion or deliberation about the research, but they are frequently brought in to answer questions about the research. The process is seen as a cooperative enterprise between the IRB and the researcher to protect the welfare of participants.

Each institution will formulate its own policies regarding IRB review categories and review criteria. As a researcher, you will usually be asked to decide if your project will be exempt, expedited, or full. However, the compliance officer, IRB chair, or a member of the IRB may change that designation if they disagree. You can facilitate the entire review process if you read through the regulations at the OHRP website (http://www.hhs.gov/ohrp/), and check your institution's website for their policies. You can also contact the institution's compliance officer or IRB chair if you need assistance.

TRAINING

People engaged in research with human participants will also have to complete some form of training. Some institutions provide training seminars, many will accept a certificate from an approved online course (for example, http://www.citiprogram.org/). Different institutions will have different guidelines for training, so you will need to consult your instructor or IRB to learn how you will be expected to meet the training requirement.

REFERENCES

American Psychological Association. (2002). Ethical principles of psychologists and code of conduct. *American Psychologist, 57*, 1060–1073. doi:10.1037/0003-066X.57.12.1060

Department of Health, Education, and Welfare. (1979, April). The Belmont Report. Retrieved from http://www.hhs.gov/ohrp/humansubjects/guidance/belmont.htm

Epley, N., & Huff, C. (1998). Suspicion, affective response, and educational benefit as a result of deception in psychology research. *Personality and Social Psychology Bulletin, 24*, 759–768. doi:10.1177/0146167298247008

National Institutes of Health Office of Extramural Research. (2008). Protecting human research participants. Retrieved from http://phrp.nihtraining.com/users/login.php.

Writing Results Sections

This appendix describes how to write a results section. The process is described from choosing the appropriate statistic to deciding how much information to include in the report. For information on preparing the rest of the manuscript, I suggest that you consult Rosnow and Rosnow (2009). Their brief introduction to American Psychological Association (APA) style focuses on the information a student would need to prepare a paper. They also include sample research reports.

CHOOSING A STATISTIC

Figure B.1 contains a decision tree that you can use to choose the appropriate statistic for your design. To use the tree, you will answer a series of questions about your design. You will start by deciding what type of statistical question you are trying to answer. You can answer questions about differences between means, frequencies, or relationships. If you are unsure of the kind of question you have, the following guidelines might be useful (however, they are only general guidelines, and violations of them are common). Experiments will generally involve questions about differences between means. Observation designs will generally involve questions about frequencies. Correlation and survey designs will generally involve questions about relationships. Once you know what kind of question you are asking, you will make decisions based on the specific design you used.

As an example, let's say I ran a version of Wiseman and Greening's (2005) study on the effect of social influence on belief in the paranormal. I had 20 participants witness a paranormal event (a psychic spoon bending video) and 20 different participants witness the same event, except that after the spoon was bent and placed on a table someone said "it's still bending." I want to know if the mean belief in the paranormal score for the group that

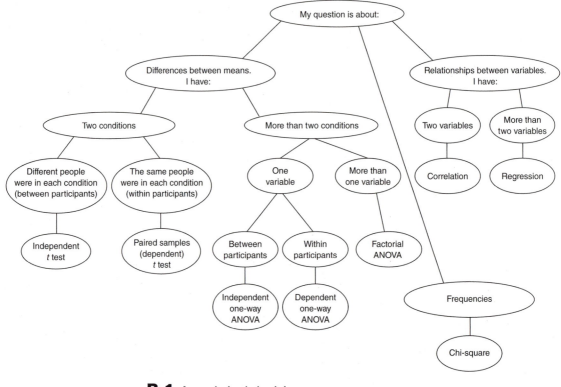

FIGURE **B.1** A statistical decision tree.

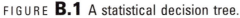

heard "it's still bending" would be greater than that for the group that merely witnessed the bending.

At the first node, I choose the "differences between means" branch. That is because I want to know if the two mean paranormal belief scores differ from one another. I have two conditions (with and without suggestion), so I choose "Two conditions." Because different people were in each group, that is the next branch I take (for between participants). That leads me to an "independent *t* test." So, the appropriate statistic for this design is an independent *t* test.

At this point, with the statistic chosen, it is time to perform some computations. You can do this by hand, using your notes from statistics, or you can use a statistics software package. Once that is done, you are ready to write.

WHAT TO SAY?

Each statistic will require a slightly different write-up. The general rule is to include enough information for the person reading your paper to understand your computations. Included here are sample results sections for each of the main statistics. (For all of these, I consulted Glenberg, 1996, to help determine what to report. Some of the results sections in the next section use his formatting. His text is an excellent source for additional information on statistics.) Note that all data presented in this appendix were generated for purposes of illustration only, and are not to be taken to be research results (some data are based on the results of published studies, but I manipulated them to illustrate various points).

Chi-square

A chi-square test can be used to find out if two frequency distributions are independent of one another. These tests are often conducted after observation designs in which frequency data are collected. For example, let's say I went to the library to stare at people to see if they could detect my staring. I stared at 40 people and then asked them if they noticed my staring. I did not stare at 40 additional people, but asked them if they noticed my staring. My data are presented in Table B.1.

A quick glance at the frequencies suggests that the two distributions (staring or not) are independent. In other words, the frequency of "detection" is approximately the same whether or not I stared at the person. The chi-square test of independence can tell me if that is the case. After computing the chi-square, I find that there is not enough evidence to conclude that the two distributions are not independent. The value for the chi-square is 0.09, $p > .90$. Here is the results section reporting that:

> The stare detection frequency distributions for stare and non-stare trials were compared using a chi-square test of independence. The frequencies are presented in Table B.1. The chi-square was not significant, $\chi^2 (1, N = 80) = 0.09, p > .90$. Participants were approximately equally likely to "detect" staring whether or not they were being stared at.

Correlation

A correlation is computed when you want to assess the strength and direction of the relationship between two measured variables. The main thing to report is the correlation itself. For the next results section, students measured magical ideation in their participants and belief in the paranormal. The students were interested in the relationship between magical ideation and belief, and expected a positive relationship (more magical ideation is associated with stronger belief). Here is a results section reporting the correlation:

> Magical ideation scores ranged from 26 to 79 ($M = 48.6, SD = 9.8$). Belief in the paranormal scores ranged from 1.0 to 6.0 ($M = 2.7, SD = 1.2$). There was a significant, positive correlation between magical ideation and paranormal belief, $r = .59$, $p < .01$. Higher magical ideation scores were associated with stronger paranormal belief.

TABLE **B.1**
Number of People Detecting Staring Based on Stare Condition

	Stared	Did Not Stare
Detected	5	6
Did not detect	35	34

t test

A *t* test is used when you want to compare the means of two conditions. If the same people are in both conditions, you will use a dependent *t* test. If different people are in the two conditions, you will use an independent *t* test. You need to report the descriptive statistics for the two conditions and the value of the *t* statistic.

For the sample results section, we will use data from an experiment similar to the projects for Chapter 10 investigating the ideomotor effect. Participants were told that red paper should lead to increased arousal and that holding their hand over red paper while rubbing on a plastic surface should make that surface feel stickier. As a control, participants also rubbed the plastic while holding their hand over green paper. The mean "stickiness" ratings for red and green paper were recorded. I wanted to know if these means would be different. The results from the experiment are presented in Table B.2.

Here is an example of how to report these results:

> The data were analyzed using a dependent samples *t* test. The independent variable was the color of the paper over which participants held their hands, and the conditions were red paper and green paper. The dependent variable was rated stickiness on a scale of 1 to 5, with 1 meaning "equal to the baseline stickiness" and 5 meaning "much stickier than baseline." The mean rated stickiness for red paper was 2.85 ($SD = 1.15$) and the mean rated stickiness for green paper was 1.70 ($SD = 0.73$). With alpha = .05, the two population means were significantly different, $t(62) = -8.05$, $p < .01$. (Report format from Glenberg, 1996)

ANOVA

One-way

This analysis is used when you have one independent variable with more than two conditions. You will need to report whether or not there was a significant difference for the independent variable. You can tell if there is a significant difference by looking under *p* (or probability or significance) in your ANOVA source table.

Imagine that we have carried out the following study based on the research discussed in Chapter 8. Participants were surveyed on their beliefs in the paranormal. The results from that survey were used to divide the participants into

TABLE **B.2**
Rated "Stickiness" Results for Red and Green Paper

Paper Color	*M*	*SD*
Red	2.85	1.15
Green	1.70	0.73

Note: "Stickiness" was rated on a scale from 1 to 5 with 1 meaning "equal to the baseline stickiness" and 5 meaning "much stickier than baseline."

three groups with 20 participants in each group: strong non-believers in the paranormal, people who are neutral about the paranormal, and strong believers in the paranormal. The goal was to see what would happen with people who do not place at either end of the more traditional sheep-goat classification scheme (sheep are believers and goats are non-believers, see, for example, Carroll, 2009). After participants were placed into the three groups, they were given lists from Roediger and McDermott's (1995) investigation of false memories. The dependent variable was the number of "lure" words recalled (words that were strongly associated with items on the list but were not actually on the list). The hypothesis was that the greater the belief in the paranormal, the more false recalls there would be. So, the sheep should have more false recalls than the goats. The important question was what would happen with the people who were neutral on the paranormal. A source table from that experiment (a modified version of a source table from SPSS) is presented in Table B.3.

The descriptive statistics for the experiment are presented in Table B.4.

The p value for belief ("Sig.") is less than .05, so the effect is significant. All I know so far is that within all possible pairwise comparisons of belief levels (sheep versus neutral, sheep versus goat, and neutral versus goat), at least one pair is significantly different. I can find out which pairs differ by conducting pairwise comparisons (also called post hoc tests). Any time you have more than two conditions of the independent variable, you have to carry out pairwise comparisons to find out which conditions really differed from one another. To find the exact procedures for this type of test, you should consult a statistics textbook. For example, Glenberg (1996) described the procedure for conducting a protected t test, the statistic I will report.

TABLE **B.3**
ANOVA Source Table for the Memory Experiment

	Sum of Squares	df	Mean Square	F	Sig.
BELIEF	343.63	2	171.82	28.88	.000
Error	339.10	57	5.95		

TABLE **B.4**
Number of False Recalls in a Memory Test as a Function of Belief in the Paranormal

Belief Category	M	SD
Sheep	9.80	3.04
Neutral	6.55	2.04
Goats	3.95	2.11

We are now ready to write the results section. As usual, we begin with a description of the analysis, then include all of the statistical information:

> The data were analyzed using a one-way, between-participants ANOVA. The mean for sheep was 9.80 false recalls ($SD = 3.04$), the mean for neutral participants was 6.55 false recalls ($SD = 2.04$), and the mean for goats was 3.95 false recalls ($SD = 2.11$). With alpha $= .05$, the means were significantly different, $F(2, 57) = 28.88$, $MSE = 5.95$, $p < .01$. Protected t test comparisons indicated that the differences between sheep and neutral participants, sheep and goats, and neutral participants and goats were all significant.

With the information provided in the results section, your readers could reconstruct the entire source table. That might be necessary if they wanted to compute post hoc comparisons with a different procedure. For example, a reader who preferred to use a more conservative test than the protected t procedure reported previously could use the numbers you have reported to compute his or her own analysis.

Factorial

This analysis is used when you have more than one independent variable. You need to report all of the main effects (the effects of each independent variable) plus any post hoc comparisons for those main effects. You also need to report any interactions (combined effects of two or more independent variables).

Factorial ANOVAs can become very complicated, so you should start with a description of the analysis. First list the factors (independent variables), then the dependent variable, then your alpha level. An example of an opening paragraph is presented as follows. The experiment involved a manipulation of the content of a text (arousing or neutral) and the direction in which that text was presented (forward or backwards). I measured participants' arousal using an arousal scale.

> The data were analyzed using a two-way, between-participants ANOVA. The factors were story content (arousing, neutral) and presentation direction (forward, backwards). The dependent measure was the participant's score on an arousal scale. For all analyses, the significance level was set at .05.

The next step is to report main effects. For that, you need to consult a source table. The source table for my experiment (a modified version of a source table from SPSS) is presented in Table B.5.

The table of means from this design is presented in Table B.6.

The best way to report main effects is to discuss them with respect to a prediction. For example, I predicted that people would have more arousal when the texts were arousing than when they were neutral. To make the results clear, I will discuss them with this prediction:

> If the hypothesis were correct, then we would expect a main effect for story content. In particular, arousal should be higher for the arousing story than the neutral story. This main effect was significant, $F(1, 79) = 15.92$, $MSE = 13.59$, $p < .01$. The means for arousing content and neutral content were 5.82 ($SD = 1.7$) and 2.90 ($SD = 1.2$), respectively.

TABLE **B.5**
ANOVA Source Table for the Story Content by Presentation Direction Experiment

Source of Variation	Sum of Squares	df	Mean Square	F	Sig of F
CONTENT	216.35	1	216.35	15.92	.00
DIRECTION	92.00	1	92.00	6.77	.04
CONTENT X DIR	105.05	1	105.05	7.73	.01
Error	1073.61	79	13.59		

TABLE **B.6**
Rated Arousal as a Function of Story Content and Presentation Direction

Content	Forward		Backward	
	M	SD	M	SD
Arousing	7.5	1.6	4.2	1.8
Neutral	2.0	0.9	3.8	1.6

Now, I repeat that for the second main effect.

The main effect for presentation direction was also significant, $F(1, 79) = 6.77$, $MSE = 13.59$, $p = .04$. The means for forward and backwards presentations were 4.75 $(SD = 1.2)$ and 4.00 $(SD = 1.7)$, respectively.

The last step is to describe the interaction. First, report whether or not it was significant. Then, choose what will be the "main" independent variable. Describe the differences in the levels of the main independent variable for each level of the other independent variable. Here is an example paragraph for the interaction in the experiment described previously:

The story content x presentation direction interaction was significant, $F(1, 79) = 7.73$, $MSE = 13.59$, $p = .01$. The means are presented in Table B.6. Simple main effects analyses indicated that when the text was presented forward, participants reported more arousal for the arousing text than the neutral text. When the text was presented backwards, participants' reported arousal did not differ.

If the design had had more independent variables, then there would have been more main effects and interactions. Simply repeat the previous steps until everything has been reported. If an effect is not significant, or if you have no prediction about an effect, you may save it until you have discussed all of the important effects. As a general rule, if an effect is significant, you need to report it, even if you had no prediction. If an effect is not significant, you might still want to report the statistical information. Your audience may want to conduct additional analyses that require all of the information from your source table.

REFERENCES

Carroll, R. T. (2009). Sheep-goat effect. *The Skeptic's Dictionary*. Retrieved from http://www.skepdic.com/sheep-goat.html

Glenberg, A. M. (1996). *Learning from data: An introduction to statistical reasoning* (2nd Ed.). Mahwah, NJ: Erlbaum.

Roediger, H. L., III, & McDermott, K. B. (1995). Creating false memories: Remembering words not presented in lists. *Journal of Experimental Psychology: Learning, Memory and Cognition*, 21, 803–814. doi:10.1037/0278-7393.21.4.803

Rosnow, R. L., & Rosnow, M. (2009). *Writing papers in psychology* (8th Ed.). Belmont, CA: Wadsworth.

Wiseman, R., & Greening, E. (2005). 'It's still bending': Verbal suggestion and alleged psychokinetic ability. *British Journal of Psychology*, 96, 115–127. doi:10.1348/000712604X15428

Presenting Your Work

This appendix describes how you should present your work. Tips are provided to help you present your work as a poster or as an oral presentation. A sample poster and sample presentation are also included.

POSTER PRESENTATIONS

Poster presentations are commonly used at research conferences because they provide a way for a lot of people to present their work simultaneously. For example, at the Psychonomic Society meetings in the fall of 2008, it took only five poster sessions to present 620 posters and two and a half days of concurrent talks to present 330 spoken presentations. A lot more people will have a chance to present if a poster format is used (Psychonomic Society Publications, 2008).

Poster presentations are also used because they allow for more interaction between the presenter and the audience. A poster will generally be seen by fewer people than may attend an oral presentation, but the people who see it will have an opportunity to discuss it with the presenter. The audience will also be composed primarily of people who are interested in hearing about the research being presented. Because of the opportunity for interaction, posters are frequently presented at undergraduate research conferences.

How Much Should Be Included?

When planning a poster presentation, you need to think about how the audience will view the poster. You will either tack individual panels to a wall board or glue them to a tri-fold presentation stand. It is also possible to create a poster using a software program and print the poster on a large sheet of paper (e.g., 4 feet by 6 feet). However, given the budget and space constraints of most undergraduate research conferences, you are most likely to glue pages to a tri-fold stand. If you are using a tri-fold stand, it will be placed on a table for presentation. You will stand near the poster to discuss it as people read it. If the poster is on a table with another poster, the scene can get very crowded. Here are some general design considerations to make it easier for the audience to see and understand the poster:

1. Do not try to fit every detail of the research onto the poster. Provide an adequate summary but try to limit how much time a person has to spend reading. If you are concerned about details, you can prepare a handout with more information that you can distribute to interested visitors.
2. Avoid pages with nothing but text in long paragraphs. A poster is not a paper, and people will not have much time to read.
3. Try not to use more than eight pieces of paper (or eight panels in a large format poster). A good mix would be one for an abstract, one for an introduction, one for a method section, two for results (one text and one figure), and one for discussion. That will allow room for a large title and your name.

To reiterate, the purpose of the poster format is to allow you to discuss your work with the audience. Provide enough detail to let your visitors understand the project and plan to convey additional information in conversation.

How Should the Poster Be Presented?

You need to make your poster visually appealing. Gluing eight pieces of paper to a poster board and standing it on a table will be very boring. In the marketplace of a poster session, few people will be interested in seeing what you have to say. But you do not want to go too far with decorating your poster. Do not make it so cluttered that the research is obscured. Here are some tips that might help:

1. Arrange the information so that a person can read each column of the poster in one pass from left to right. If there is a crowd, people will not be able to move back and forth in front of the poster.
2. Make the print large enough to be read at a distance of at least three feet.
3. Be sure that the title can be read from an even greater distance than the rest of the poster. People will be looking for particular posters if there are time constraints. Help them find your poster if they are looking for it.
4. Use bullets and space out the information. Try to write in bite-sized chunks. This makes the poster easier to read at a distance.
5. Convey as much information as possible in figures and illustrations. Make sure these are also large enough to be read at a distance.
6. Glue each piece of paper to colored backing paper. My students usually use two colors. For example, you may use a bright blue and a bright yellow. The colors you choose should make the poster text stand out.
7. Apply some decoration to give the poster visual appeal. For example, one group of students conducted a memory study for real-world information.

They asked people for memories from the movie *Titanic* and the movie *As Good as It Gets*. They proposed that the emotional content of *Titanic* would lead to more memories than *As Good as It Gets*. For the poster, the students downloaded pictures of the *Titanic* and the movie poster from *As Good as It Gets*, and they placed the pictures around the text panels.

8. You should dress up for the presentation.

A good rule of thumb is to try to imagine yourself as a member of the audience at a poster session. What would make you interested in reading a poster? How would you want the poster to be designed so that it was easy to understand?

A Sample Poster

An example of the amount of material that you will need to include is presented in Figure C.1. This poster was presented at the fall 1998 Middle Tennessee State University Psychology Day. The poster won a research prize in its category. Each section was presented on a separate piece of paper.

Note that this experiment won a research prize even though the hypothesis was not supported. You may be concerned about reporting research that did not work out, but those concerns are unfounded. Many experiments do not support the hypothesis; this is especially true of experiments conducted in research methods laboratory classes. You have a very limited amount of time to design the experiment, and you only get one chance to collect data. If the experiment was well designed, and if you present it well, your audience will still have an opportunity to learn something from your results.

The Effect of Room Color on Mood

Tracey Fox, Patti Saulter, and Neil Norman

ABSTRACT

The question was, Does the color of a room affect people's mood? Previous research results have been mixed, but blue tends to be calming and red tends to cause anxiety. We manipulated room color using colored lights in a white room. One group of participants was in a red room; the other was in a blue room. We measured mood by looking for Stroop interference for mood-congruent words. We found no main effect of room color for percent correct or reaction time on the Stroop task.

FIGURE **C.1** A Sample Poster Presentation.

(Continued on next page)

INTRODUCTION

- How does the color of the environment influence mood? Jacobs & Suess (1975) found that manipulating room color using colored lights affected anxiety. Red and yellow lights produced more anxious moods than blue and green lights. However, research on this topic has been mixed. Some studies find no effect, others find the opposite effect. Our goal was to attempt to develop a more reliable dependent variable to see if we could clarify the relationship between room color and mood.
- Research has shown that Stroop interference occurs for words that match a person's psychological state. For example, Cooper and Todd (1997) found that anorexics have more interference for shape words (e.g., "thigh") than control words.
- Richards, French, Johnson, Naparstek, and Williams (1992) found more Stroop interference for anxiety words in people who score high on a trait anxiety scale.
- Our goal was to use a Stroop interference paradigm to measure anxiety after participants sat in a blue or red room.

METHOD

- There were 32 participants; 16 were in a blue room and 16 were in a red room.
- Room color was manipulated by placing gels over can lights in the room. We used 40-watt bulbs. The room was saturated with the light, but the overall lighting was dim.
- Participants started by sitting in the appropriately colored room for 10 minutes. To occupy their time, participants attempted to solve as many tangram puzzles as possible. The puzzles were pictures of people that participants had to recreate using seven shapes.
- Participants then completed a Stroop interference task. They saw three sets of words, 48 in each set. The sets were randomly ordered for each participant. One set contained anxious words ("tense," "aroused," "excited," "hostile"). One set contained soothing words ("soothed," "relaxed," "serene," "peace"). The last set contained neutral words ("one," "two," "three," "four"). The words were red, green, yellow, or blue. The room for the Stroop test was white.
- We compared average response time and error rate for the three word types for people in the two room colors.

FIGURE **C.1** A Sample Poster Presentation. (*continued*)

RESULTS

- Data from the neutral words were not used in the analysis because participants did not differ on these words, and this condition did not differ from either of the other conditions.
- For the reaction times, there was no main effect for room color. The main effect for word type was significant. Tense words ($M = 831$ ms) were responded to more slowly than soothed words ($M = 780$ ms), $F(1,30) = 5.83$, $MSE = 7011.54$.
- We were expecting a room color X word type interaction. We expected participants in the blue room to take longer to respond to soothed words, and participants in the red room to take longer to respond to tense words. This effect was not significant. However, participants in the red room did take longer to name the colors of tense words than participants in the blue room. These data are illustrated in Figure 1.
- The results of the accuracy data were similar. There was no main effect for room color. Participants were marginally more accurate for tense words ($M = 96\%$) than for soothed words ($M = 95\%$), $F(1,30) = 3.00$, $MSE = .001$, p $= .09$. The interaction was not significant. The accuracy data were less meaningful due to a ceiling effect.

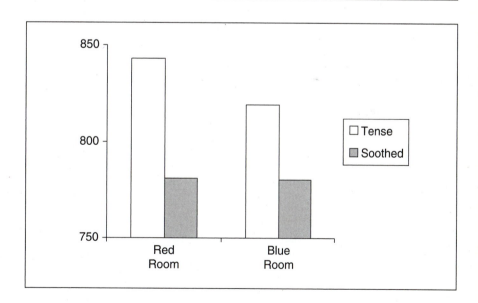

FIGURE **C.1** A Sample Poster Presentation.

(*Continued on next page*)

> ### DISCUSSION
> - We did not find a difference in naming time for the colors of the words based on room color. It may be that there was no difference because room color has no effect on mood.
> - However, a number of alternative explanations are also possible.
> - The Stroop test did not take place in the colored room. This might have reduced differences due to color.
> - The colors were not intense enough. The red gels were more intense than the blue gels. This meant the red room was more red than the blue room was blue. This lack of color may have reduced any differences.
> - The tangram puzzles may have produced anxiety in all participants. Overall, the anxiety words took longer, regardless of condition.
> - Running participants in groups may have increased anxiety. Some participants reported being frustrated with their partners because they weren't allowed to use the puzzle.
> - In conclusion, even though Stroop interference has been shown to be sensitive to changes in anxiety, we found no changes in Stroop interference based on the color of the room.

FIGURE **C.1** A Sample Poster Presentation.

Source: Saulter, P., Fox, T., & Norman, N. (1998, November). "The Effect of Color on Mood". Poster presented at the Middle Tennessee State University Psychology Day, Murfreesboro, TN.

ORAL PRESENTATIONS

Oral presentations give researchers an opportunity to share their latest research with a large audience. An oral presentation is more formal than a poster presentation, and there is less opportunity for audience participation.

How Much Should Be Included?

Most of the suggestions for a poster presentation also apply to an oral presentation. Here are some tips:

1. Do not try to fit every detail of the research into the presentation. Provide an adequate summary, but remember the limitations of oral presentation formats. People will only be able to digest a certain amount of material in 10 to 15 minutes. If you stick too closely to details, the audience will lose the thread of the presentation.

2. Focus on questions. Pose a research question and answer it. Help the audience to understand your motivation for each part of the experiment. Why is this an interesting question? Why are you using this methodology to answer it? Why are the results important?

3. Use a lot of slides. Let the audience follow along the outline of the presentation as you go. Someone who temporarily loses track of the presentation can always catch up by looking at the visuals you provide.

4. A standard format is 15 minutes for each presenter. Plan for 12 minutes of presentation and 3 minutes of questions. In your 12 minutes, spend around four setting up the problem, two discussing the methodology, two discussing results, and four for the discussion.

How Should the Talk Be Presented?

You have sat through boring presentations. You have also seen interesting presentations. Avoid the characteristics of boring presentations and copy the characteristics of interesting presentations. You can deliver a professional presentation and still be a stimulating speaker. Here are some tips that may help:

1. Memorize the beginning of the presentation word for word. A good opening is to read your title and mention all of the people who participated in the project. This will get you started and help with the initial nervousness.
2. Do not read your talk. You will bore your audience, and you will make it impossible for them to pay attention. Instead, use visuals as a memory cue and speak spontaneously. For example, you may put the number of participants on an overhead. This will remind you to mention the number of participants, and give you an opportunity to describe them in detail.
3. Do have notes prepared for each section. You may panic and be unable to remember what you wanted to say. If you have notes, you can use them for backup. You can consult your notes without reading them to the audience. It is acceptable to pause between sentences and think about what you want to say next.
4. Speak slowly enough that the audience can follow your ideas, but do not talk in a monotone.
5. Anything you show on a slide should be printed neatly in large, bold type. There is nothing more frustrating than struggling to read the visuals during a presentation.
6. Keep your visual aids simple. The audience has a limited amount of time to read and understand them. If everyone is struggling to understand what is being projected, nobody will be listening to you.
7. Never present a page full of statistics or text and tell the audience to read it for themselves. If it is important for the audience to read something, read it to them. If doing this makes you feel as though you are spending too much time reading to the audience, you are. Cut back the amount of material that you are presenting.
8. Do not assume that the audience will be able to see something just because you project it on a slide. There may be obstructions, or it may be hard to see from the back of the room. Always describe what you are presenting.
9. Feel free to move around, but do not move so much that you distract the audience.
10. Rehearse the whole presentation at least once and try to rehearse in front of an audience. Let the test audience help you decide if the talk is clear.
11. Dress up for the presentation.

12. Try to avoid "PowerPoint-itis." You do not want to become mesmerized by your presentation and begin to read quickly through the slides and advance rapidly through the presentation. The visual aids are only aids, you are presenting the ideas verbally.

You will probably be nervous before the presentation. Here are some tips to help settle your nerves:

1. Rehearse thoroughly. If you know what you want to say, you will feel better about saying it.
2. Get the audience to do something. This will distract them temporarily, and it will put you in control of the room. For example, one presenter I saw surveyed the audience to see if they believed various "facts" (e.g., you will do better on a multiple choice exam if you do not change your answers). After getting the audience to express an opinion, he pointed out that the "facts" were all wrong. The audience was then very eager to hear why the facts were wrong, and the speaker got a moment at the beginning of his talk to take a deep breath and let the audience do some of the work. Another nice feature of this presentation was that the audience was embarrassed for expressing belief in ideas that were false. The awkwardness shifted from the speaker to the audience.
3. An interested audience is easier to talk to than a bored audience. Get the audience interested by giving them something to do (as outlined previously). You can also make a provocative statement. I once saw a presenter who started by saying that there was no such thing as memory. Then he set out to prove it by giving the audience a memory demonstration. That combined two elements to build interest, and the audience was very involved by the time he got down to the main part of the talk.
4. Keep these things in mind:
    a. Fifteen minutes goes by very quickly when you are speaking.
    b. Nobody will try to ask you a question that you cannot answer.
    c. If you do not know the answer to someone's question, you can say, "I don't know." You can also try to involve the person asking the question in speculating about the answer.
    d. You can direct the audience's questions to topics you know. For example, you might say, "The exact details of this procedure are not essential, but if you would like to know them, we can discuss it in the question period." Try not to do this too much because it can be annoying.

A Sample Presentation

Given the rules, it is not possible to show you a sample talk. I have never written a talk in my life, and I would not want you to write a talk either. If I were going to present the room color experiment in the poster mentioned before, I would make notes similar to the poster. Then I would memorize most of the information on the notes and prepare a series of slides to help me remember what I wanted to say. Sample slides from this talk are presented in Figure C.2.

INTRODUCTION

- How does the color of the environment influence mood?
  Jacobs & Suess (1975)
  Other studies
- Stroop interference occurs for words that match a person's psychological state.
  Cooper and Todd (1997)
  Richards, French, Johnson, Naparstek, and Williams (1992)
- Our goal was to use a Stroop interference paradigm to measure anxiety after participants sat in a blue or red room.

METHOD

- 32 participants; 16 in a blue room and 16 in a red room.
- Participants sat in the appropriately colored room for 10 minutes completing tangram puzzles.

  [I would show some tangram puzzles here and ask the audience to solve the puzzles. I would pick one easy puzzle and one hard puzzle to let the audience get some idea of the task.]

- Stroop interference task.

RESULTS

- No main effect for room color.
- Main effect for word type.
  Tense words $M = 831$ ms
  Soothed words $M = 780$ ms [The statistics would be in a smaller font size.]
  $F(1,30) = 5.83$
- No room color × word type interaction.

  [I would show the figure from the poster.]

DISCUSSION

- The hypothesis was not supported.
- Possible explanations:
  1. The Stroop test did not take place in the colored room.
  2. The colors were not intense enough.
  3. The tangram puzzles may have produced anxiety in all participants.
  4. Running participants in groups may have increased anxiety.

FIGURE **C.2** Sample Oral Presentation Visuals.

Obviously, the slides do not contain enough information to fully understand the experiment. I would flesh them out with the talk. For the opening, I would find a provocative statement in the literature or find an anecdote about room color and mood. For example, statistics on how the environment influences productivity might help motivate the audience to be interested in my research; or an anecdote about putting prisoners in pink holding cells may be good for a laugh.

I would bring to the presentation my PowerPoint, plus cards with the detailed information to flesh out the talk. I do not usually rely on the cards, but they are nice when you forget what you want to say. I would also bring additional information that I did not plan to present. I like to be prepared in case someone asks a question that I did not anticipate. Again, feeling prepared makes you less nervous.

When you are making a presentation that involves PowerPoint, it is a good idea to have several backup plans prepared in case of technical difficulty. An experienced presenter can improvise through almost any circumstance, but avoiding trouble is best for inexperienced presenters. If you have your own laptop, be sure that you have the appropriate cords to connect it to whatever projector may be available. This is a likely source of interface problems, but if you have your own computer, you know that your slides will present accurately. It is more common to bring your talk on a thumb drive. If there is a chance that you will be using a different type of computer or operating system for the talk, you may want to check the format before you arrive. It is also common to e-mail the talk to yourself, or to post it on a web page. I also save mine as a PDF file with one slide per page. If nothing else works, you can at least scroll through the talk. In general, technical difficulties can be a killing blow to your confidence. You want to be as prepared as possible to deal with these difficulties so that you can focus on the content of what you want to say rather than the technology you are using to support your presentation.

REFERENCES

Fox, T., Saulter, P., & Norman, N. (1998, November). *The Effect of Room Color on Mood.* Poster presented at the Middle Tennessee State University Psychology Day, Murfreesboro, TN. Used with permission of the author.

Psychonomic Society Publications. (2008). *Abstracts of the Psychonomic Society,* 13.

Evaluating Sources

Information is everywhere. Much of that information could have important implications for the way you live your life. You might also be interested in incorporating information from various sources into your research project. This appendix is designed to give you some guidance in evaluating those sources.

KINDS OF SOURCES

I will consider five types of sources. The information provided here is intended to be a guide to help you evaluate the credibility of the information contained in any particular source. On average, some sources are going to be more reliable than others. However, there are no clear-cut rules (e.g., that you should only use peer-reviewed sources in your research). In addition to the kind of source, you should also evaluate the information itself (Appendix E has some suggestions to help you do that).

1. Peer-reviewed journals. When an author submits an article to one of these journals, that article is subjected to a thorough review. Articles are usually first reviewed by an editor who will determine how the article should be handled. With some journals, the editor will evaluate whether or not the article is up to the journal's standards, whether or not the content is appropriate for the journal, and whether or not the article has a chance at publication. If the article makes it through the initial evaluation, it will usually be sent to an action editor who will ultimately make the decision on publication. Even though most journals have a relatively narrow focus (e.g., *Personality and Social Psychology Bulletin* obviously contains articles related to personality and social psychology), there are usually sub-disciplines that are more specialized. The action editor will be someone with expertise close to the article's content area.

The action editor will select reviewers. The reviewers will be people whose research programs and expertise are close to the content of the article. There are usually between three and five reviewers. Reviewers will check the quality of the article. Some things they will evaluate:

a. Does the article make a contribution?
b. Is that contribution big enough to warrant publication?
c. Is the methodology of the experiment(s) sound?
d. Have the right statistical procedures been selected?
e. Have the statistics been used properly?
f. Can the conclusions be drawn from the data?
g. Are there alternative explanations?

The action editor will collect the reviews and make a decision. The possible outcomes are:

a. Reject the article. Manuscripts can be rejected for a variety of reasons. Sometimes they are of poor quality, sometimes the reviewers think the research is fine, but it just is not "big" enough to merit publication.
b. Revise and resubmit. The article has merit, but the current form is unacceptable. Sometimes a new analysis or a brief rewrite will suffice (like including something in the literature review). Sometimes more experiments will need to be conducted.
c. Accept as is. This is rare.

If the author has been encouraged to resubmit, the author will try to make the revisions requested and send the paper back. You can see that most papers in psychology go through at least one revision by looking at the publication history that is included at the end of most articles. Many articles that are resubmitted are still rejected for publication.

Top journals have rejection rates in the 80%–90% range (Suls & Martin, 2009). Lower tier journals may accept more papers, but most peer-reviewed journals still have high rejection rates. (Many articles rejected by one journal may eventually be published somewhere else, so high rejection rates may be slightly inflated.) "Good" work can sometimes be rejected. (In a recent special issue of *Perspectives on Psychological Science* devoted to improving psychological science, 9 of the 26 articles were about peer-review, including a debate about whether or not the current peer-review system would allow important science papers from the past to be published.)

Note that peer-review does not guarantee that something published is "good," it just lets you have confidence that the work has been carefully reviewed by experts. There may be alternative viewpoints and continued debate. For example, Mangan, Armitage, and Adams (2008) presented a validity study for a lie detection technique. Verschuere, Meijer, and Merckelbach (2008) took issue with their results (the phrase "it's just not science" was in the title of Verschuere et al.'s article). In their abstract, Verschuere et al. described the publication of Mangan et al. as "an example of the failure of the peer-review procedure" (p. 27). Vul, Harris, Winkielman, & Pashler (2009) published a paper critical of methods used in fMRI research. This article was published along with a number of commentaries due to its controversial nature (Diener, 2009). In fact, the editor (Diener, 2009) wrote an introduction explaining the article's history (and mentioning that the word "voodoo" had originally been in the title, but that it was removed to set a better tone for the debate). The point of this discussion is that science is a living enterprise, and the best we can do is get as close to the truth as we can. There will always be debate and differences of opinion, regardless of the quality of the source. It is up to you as the consumer of information to be sure that you have properly surveyed the literature.

Evaluation. If the journal is peer-reviewed you still need to think critically about the content, but you can have strong *a priori* confidence in the source. One thing to keep in mind about peer-review is that it takes time. By the time an article appears in print, the actual research may be several years old. Whereas other sources may not have been subjected to the same rigorous review process, the information in those sources may be more current.

2. Non peer-reviewed journals/ultra-low rejection rate journals. These sources may subject articles to a slightly less rigorous review process, or they may not review articles at all. One way to identify these kinds of sources is to look at the instructions to authors (in the printed journal or on the web page). The review process is usually described there. In psychology, most top journals do not expect authors to pay to publish in them, so one clue to non peer-reviewed journals is to look for charges to publish (note that in many disciplines top journals do have page charges, so this is not a defining feature).

Evaluation. Keep in mind that "good" research can still appear in these journals. However, the quality can be more variable than in peer-reviewed journals. Approach the articles with a slightly higher level of skepticism and consider the issues considered by reviewers described previously.

3. Conference presentations/proceedings. You might get a copy of a paper derived from a talk or poster presentation at a conference. Some conferences allow all presenters to publish a brief paper in conference proceedings. Many people presenting at conferences also post a copy of their presentation on their website. Some conferences use peer-review. However, the process is usually less rigorous than for a journal because conferences exist to disseminate newer, less polished research. Conferences also get a large number of submissions and only have a short amount of time to make a decision. Finally, conference proposals are usually shorter than papers, so some of the information needed for a full review is not sent to reviewers.

Evaluation. If possible, try to find a published version of information presented at a conference. If you rely on a report from a conference, be sure to subject the information to the skeptical reading suggested previously. Again, conference presentations are going to be your source for the most recent research results.

4. Books and book chapters. I will divide this into three sorts: Edited volumes, reviews, and topical books.

a. Edited volumes. Usually a person with a reputation in an area will ask experts in the field to contribute chapters for an edited volume. Many edited books cover recent research or special topics, and are designed to bring a variety of research together in one place. Books and chapters are frequently based on peer-reviewed research, but the books and chapters themselves are frequently not peer-reviewed. For edited books, the editor usually decides whether or not a chapter is "good" enough. When original research is reported in books or chapters, it could be that the research was new and the author wanted to tell people about it. On the other hand, the research might not have been able to withstand scrutiny.

b. Reviews. Some books are part of series that provide reviews of research areas (e.g., *The Psychology of Learning and Motivation: Advances in Research and Theory*). These books can be especially useful when you are beginning your project because review articles survey the entire published literature on a particular topic.

c. Topical books. One person may write an entire book. These kinds of books are usually written from a particular perspective. Journal editors usually try to remove slanted language or reject clearly biased articles. Book authors might actually be presenting their side of the story.

Evaluation. Books and chapters can be a valuable resource, but as with any source, you should still evaluate the quality of the content for yourself.

5. Internet pages. Basically, somebody posts something on the Internet. Keep in mind that books cost money to produce, so publishers generally check them for merit before allowing them to be published. Compared to publishing, web pages are cheap. Also, most of the time, nobody checks the content of web pages. You should not take information presented on the Internet at face value. If research results appear only on the Internet, be suspicious. If a website includes a summary of other people's research, find some of the original research. Compare the website's summary of the research to the original research. If the summary appears unbiased and accurate, you can gain confidence in the rest of the site.

Some sites are peer-reviewed, provide discussion forums for experts, or are the web-based portion of more reputable sources. You may place more confidence in these types of sites. For discussion forums, be sure to read enough to find out both sides of the issues being debated.

Keep in mind that sites claiming to be skeptical are not necessarily above suspicion. Unbridled skepticism is also unscientific. Evaluate the claims of sites designed to debunk in the same way you would evaluate sites designed to promote.

Evaluation. When you consider Internet sources, be very cautious. Assume the role of reviewer. In general, you can use the Internet to find a direction, and then turn to stronger sources for the foundation of your research.

REFERENCES

Diener, E. (2009). Editor's introduction to Vul et al. (2009) and comments. *Perspectives on Psychological Science, 4*, 272–273. doi: 10.1111/j.1745-6924.2009.01124.x

Mangan, D. J., Armitage, T. E., & Adams, G. C. (2008). A field study on the validity of the Quadri-Track Zone Comparison Technique. *Physiology and Behavior, 95*, 17–23. doi:10.1016/j.physbeh.2008.03.001

Suls, J., & Martin, R. (2009). The air we breathe: A critical look at practices and alternatives in the peer-review process. *Perspectives on Psychological Science, 4*, 40–50. doi:10.1111/j.1745-6924.2009.01105.x

Verschuere, B., Meijer, E., & Merckelbach, H. (2008). The Quadri-Track Zone Comparison Technique: It's just not science. A critique to Mangan, Armitage, and Adams (2008). *Physiology and Behavior, 95*, 27–28. doi:10.1016/j.physbeh.2008.06.002

Vul, E., Harris, C., Winkielman, P., & Pashler, H. (2009). Puzzlingly high correlations in fMRI studies of emotion, personality, and social cognition. *Perspectives on Psychological Science, 4*, 274–290. doi:10.1111/j.1745-6924.2009.01125.x

Discriminating Science from Pseudoscience

Discriminating science from pseudoscience is sometimes challenging. The desire not to be "tricked" into believing something that is not true competes with the desire to understand how the world works. A number of systems have been proposed to assist in separating science from pseudoscience. This appendix reviews several of those proposals.

SCIENCE VERSUS PSEUDOSCIENCE

Telling science from pseudoscience is a tricky business. Popper (1962) discussed these issues at length and proposed risky prediction as a criterion. The notion behind risky prediction is that real scientists make predictions that can be proven false. When falsification happens the hypotheses leading to those predictions are modified or discarded. This makes science self-correcting. For example, when the Piltdown man fossil was discovered, it fit nicely into then current thinking about human evolution (Scott, 2004). Eventually, as more fossils were found, Piltdown man became increasingly difficult to "fit in." Finally, problems reconciling the Piltdown fossil with the rest of the fossil record led to the discovery that it was a hoax (Scott). Not only was the "fossil" itself removed from the scientific record, but what prompted this was the gradual abandonment by scientists of the hypotheses that made the Piltdown fossil such a "perfect" specimen of the missing link in the first place.

Contrast this with astrology. Whereas astrology has aspects of empirical science ("its stupendous mass of empirical evidence based on observation," Popper, 1962, p. 34), most people would not classify it as science. Popper's explanation for this is that it does not make risky predictions. What observations would cause an astrologer to conclude that the theory behind astrology was wrong? What "cases" would an astrologer encounter that could not be accounted for by astrology?

Popper's (1962) thinking about the difference between science and pseudoscience led him to several conclusions that he summed up in this way: "*the criterion of the scientific status of a theory is its falsifiability, or refutability, or testability*" (p. 37, italics in the original). (Note that in reality the picture is not as clear as I am painting it here. For a more complete discussion of Popper's theories, and problems with them, I suggest the *Stanford Encyclopedia of Philosophy* entry on Popper, http://plato.stanford.edu/entries/popper/)

Another way to try to make the distinction between science and pseudoscience is to look for clues that might distinguish one from the other. No set of clues will necessarily decide all cases, but when something has many of the features of a pseudoscience, that is a warning to you to look more closely. The rest of this appendix will be devoted to various approaches and their application.

POPPER'S (1962) CRITERIA

Popper (1962) drew several conclusions about the difference between science and pseudoscience. I am summarizing them as three main principles:

1. "Confirmations should count only if they are the result of *risky predictions*" (Popper, 1962, p. 36, italics in the original). This can be paired with Popper's assertion that confirmations are easy to find if we are looking for them. The quality of the evidence is a function of how much risk the study presented to the theory.

2. "Every genuine *test* of a theory is an attempt to falsify it" (Popper, 1962, p. 36, italics in the original). Again, Popper is discounting "tests" that had no chance of falsifying the hypothesis. If the hypothesis would be supported no matter how the data came out, why collect the data in the first place? This can be connected to Popper's assertion that "a theory which is not refutable by any conceivable event is non-scientific" (p. 37).

3. When a theory is falsified but not rejected because of *ad hoc* assumptions that are added to it, that procedure "rescues the theory from refutation only at the price of destroying, or at least lowering, its scientific status" (Popper, 1962, p. 37).

Here is a list of questions that you can ask of any research:

a. Is the primary aim of the research confirmation? ("No" is preferred.)
b. Were confirmations the result of risky predictions? ("Yes" is preferred.)
c. Does the theory prohibit things? ("The more a theory forbids, the better it is," Popper, 1962, p. 36.)
d. Is the theory irrefutable? ("No" is preferred.)
e. How much exposure to falsification was there? (More is preferred.)
f. Is evidence counted that is not the result of a genuine test? ("No" is preferred.)

g. Are there *ad hoc* assumptions added to the theory that prevent it from being falsified? (Assumptions are bad.)

An analysis of reports of alien contact experiences with respect to these questions was presented in Chapter 8 in Science Note 8.1.

LANGMUIR'S (1989) PATHOLOGICAL SCIENCE

Langmuir was a physicist who initially presented his ideas about pathological science in a talk in 1953 (Langmuir & Hall, 1989). This talk was recorded and a version of the talk was published in *Physics Today* in 1989. Langmuir's approach to the definition of pseudoscience was prompted by a different question than Popper's. Langmuir found that there were instances in the history of physics in which some phenomenon seemed to be supported by the data but then turned out to be false. What interested Langmuir was that during the time the phenomenon was supported, reputable scientists, following the standard procedures of science, were producing data consistent with a phenomenon that did not really exist. Obviously they had been "tricked," but how did this happen, and how could it be prevented in the future?

Pathological science was Langmuir's (Langmuir & Hall, 1989) answer to these questions. He concluded that there were certain features that these phenomena had in common, and that science with these features has a good chance of being pathological. Note that there is nothing in the description of pathological science intended to indicate conscious fraud on the part of scientists. Instead, the hypothesis is that pathological science is "science gone wrong." One nice feature of the pathological science hypothesis is that it explains why some phenomena will not go away, regardless of how much negative evidence is collected. Because data can be collected to support the hypothesis, and the proof stays *just* out of reach, researchers receive just enough reinforcement to keep going. The features of pathological science are:

1. "The maximum effect that is observed is produced by a causative agent of barely detectable intensity, and the magnitude of the effect is substantially independent of the intensity of the cause" (Langmuir & Hall, 1989, p. 44). Usually, the more of something that you add, the stronger its effect. Pathological sciences tend to not work this way.
2. "The effect is of a magnitude that remains close to the limit of detectability, or, many measurements are necessary because of the very low statistical significance of the results" (Langmuir & Hall, 1989, p. 44). The biggest danger here is when human observers are making the observations. When the actual effect is small, the effect of "wishful looking" becomes more pronounced.
3. "There are claims of great accuracy" (Langmuir & Hall, 1989, p. 44). People engaged in pathological science believe that they will be able to measure things to a greater precision than traditional scientists, or that their new data will turn science on its head.
4. "Fantastic theories contrary to experience are suggested" (Langmuir & Hall, 1989, p. 44).

5. "Criticisms are met by *ad hoc* excuses thought up on the spur of the moment" (Langmuir & Hall, 1989, p. 44). Langmuir shares this concern with Popper (1962). A genuine scientific hypothesis should not require for its support untested assumptions added every time the data do not come out right.

6. "The ratio of supporters to critics rises up to somewhere near 50% and then falls gradually to oblivion" (Langmuir & Hall, 1989, p. 44). Eventually, the facts come out, but before they do the novelty of the claims seduces many researchers into the pathological science.

An evaluation of research on staring detection as pathological science was presented in Chapter 2 in Science Note 2.1. Langmuir (Langmuir & Hall, 1989) applied his analysis to ESP research and flying saucers. For example, regardless of the kind of ESP task (predicting how a deck of cards would be shuffled in the future or how one had just been shuffled), the effect was always the same. Rather than being evidence for the effect, Langmuir believed that that showed that the effect was the result of pathological science.

BOGUS SCIENCE

Park (2003) was a little less charitable in his characterization of non-science. His list was generated as a suggestion for judges to use when deciding if expert testimony represents scientific consensus, or if it is the opinion of "an expert for hire" who will say whatever is required for a particular case. Park provided a list of seven criteria, the more of these you find, the more concerned you should be.

1. "The discoverer pitches the claim directly to the media" (Park, 2003). In Appendix D we discussed various types of sources. Scientists generally publish in peer-reviewed journals (the content is reviewed by experts prior to publication). Peer-review is no guarantee of quality, but it is suspicious when researchers proclaim their results to the media prior to going through that step.

2. "The discoverer says that a powerful establishment is trying to suppress his or her work" (Park, 2003). One side effect of peer-review is that people can feel as though their ideas cannot get a fair hearing. However, as we saw with the case of pathological science, scientists are just like everyone else. They are captivated by the lure of the new, "big" idea. If anything, the "conspiracy" in science is towards publishing exciting, new ideas, not in suppressing them.

3. "The scientific effect involved is always at the very limit of detection" (Park, 2003). Again, tiny effects open the door for "wishful looking."

4. "Evidence for the discovery is anecdotal" (Park, 2003). Anecdotal evidence is someone presenting one (or a few) cases collected under uncontrolled conditions to convince you of something. For example, the people appearing in weight loss commercials are providing anecdotal evidence. The fact that most weight loss commercials also have a disclaimer saying

"results not typical" can help explain the problem with anecdotal evidence. The anecdotes might have been carefully chosen (who would put someone in a weight loss commercial who did not lose weight?), or they might represent a special circumstance, or even an accident that cannot be repeated.

5. "The discoverer says a belief is credible because it has endured for centuries" (Park, 2003). If so, then it should be easy to produce experimental evidence to support the claim.

6. "The discoverer has worked in isolation" (Park, 2003). Science is a social enterprise. Progress in science is slow and science is done by many people working in a variety of settings. It is unusual for a person working alone to produce a unique discovery.

7. "The discoverer must propose new laws of nature to explain an observation" (Park, 2003). When someone pits the theory of gravity against their observation, the chances are that the observation is wrong, and not the theory of gravity.

We can evaluate the claims made by graphology against Park's (2003) list. Pro-graphology research is far more likely to be published in mass media sources than in peer-reviewed journals. In fact, many details of graphology systems are kept secret (Greasley, 2000), making it difficult for independent evaluation to be done, and making it difficult for peer-review to work. Graphology is widely accepted in the mainstream (e.g., Thomas & Vaught, 2001), so there are few claims of suppression by the establishment. Validity studies of graphological predictions suggest that effects are very small (if there are any effects, Neter & Ben-Shakhar, 1989). Graphology reports are packed with anecdotal evidence (e.g., Goodwin, 2009). Part of the justification for graphology's effectiveness comes from claims that it has been used for centuries (e.g., Handwriting Research Corporation, 2009). Many graphological systems are the unique product of their creator, working in isolation. Finally, the idea of coordination between motor areas and personality areas in the brain has not been demonstrated empirically. This analysis does not prove that graphology is not science, but it does raise a lot of issues that are cause for concern. In these kinds of cases, the best course of action would be to look for top-quality data to support a claim.

SKEPTICAL EVALUATIONS

Sometimes the work has been done for you. When you find yourself confronted with an extraordinary claim, turn to the data. For example, Silver (1987) presented a critical evaluation of various proposals to treat learning disabilities. He compared controversial approaches to generally accepted therapies. For each controversial approach he described what it was, how it was supposed to work, and what the evidence was that supported it. He also provided a frank evaluation of each approach. For example, for "ocular lock" and its treatment, Silver says "they report a theory and suggest that it is based on research facts. If one makes the effort to seek out the references cited, it is found that no such research facts exist" (p. 502). Silver goes on to say:

> Parents and professionals should know that this proposed chiropractic treatment for dyslexia and learning disabilities is not based on any known research; that some of it is based on anatomical concepts that are not held by the majority of anatomists; that there is no research done by others that replicates the proposed cures; and, that there are no follow-up research studies to document the claimed results. (Silver, 1987, p. 502)

That seems to sum it up.

Some reports also explicitly analyze a research enterprise (or other area of endeavor) using a checklist of potential features of pseudoscience. For example, Lilienfeld and Landfield (2008) presented an analysis of pseudoscience in law enforcement based on ten possible features of pseudoscience. There was some overlap with the systems discussed previously, but Lilienfeld and Landfield also considered additional features (such as the use of overly technical language).

REFERENCES

Goodwin, C. (2009). Retrieved from http://www.toughcases.net/graphology.html

Greasley, P. (2000). Handwriting analysis and personality assessment: The creative use of analogy, symbolism, and metaphor. *European Psychologist, 5,* 44–51. doi:10.1027//1016-9040.5.1.44

Handwriting Research Corporation. (2009). Retrieved from http://www.handwriting.com/facts/history.html

Langmuir, I., & Hall, R. N. (1989). Pathological Science. *Physics Today, 42,* 36–48. doi:10.1063/1.881205

Lilienfeld, S. O., & Landfield, K. (2008). Science and pseudoscience in law enforcement: A user-friendly primer. *Criminal Justice and Behavior, 35,* 1215–1230. doi:10.1177/0093854808321526

Neter, E., & Ben-Shakhar, G. (1989). The predictive validity of graphological inferences: A meta-analytic approach. *Personality and Individual Differences, 10,* 737–745. doi:10.1016/0191-8869 (89)90120-7

Park, R. L. (2003). The seven warning signs of bogus science. *The Chronicle of Higher Education, 49,* B20. Retrieved from http://chronicle.com/article/The-Seven-Warning-Signs-of/13674

Popper, K. R. (1962). *Conjectures and refutations: The growth of scientific knowledge.* New York: Basic Books.

Scott, E. (2004). *"Scientific creationism", evolution & race.* Retrieved from http://skepticreport.com/sr/?p=474

Silver, L. B. (1987).The "magic cure": A review of the current controversial approaches for treating learning disabilities. *Journal of Learning Disabilities, 20,* 498–504, 512. doi:10.1177/002221948702000808

Thomas, S. L., & Vaught, S. (2001). The write stuff: What the evidence says about using handwriting analysis in hiring. *SAM Advanced Management Journal, 66,* 31–35.

INDEX

Boldface page numbers in the index indicate pages where the term is defined.